HONORARIUM: ESSAYS 2001–2021

HONORARIUM
ESSAY$ 2001—2021

NATHANIEL g. MOORE

PALIMPSEST PRESS

2021

Copyright © 2021 Nathaniel G. Moore
All rights reserved

Palimpsest Press
1171 Eastlawn Ave.
Windsor, Ontario. N8S 3J1
www.palimpsestpress.ca

Printed and bound by Rapido Books in Ontario, Canada.
Edited by Jim Johnstone.
Cover image by Will Rendall.
Cover design by Ellie Hastings.
Typesetting by Carleton Wilson.

Palimpsest Press would like to thank the Canada Council for the Arts and the Ontario Arts Council for their support of our publishing program. We also acknowledge the assistance of the Government of Ontario through the Ontario Book Publishing Tax Credit.

LIBRARY AND ARCHIVES CANADA CATALOGUING IN PUBLICATION

Title: Honorarium : essays, 2001-2021 / Nathaniel G. Moore.
Other titles: Essays. Selections
Names: Moore, Nathaniel G., author.
Identifiers: Canadiana 20210101504 | ISBN 9781989287804 (softcover)
Classification: LCC PS8626.O595 A6 2021 | DDC C814/.6—dc23

For the gang at 520: Amber, Richard, Finny

CONTENTS

11 Introduction: Paid in Books

PART ONE: ENTER THE CANON

19 The Catullus Lot ($0)

31 Is Evil Just Something You Are or Something You Do? (Or Something You Decide to Write About Because You Want to Be Edgy?) ($100)

36 The Wolves of Bloor Street ($100)

39 Who Killed the Third Person? ($100)

43 Fully Loaded ($125)

47 So You Think You Can Dance Write? ($100)

PART TWO: HYPE, HUSTLE, HELVETICA

53 Heather Birrell: *Mad Hope* ($100)

64 Jen Sookfong Lee: Idaho Revisited ($0)

67 Camilla Gibb: The External World ($50)

71 Sheila Heti: How Should a Novelist Write? ($100)

78 Zsuzsi Gartner: The Crafty Wick ($125)

81 Chuck Palahniuk: Migration Patterns in 21st-Century Big-Box Retail ($100)

86 Derek McCormack: To Be Gay and Get Fucked Up ($125)

91 Julie Booker & Jessica Westhead: *Up Up Up + And Also Sharks* ($125)

95 Vivek Shraya: The Earnest Expression of Self ($125)

98 Ibi Kaslik: Demystifying Clichés about Anorexia ($50)

101 Sonja Ahlers: Greetings from Lake Cowichan ($50)

107 Randall Maggs: The Sawchuk Sessions ($125)

113 Lynn Crosbie: Forgot about Lynn: 72 hours with *Life Is About Losing Everything* ($125)

118 Michael Turner: Everything I Have Goes into Everything I Do ($100)

PART THREE: THE HARD SELL

123 Kingpin of Fear: Loathsome Secrets of an Adolescent Bowling Star in the Dying Days of the Nineties ($0)

134 Heart-Knocked Life ($275)

139 Parts Unknown: An Interview with Michael Holmes ($50)

146 It's Still Real to Me, Dammit ($0)

148 The Steel Cage ($0)

PART FOUR: BLOOD IS THICKER

153 Montage of Heck: Write What You Fear You Know... *and Are... and Have Been All Along* ($0)

172 My Grandfather's Cult ($100)

186 Fear and Loathing on Protection Island ($200)

PART FIVE: NO ALGORITHM, NO OVERTIME, NO MERCY!

199 Mark Leyner: The Hoboken Knight ($100)

202 Sina Queyras: Twenty-Four Hours ($175)

204 Lynn Coady: *The Antagonist* Is the Anti-Buddy Film We Can All Use ($75)

207 Alisha Piercy: 2010: The Year She Makes Contact ($100)

210 Rachel Zolf: A Tormented History ($177)

212 Joey Comeau: A Nihilistic Parody for Our Troubled Times ($175)

214 Robert Rotenberg: Toronto the Bad ($250)

216 Buried Treasures ($0)

219 Rated "R" ($50)

223 Sarah Edmondson: Hitting the Reset Button ($0)

PART SIX: EXIT THROUGH THE GIFT SHOP

229 How to Be Your Own Book-PR Dream Team ($125)

247 Amazon Isn't the Antichrist. Still, I Wouldn't Invite Them to My Book Launch ($100)

252 Viewer Digression Advised: Netflix Is Not a Publishing Course ($0)

257 Creation Myths: How to Shape Your Work-in-Progress ($0)

260 R. M. Vaughan: The Selfless Giant ($300, donated to The ArQuives)

265 ACKNOWLEDGEMENTS

267 ABOUT THE AUTHOR

INTRODUCTION: PAID IN BOOKS

> Look at this. It's worthless. Ten dollars from a vendor in the street. But I take it, I bury it in the sand for a thousand years, it becomes priceless... Like the Ark.
>
> —Doctor Rene Belloq, *Raiders of the Lost Ark*, 1981

One of my esteemed colleagues in the cultural arts hangs out on social media with a bio that simply reads "paid in books," which is a hyperbolic economic forecast for most critics who ply their trade outside of the remaining forces that cover mainstream publications. Those with more balanced lives might not get the joke as much as those who work in the arts, but the sentiment isn't lost on anyone. The general reputation of the book business is that it's not at all about the money. But I don't buy that completely. While book sales may not be what every author hopes for and dreams of, there is a lot of unsung privilege in working in publishing, and I would like to state emphatically that although I dabble in clowning, I do recognize the extreme privilege I have been gifted over the last two decades. No one sets out to build an empire by working for $100 a pop for their "cultural insight," but over the years I've been allowed to live in multiple provinces, work with countless authors, publishers, and magazines, and paid or unpaid, it remains a privilege, one that I understand isn't the case for others who don't have it as easy. And I made it look easy; whether it was or not, I'm not exactly sure. Whether or not it was always needed, well, that's entirely up to readers to decide.

A random piece from my online oeuvre, circa 2007, nicely nestled in amidst my twenty years of lexical hijinks, demonstrates my stride at presenting the facts with an overdose of special effects:

> "Who's holding?" That's all I ever hear at literary events these days. As *The Danforth Review* watches you watch the closing season credits roll over for our illustrious online 2006–2007 season, you, the literary desperate, needing a fix but not sure where to turn, not sure who's holding this summer, still try to cop the VIP Bib/Bookmark Dinner Platter Combo ($1,949) which comes with the "Got Griffin?" limited-edition diamond-encrusted tiara. No, these are not the drunk ATM ramblings of an overworked cultural enthusiast, though they sure sound like it... As summer swells out of its Ugg boots and into its deadbeat sandals, the Canadian literary scene prepares to Scream. I know I've been screaming for the past twenty-four hours after looking at the star-studded lineup for the Main Stage. I mean, come on! It's going to be great. Really great. Toronto favourites Zoe Whittall, Rachel Zolf, and more. It's the who's on first of Canadian poetry, and it's coming like the weather.

It's weird to think that writing such as this would equal a hundred dollars in Canada Council money, as appointed to my bank account by *The Danforth Review* in 2007, but as the saying goes: what's good for the cultural worker is good for the sassy barista whose eyes roll at dawn. Yet at the same time, I can see that I was attempting to emulate certain literary heroes of mine, while at the same time offering a close facsimile of the writing community I knew and loved.

When I began this career as a cultural worker, private citizen of book and magazine publishing, I was living in Waterloo, Ontario, and the first piece of non-fiction for which I was paid came by way of an interview with Erina Harris in *The Danforth Review*. Erina, at the time, was an arts and culture staffer for the Kitchener-Waterloo region and had just published a chapbook called *the 82 short poems of eliza* (Circus Press). I seem to recall there being some funding drama at *The New Quarterly*[1] at the time, and I myself was starved for any like-minded creative writing people to connect with. As I would do for the next two decades, I ransacked the author bio of my subject and put together a crude editorial lead-in, stating the various periodicals the poet had been published in.

It was the spring of 2004 when I began to frequent literary readings on a fanatical level in Toronto. After an internship at *Quill & Quire*, I accidentally got an invitation to the Griffin Poetry Prize fancy-dress affair and found myself surrounded by the who's who of Canadian publishing as it was during the mid 2000s. I got the nerve to talk up Michael Ondaatje on the dance floor and told him about my exciting new novel and how his cowboy of a poetry book, *The Collected Works of Billy the Kid*, was a real inspiration. Ondaatje turned to me and said, "It's very loud."

And so I continued to pound the pavement looking for a humble landing platform for my weary TIE Fighter, or however the expression goes. Toronto Small Press Fairs, Canzines (including that time I saved one of the editors of a local magazine from being flashed by a vagrant), that fun puppet show I concocted with Ibi Kaslik, Jessica Westhead, Sarah Selecky, Paul Vermeersch, and others. The *Bowlbrawl* noise from the bowling-alley gutter. It seems like a lifetime, or at least a Main Event Era, ago—the kind of creative peak that never comes again. But I'm sure it will.

Toronto in the first decade of the 21st century was a very special place. At one of my first readings, I looked out in the audience and saw Tony Burgess, who became a close ally years later. That night, I remember him turning to a friend he was sitting with and asking, "Where's his boa?" He was referring to the promotional photos I had done for my website, in which I sported a pink boa as an homage to the ex-wrestler Jesse "The Body" Ventura. At that time, I worked as a bookseller at Chapters at 110 Bloor and then at the Yonge and Eglington Indigo after the Chapters on Bloor was sold to Winners. Rumours suggested that Indigo had agreed to pay the first year of Winners' rent as

---

[1] The year 2021 marks the twentieth anniversary (celebrated by myself and perhaps *The New Quarterly*) of my first submission to the magazine. I have been rejected by this incredible literary journal for a fifth of a century, during the first five years of which, I actually lived a few kilometres from their alleged offices.

part of the deal. The highlights of that stint as a bookseller were hand-selling nearly 90 copies of *Bowlbrawl* to Christmas shoppers that holiday season and being invited to the paperback party for Camilla Gibb's *Sweetness in The Belly* at Random House, where I was not only allowed in the building, but given champagne and strawberries.

Like a man in a zip-up cardigan, I fondly remember bike riding with my poet-friend angela rawlings in the Annex, and on another occasion, going to see the large Morrissey display for *You Are The Quarry* at Sonic Boom (where the Dollar Store now resides) with a certain anxious Montreal poet. I remember meeting a grade school–looking Spencer Gordon for only the second or third time at the launch of *Toronto Noir*, where I played "The Janitor" on stage in my first non-speaking part at my own book launch.

History is hard to come by, mainly because you don't know it's happening. But four years later, at that young man's book launch for *Cosmo* (Coach House Books), I'd meet the woman of my dreams, who up to this point hadn't existed, as far as I could tell. (Though she had attended a reading I'd given four months earlier at The Art Bar Reading Series, where we weren't introduced.)

Besides puppet shows, there were Ice Scream Socials, 18-poet readings at the Ossington (aptly titled No Way Out), and literary-themed Olympic Games (Canzine) at which I was presented with a championship title by Conan Tobias for finally breaking the seven-year curse of being rejected by *Taddle Creek* when an excerpt from *Savage* was published in the 2009 Christmas issue. Memories to last a thousand launchtimes!

When *Open Book: Toronto* first started out, I desperately wanted to be a part of it because I felt as though I had my finger on the pulse of the energy of a whole generation. I spent a good decade in Toronto hunting down all that was poetry and fiction for various interviews, reviews, promotional ideas, and other triumphant hype. During this time I also helped write a short film (*Sahara Sahara*), was on editorial boards for a couple of magazines, and in general tried to keep the streets safe from apathy as it related to books and the people making them.

Now, more than ten years later, you can go up on a vague hill in Trinity Bellwoods Park, onto a field on St. Thomas University's campus, in the stacks at The Paper Hound on West Pender Street, to The Word bookstore on Milton Street in Montreal, or into the refreshing innards of the Halifax Central Library, and with the right kind of sunglasses you can almost see the dog-eared shadow—that place where the page was finally read and turned over, one page closer to finishing one book and starting another.

PART ONE:
ENTER THE CANON

THE CATULLUS LOT ($0)

1. LUST IN TRANSLATION

It could be said that Catullus devoted his life to eroticizing pain rather than exorcising it. Have I read too deeply into his romantic crime-scene after-gashes? Perhaps. Upon hearing I was into Catullus, my octogenarian grandfather wrote me in 1997: "And what is your interest in Catullus? I read his poetry in 1932 and thought little of it." My identity at the time, that of a know-it-all outsider who left his family and his much-beloved younger brother to become a poet—a romantic poet, no less—was too delicious an ego crutch ever to consciously abandon. But unlike Catullus, whose death before thirty remains a mystery to this day, I press onwards, nearly twenty years older than he was when he expired.

Anne Carson's poetry book *Nox* is based on her older brother who died suddenly in 2000. Michael was a sibling who, having run away in the late 1970s, barely kept in touch with the award-winning innovator of the dead. This dead brother gets minced with the infamous dead brother of Catullus's poem, which was the catalyst for the book. Innovation is key with all of Carson's work, and the accordion-like reprint of her Michael notebook stands in for a traditional book, held as it is inside "a box about the size of the New Revised Standard Version of the Bible," according to *The New Yorker*.

From a "publicity" (is that a word familiar to poetry?) standpoint, the work is marked as a dead-brother tribute with a side of Catullus (and his infamously sad fraternal "Poem 101"). "Poem 101" has been read at funerals around the world. What I admire about Carson's book is that she writes her own brother into the dust and dirt of Catullus' infamous brother farewell.

I would like to admit two things: First, I'm no Anne Carson; but second, nor am I a hack. Okay, I want to admit a third thing: it wasn't until I was two years deep into my as-yet-still-unpublished Catullus novel that an editor at Beach Holmes Publishing wrote saying my work reminded her of Anne Carson. Who? Then I realised what I was up against. Then I realised how many other poets had written about Catullus before me. Then I didn't care. It was too late.

As the twentieth century died, Catullus was the poet on whom I had no intention of giving up. He was someone I didn't particularly want to lose to another. By any means necessary, I would be his and he would be mine. That's the thread of this storyline. *Identidem* means "again and again" in Latin and is found in Catullus's landmark piece in which he reveals a secret and married lover, Clodia Metelli, as Lesbia ("Carmen LI"). In *identidem* I hear the words *tandem, identity,* and of course *dent.* I also hear the word *identical,* as in *identical acts*: *I feel this again and again, I see this happening again and again.* I picture someone saying softly, "I dented him." This takes my breath away. An obsessed congregation of one, talking in tongues.

Perhaps two tongues. In Catullus's work, duality is a theme, the voice simultaneously loving and hating, expressing remorse and detachment, curiosity and apathy, without commitment to remain in either field, without commitment to an absolute. His most notable poems (outside of those devoted to his beloved Lesbia) are the aforementioned "Poem 101" and the gender mash-up epic known as "Poem 63," about the myth of Cybele and Attis, which demonstrates the poet's dedication to craft and intent.

Catullus's Attis poem, a concept album of a mini-epic if there ever was one, goes out of its way to be relative, even by 21st-century standards. Attis opens up the debate, now a regular topic amongst the aging icons who, in their twilight, are as foggy as Attis himself. In the poem, after Attis castrates himself, all the pronouns associated with him switch to feminine. The mini-epic, with its mythological high theatre, its domestic, sexual alchemy, is a feat that Scottish classics professor W. Y. Sellar famously called "the most remarkable poetic creation in the Latin language."

Building on an earlier article in which he discusses the promise and perils of reception theory in his "Catullus 63 in a Roman Context," Ruurd

Nauta proposes to reconstruct the horizon of expectation of the original audience, showing that the poem would have unsettled readers' expectations about marriage, masculinity, *pietas*, and Roman-ness in general: "Attis is a *gallus*, a castrated devotee of the Mater Magna, and thus a reconstruction is attempted of the mental picture that Romans of Catullus's time had of galli." Examining the protagonist's sexual and cultural identity from the perspective of a contemporary Roman reader, Nauta points out that Attis's behaviour stood in sharp conflict with conventional norms and values. By converting himself into a woman, he has disrupted the normal passage to heterosexual adulthood from homosexual youth (*ego iuvenis, ego adulescens, ego ephebus, ego puer*, 63); his present condition thus stands in striking contrast to the more conventional state of marriage celebrated in the other *carmina maiora*. Attis also abandons the social and economic order: a study of the allegorization of the Magna Mater myth in other Roman authors, particularly Lucretius, shows that a contemporary audience would have seen the self-castration as disrespectful of *pietas* ("duty," "religiosity," or "religious behaviour") towards parents and one's country of origin. Nauta speculates that Catullus's audience might have read his poem as an implicit discourse about national identity.

Of his 116 poems in total, Catullus's epics tend to be neglected, which is unfortunate, as they offer a glimpse into the painstaking efforts this young poet made to write beyond his Lesbia cycle and his angrier, accusatory, dare I say *bitchy* poetics. I believe these more involved poems were playing off the poet's own romantic life and its disintegration. In the dense worlds of his epics, Catullus drew on influences and imagery both from traditional modes of literature and from his own take on love from the perspective of manic youth.

2. "ASK ME WHO I WAS"

Posing as an ancient-Roman literary journalist, I made some calls to publishers in Toronto to see if they'd ever published posthumous writing—you know, would they be interested in publishing the dead? It was the early 2000s. The responses were curious. "I would like to see manuscripts from dead folks. To see if they've changed and modernized themselves in any way," said one beloved publisher. Another said, "The reason we've never published posthumous writing is that we've never had any submissions. But an added detriment is this—certain funding bodies (Ontario Book Publishing Tax Credit, I think, for one) only fund books by living authors." Added another, "If somebody pulls a Lazarus? Depends on the writer. The new work would have to do something for me." And further still, on the chance of publishing a favourite writer's work after death, one publisher beamed, "Should one of our favourite poets return from the grave, we would probably want new stuff. Assuming she or he died in an interesting way and could write about that. But if they get all maudlin and sentimental, well, there's no additional room for that in CanLit. As long as it isn't light-at-the-end-of-the-tunnel crap, I think it might be more fun to publish post-humously written verse."

In a way my second Catullus book, *Goodbye Horses*, is like this with a twist; I see it as my autobiography of writing his biography through his poetry. I spent countless years researching individual poems and their subjects, locations, myths, and backstories. There was a lot of ground to cover. When I pitched it to Mansfield Press, I explained to publisher Denis De Klerck that this was me doing Catullus at 43, while *Let's Pretend We Never Met* was me doing Catullus at 32. In the time between the two books I've become a father and less of a hooligan. Catullus desperately wanted domestic virtue—a family with children. He died without achieving that, which to me is a large part of his tragedy. I want to write him an ending.

For a long time, I thought *Let's Pretend We Never Met* was my masterpiece. It wasn't. I should know—I provided the cucumber sandwiches! But seriously, as the book's tenth anniversary approached in 2017, I thought of re-releasing it. Beth Follett at Pedlar reverted the rights to me. When I went to read the book, though, I realized how uneven it is, how most of it seems to be meta-fiction, and how dated the poetry felt/read to me. It was chaotic and turned me off. My new work reflects a calming down, both in life and on the page—though I'm still wild and irreverent compared to the quotidian parasol-twirling Canadian writer in khakis.

3. "I KNEW HIM FIRST AND I KNEW HIM WELL"

My 2019 Catullus poetry is archaic with a bit of New World, but I try to stay pure. It's a different situation, writing Catullus in my forties versus writing him when I was in my late twenties, as I have no romantic conflict in my life now thanks to my wife. So in my forties I approached his troubles from a more centred realm, which I think helped overall. I was able to be jaded, happy, moody, flirty, and disgusting, and then return to form. I trawl #Catullus on Twitter, but only to see how he's being remembered; for the most part it's for his infamous (and possibly worst) poem, old number 16. I think students like to refer to it online so people will Google it and say, "Oh my!"

While writing *Goodbye Horses*, I made a concerted effort not to Sophia Coppola things with shots of high-tops in Lesbia or Ipsithilla's closet à la *Marie Antoinette*. I wanted the book to refer to the past, not the contemporary world. So I researched things like the types of foods people would have eaten at food stands, which became an overriding obsession. I've always been curious as to how Catullus and the gang spent their time. It must have been a tiring life: half-blocks of apartments on fire in the poor neighbourhoods, walking to the market, rancid streets, the congested populace. And forget traveling quickly. Verona to Rome would be a two-week trip at the least. (It's roughly the distance from Montreal, Quebec, to London, Ontario).

Catullus couldn't chill out to Belle and Sebastian, drink herbal tea, and process things for very long. His lifespan wouldn't allow it (he died at twenty-nine), and he didn't have the emotional tools or access to therapy to figure everything out. So maybe that's my job. I'll take his place in the showdown, but with a family and without the need to end his/my life with a big question mark at the end. As readers, we get these raw glimpses of hatred, love, lust, and disgust, but we don't know what poems he liked or hated or how he would have curated his work had he lived to be 60 or 70.

4. GOTTA HAVE TRUE FAITH

I first tripped over poetry as a teenager. I had spent about half a decade mourning my early romantic burglary year (1987–88) and my perceived eleven months of high-octane popularity at age thirteen. Like Catullus, I read traditional poetry from the time of my existence (and a little before) but was equally influenced by music (everything from The Beatles to George Michael to Simon & Garfunkel to New Order, Pink Floyd, and Allan Sherman.) Pop lyrics and poetry were better than real-time dialogue; they were drenched in passion and had a directness I didn't know could be obtained. At the cusp of my second decade, poetry was the true filter; however crudely I was constructing my voice, this voice was the loudest. I had a healthy outlet for my fantasies.

These days, as I walk through the valley of my shadowy cerebral cortex, I can pinpoint the exact moment I first read the name *Catullus* and discovered his lexical attachment to the woman he loved and her infinite capacity for sexual inspiration. Spiritual inspiration too, as Catullus was not just a windup penis, hopping from bed to bed. It was a rainy evening in November of 1995, and I had stepped into a used bookstore near the university to find a tattered book with the title *Roman Civilization*. As I read from it in snacking portions over the next several weeks, I found myself returning to the short passages describing Catullus and how he was different from the traditional poets of the Late Republic, how he disguised his secret love, Clodia Metelli, by calling her Lesbia, a tip of the proverbial hat to the Isle of Lesbos and Sappho, whom she admired.

Two months later, as if I'd conjured up some lost love, I found a new book in Coles at the Eaton Centre in Toronto that I bought for a couple of dollars: *From Bed to Bed* (an abridged version of James Michie's *The Poems of Catullus*). At the indoor fountain adjacent to Orange Julius, I began to pore over Michie's versions of Catullus's greatest hits. His druggy words had taken hold of my 21-year-old mind. Thinking of Catullus as a musical band (which technically it *is* in New Jersey), the young poet started out as a Sappho cover band and, much like The Beatles, soon stopped covering the hits of a previous generation and started working on his own material. As in the work of many poets of his day, the influence of Greek mythology and poetry is entirely obvious. And as Ezra Pound said in *The Egoist* in 1917, "The Greeks might be hard put to find a better poet among themselves than is their disciple Catullus."

Through Catullus, from the first day until now, I find myself both creator and excavator. My archaeology of Catullus is necessary for me to maintain passion. For example, I've recently discovered that Lesbia's true identity wasn't known until she was identified by the North African writer Lucius Apuleius, who wrote the Latin novel *The Golden Ass* in the second century. When Ovid wrote *Trista* a few decades after Catullus's death, the poet did not know who Lesbia was, simply that she had existed.

Perhaps the biggest Catullus fanboy in all of ancient writing is Martial, a Spanish poet from first-century Rome, who mirrored and imitated Catullus's style. In fact, Martial almost treated Catullus like a god he was constantly trying to both impress and outdo (more of the latter) with his own brand of bawdy, petty epigrams, while his less carnival barker–type histrionics were considered "tributes," their flattery designed to get return invites to dinners. Like me and hundreds before me, Martial felt an ownership over Catullus's energy, wanting to be the poet who answered the metaphoric impossibility of Catullus's infamous math problem, "how many kisses?" I'm not a huge Martial fan. There are moments of great control and humour, but to me he's a pale imitator. Though I'm not about to *ceremonially burn* a *copy of Martial each school year like some university professors who shall remain nameless*.

5. "HOW DID YOU DO THAT? THE INTERNET?"

One could easily spend a quarter-day trawling journals, online forums, used books, and PDFs of texts culled from the nineteenth through to the twenty-first century and find convivial Catullus chatter, shards of intellectual inquiry such as the "ethnic phonetic play in Catullus," and other esoteric fodder that makes my Catullus cup run over with joy. As my years of research piled on, I would get word of new (at least to me) versions of Catullus lingering on the page. In the fall of 2001, my poetry best friend, Tavis E. Triance, wrote to say, "You need to go to the library and find Louis Zukofsky's *Catullus*. I don't know what it's like, but Zukofsky has some amazing stuff; the Catullus bit you can figure out." While I saw Zukofsky's radical phonic/sonic transliteration of Catullus as an inventive and important addition to his post-mortem, it didn't inspire me; Zukofsky's renderings leaned too heavily on the experimental and didn't offer any breathing room into the lyric. Reproducing the assumed sound of Catullus' Latin into English above the literal meaning seems to me to be an overextended gimmick.

In another message from 2001, Tavis suggested the ingredients of my creative veneer. "I think that Catullus is you in imagination/mind mode taken literally. As if all the poems/ideas for art stunts/delusions/fantasies could materialize and be a person in your life. Sort of like the Snuffleupagus on sex, drugs, scandal, murder, lechery, literature, slander, illness, and artifice. Basically doing all of the things that you think of and aren't always able to do because of societal limitation/obligations." The feeling I get is this: not to complete my Catullus mission would render me flat, starved of mirth, and with a digest of apocalyptic portents, highly unhappy, unable to dance. Twelve years after first reading his name in that paperback, I published the aforementioned *Let's Pretend We Never Met* (Pedlar Press, 2007), a poetry-prose hybrid (now out of print, email me and I'll send you the PDF) dealing with my obsession with the dead Latin bard up to that point. While I moved onto other projects, dozens of Microsoft Word files with "Catullus" in the title remain entombed in my hard drives and email archives, gaining age and their own unique vintage.

"Catullus intended to offend, which is why he is so loved and hated," said Carl Sesar, who first published his *Catullus* in 1974. What is it about Catullus that makes me keep coming back to him like a favourite vampire, knowing full well he's about to appear in my bedroom from a lightning storm–lit terrace and parse familiar phraseology in a family cadence? It's the mystery, the obsessive academia, the ethereal moments such as when I sat in a movie theatre a decade ago watching a cowboy film about Jesse James (which takes place in the 1880s, filmed in Calgary, starring Brad Pitt and Casey Affleck) and a supporting character/cowboy cocksmith named Dick Liddil, of all names, quotes Catullus to demonstrate his bravado as it relates to fellow cowboy and hired hand Ed Miller, while referring to a prostitute whose words he mistook for love:

> Ed Miller: Yeah, sure, she has been with other people. But the kinds of things she said to me, people just don't say unless they really mean it.

THE CATULLUS LOT ($0)

Dick Liddil: "My love said she would marry only me, and Jove himself could not make her care, for what women say to lovers, you'll agree, one writes on running water, or on air."

After learning the infamous marriage poem about Jove/Jupiter, Ed Miller, giddy, suggests they use these lines in a note to the woman, and, like a classic Catullus punchline—derogatory, satirical, and harsh—Dick Liddil replies, "Naw. Poetry don't work on whores."

The truth is, Ph.D. candidates continue their witchcraft on Catullus; podcasts on him are being recorded and shared online; terrible and terribly-acted high school–level Catullus-based history projects pop up on YouTube every year; new biographies, essays, and emo children of the Internet are quoting the poet on Twitter as they guide their paper hearts through this cruel world. When I read a Leonard Cohen poem from forty years ago, I see the lineage of Catullus's own sad state of romantic affairs. Take "I Heard of a Man" from *Let Us Compare Mythologies*. Perhaps it's a unique reaction I've forced myself to see, but I hear Catullus's own "Poem 51," which begins, "To me that man seems like a god..." and becomes a poem of quasi-acceptance, of frustration, longing, anger, and spiritual unrest.

When I listen to a six-week-old pop song sung by a twenty-nine-year-old pop diva, I think of cultural theories that examine Catullus's riffs on Lesbia as a literary construct, while the person she is in reality lives free of his literary garrison, free of his poetical and abject constraints on her person. She is a character who, through the ages, has been slut-shamed, nearly deified, and perhaps aptly described by Camille Paglia (who I realise is a polarizing icon in 2021—one who has clearly expressed less-than-supportive, if not cold and hostile, opinions about sexual assault victims) as "cynical Lesbia, adulteress and dominatrix...vampiristically draining the strength of all." Hardly the type of personal information one would use on an online dating profile. Lesbia is a character, but Clodia Metelli gallops past this sketch of a woman. When I see a tearful sibling interviewed on the news about his dead brother, I think of Catullus's lasting "Poem 101" (*ave atque vale*—for all time, hail and farewell), a poem so lasting, in fact, it's an online sample poem to read at a funeral. But my job is not to fill in the blanks for you, sing you a Catullus jingle, or tell you anything more about Catullus than what I wish to say. He existed long before me, and will exist, outside of me, long after you read any of the books his poetry appears in.

6. ARCHAISM BEGINS AT HOME

I've often wondered: if Catullus had not died so young, would he have culled his more malignant poems, or perhaps placed them on their own, away from his more beloved ones? Sesar wrote, "No matter how nasty or repellent he gets in certain of his poems, he manages to do it with such great impact and such style you're forced to swallow them as art." It's all about context, really. When I asked about this stream of thought on Catullus in an interview I conducted with translator Daisy Dunn, the author of *Catullus' Bedspread: The Life of Rome's Most Erotic Poet*, she said, "There were aspects of Catullus which were very difficult to write about from an emotional perspective. How does someone in the twenty-first century talk about Catullus's jokes about rape, for instance?" This question contrasts with the many translations into English that have made Catullus feel like a contemporary poet. "Translation is a highly subjective art," Dunn offered. "There are some popular modern Catulluses out there which make me cringe," she says, adding, "I really dislike anything that tries too hard to parallel Catullus's urbanity with slang which soon feels dated. Having said that, I don't want to be reading *copulations* and the like in a modern translation either. English archaisms are too often used to veil the fruitiness of Catullus's Latin. Why shy away from that today?"

Despite gender and orientation labels being nonexistent when he wrote (the time was more about class and power than sexual freedom and identity), Catullus is admired, along with Sappho, for accessibility to the modern reader. In her book *Catullus*, Julia Haig Gaisser writes, "Catullus is the most accessible of the ancient poets. His poems convey an emotional immediacy and urgency that claim readers' sympathy." Dr. Maxine Lewis, with whom I've corresponded, has devoted much of her adult life to everything Catullus. In one of her many essays on this subject, Lewis compares Catullus's lasting impression to that of Barthes, an author who "died but still haunts us, brought back to a semblance of life by his readers' desire." Lewis believes that modern readers' reception of Catullus is dominated by "an unusually intense desire to find the poet inside his work and to tell the story of his life."

Catullus wrote about things both highly accessible and deeply personal; he was an obsessive poet who wrote of the beautiful and the abject. Camille Paglia wrote of Catullus in her 1990 book *Sexual Personae*: "Catullus, like Baudelaire, savours imagery of squalor and filth. His moral assumptions remain those of republican Rome, which he jovially pollutes with degeneration and disease. His poetry is a torch-lit descent into a gloomy underworld where we survey the contamination and collapse of Roman personae." It's my assumption, based on the evidence, that Catullus was obviously gifted with a scholarly upbringing to gain such a permanent interest in poetry. He must have, at some point, found the traditional poets of his day a complete bore. His breadth of taste—encompassing traditional marriage hymns, the sonnet, the vulgar epigram, the lust poem, the love poem, and the myth-based epic—demonstrates a constant survey of terrain, taboo, and experiences from real life, from mythology, and from that poetic mood which can't fully express what the mind craves to deliver. There were, after all, only so many words back then. Catullus continually borrowed and gnawed at the norms. I would imagine that his reading and appreciation of art were not limited to the traditional outlets, or else he never would have bothered to use poetry as a medium to chronicle the highs and lows of public love. He would have married and started a family. Catullus was biding his time for what he perceived to be true love.

Besides love poems, Catullus wrote numerous political lampoons and, at times, hysterical portraits of depraved, incest-obsessed individuals, or the romantic impulses of men who smelled like goats. Catullus was an instigator and also very wealthy. We know nothing of his upbringing other than he would have been upper-class and well connected in Rome. He arrived there in his early twenties and never really left. For most of his final decade of life, Catullus was ensconced in Rome's social decadence and, of course, obsessed with Clodia Metelli, a married woman of power. Metelli, a poet herself, would have seen Catullus's gesture to disguise her as Lesbia in his writing as quite clever. Though she's easy to see as a literary construct, and an abject one at that, Marilyn Skinner's book *Clodia Metelli: The Tribute's Sister* provides insight into Lesbia as a person.

7. SCROOGED

It's been a quarter century of Catullus thump, thump, thumping at my door, a Jacob Marley-type haunting, but today I'm more interested in honouring him than pretending to be him or pretending to be haunted by him. The Catullus versions (poetry and fiction) I am writing now are attempts to understand, to know, and to reflect him as best I can. While a new crop of Catullus fans may rise and begin their own versions of my entry into Catullan obsession (oblivion), I'm still jogging on pace for whatever goal Jupiter has dared me to accomplish in my lifetime. And I know who will be waiting for me at the finish line, eating a tofu sparrow sandwich.

IS EVIL JUST SOMETHING YOU ARE OR SOMETHING YOU DO? (OR SOMETHING YOU DECIDE TO WRITE ABOUT BECAUSE YOU WANT TO BE EDGY?) ($100)

Fucking Morrissey. Stephen Patrick Morrissey—the former frontman of The Smiths. The man who turned millions into vegetarians overnight with 1985's *Meat is Murder*. The man who, over the last two decades, has distanced himself from all that he once allegedly stood for to become evil himself.

For years I thought he wrote the line, "Is evil just something you are? / Or something you do?" from his 1988 Irish dance hall classic, "Sister, I'm A Poet." But it wasn't him. The fragment belongs to Brett Easton Ellis, author of *American Psycho* and other novels.

I've been thinking a lot about genre and intent. Does poetry go through the same scrutiny that fiction does? Is Sylvia Plath's "Daddy" autobiography?

"I find that people are not usually all good or all bad. Instead of thinking about whether I like a character or not, I look for complexity," says novelist Barbara Langhorst.

> Even in truly despicable characters, such as Martha Ostenso's Caleb Gare, from her novel *Wild Geese*, we can see reasons why he is the way he is—so terribly hateful to his family. He is driven by his devotion to the land and his feelings of resentment about his wife's pregnancy by a man she truly loved. Instead of writing about heroes and villains, I find it is much more difficult and interesting to show characters who

feel one way about themselves, yet are perceived by others in a different light.

Even the most typically blissful moments can be darkened by poetic imagination. In her debut collection of poetry, *The Panic Room*, poet Rebecca Papucaru explains how her poem "I'll Start Tomorrow" had elements of evildoing in its conception—pun intended.

> It began as a short poem based on a story my mother told me about my birth. In the hospital, when the nurse brought me to her all swaddled up, she briefly mistook me for a loaf of bread, and not just any bread, but sourdough, which she loved. I don't know how long the hallucination lasted, not long enough for my mother to ask for a knife and some chopped liver, certainly, but in that first draft that's what she does.

Morrissey, who by all accounts is a card-carrying member of PETA, reserves all his hatred for human beings and their life choices. I became outraged while putting this essay together, because, as Tim Jonze's article in the *Guardian* states, Smiths fans feel cheated in the 21st century by Morrissey's accruing tirades about race and immigration. From that same article, published in 2019: Morrissey "has claimed Sadiq Khan, London's first Muslim mayor, 'cannot talk properly,' and declared 'Even Tesco wouldn't employ Diane Abbott,'—the Cambridge-educated shadow home secretary and Britain's most prominent black MP."

For someone who was so beloved and spoke on behalf of callow youth while giving home to the lonely, it's heartbreaking. Maybe that's why some fans have refused to meet Morrissey, even before the mainstreaming of his controversial ways. They didn't want to be destroyed by meeting someone so influential. That's what this betrayal is, though; Smiths fans are irate because the person who informed their youth, who inspired them to read (I can't tell you the number of books I picked up or authors I discovered by following the cryptic references Morrissey peppered through his interviews and lyrics) has turned into the golfing buddy of Donald Fucking Trump.

Morrissey's evil comes in all shapes and sizes. In March 2006, he globally vilified Canada for continuing to hunt seals, refusing to play in the country despite the millions of dollars his tours generate. In 2019, he lifted the ban to collect his Canadian payday.

During this time Morrissey also published two books, putting the long debate about the lyricist's ability to write well in other genres to rest. While his autobiography was mildly controversial (mainly because the singer demanded it be a Penguin Classic), his novel was so bad, my doing anything but providing you with enough of a taste of the hilarious reviews…well, I'm sure you might find yourself trawling the novel's entertaining criticism. Here's the tail end of the *Guardian*'s caustic caveat:

> Morrissey can't be blamed for believing in his own brilliance. But the spineless mandarins at Penguin who brought this to print should be ashamed of themselves. At a time when the traditional fiction market is under attack from all sides, publishers need to reassure us that their judgment is still valuable. This fiasco of a novel does precisely the opposite.

By societal standards, Morrissey is evil simply for positioning himself on the opposite side from good. But in writing, evil is sometimes a necessity. For what hero could exist without a villain to play off of?

Hamlet once said, "There is no good or evil, but thinking makes it so."

Worked away at over and over again for months, one's emails—turned into poetry and fiction—can wind up becoming something darker in their final resting place. Your once biographical, personal brain matter, channelled into a lexical prison, is now unleashed for public consumption under the guise of "literature." Are pop songs autobiographies? Is "Stan" by Eminem based on an actual person who imitated the abject tropes of a rap song? Did Phil Collins really see someone not help someone drowning and then invite him to the first row of the concert and sing "In the Air Tonight?" If so, is this song non-fiction? How about something more obvious, like Side A, Song One of Michael Jackson's *Thriller*. "Gotta Be Starting Something" is clearly a domestic recreation of the artist's mother making him poached eggs and sausage one morning in 1962, a celebration of the infinite power that exists between mother and son. Are there any similarities between the process of writing a book and of writing a pop song?

When I interviewed novelist Rob Benvie for Music Week one year, the Halifax author and member of the band Thrush Hermit outlined the differences between writing music and writing fiction:

> For me, the only similarity between writing music and a book is in the process of conceptualization and translation—that is, turning dumb ideas into less-dumb actual results. Beyond that, they couldn't be more different. Making music usually involves collaboration at some level, while writing is a profoundly solitary activity. Writing is usually excruciating, while making music is often fun. Playing in a band you receive applause and get your picture taken and have drinks provided, while writing just leaves you spiralling into misery alone at your desk. But the rare, electric joy of knowing you've written something good is, for me, far more rewarding on a creative plain. Both involve long stretches of self-doubt and financial anxiety, then fleeting eruptions of reassurance.

For the release of Michael Lista's sophomore collection, *The Scarborough*, the poet leaned towards standoffish answers as to how autobiographical the work in the book actually was. Compare this to the reaction decades earlier to Lynn Crosbie's *Paul's Case: The Kingston Letters*, for which the esteemed author received a fair share of death threats. The *Quill & Quire* review of *Paul's Case* teased at revealing that we are now living in a world where horrific crimes and the personalities involved are simply too much for us to not become slightly intrigued by them—if not, at times, completely fixated. Crosbie "also portrays a society fascinated by crime, implying that the media coverage of Paul Bernardo's trial turned it into a kind of sick celebration of his deeds."

For Lista it seems, from all evidence, that the poet was concerned about aligning himself too closely with the subject of his poetry. My interpretation, then, is that the poet made some effort to distance himself from a subject he says the book isn't even about. Yet the book's title, despite the absence of the word *Rapist*, implies the poetry was inspired by the Scarborough Rapist, who became a full-blown terror in southwestern Ontario in the early 1990s.

Reviews of the book never veer from this thread. Take *Maisonneuve*'s spin, which tries to balance the poet's intent and the subject's abject realism:

> In Michael Lista's capable hands, "Scarborough" is a play on words, an allusion to a psychic injury his hometown sustained about twenty years ago. In the late 1980s and early 1990s, while Lista was growing up, Paul Bernardo—often assisted by his wife, Karla Homolka—attacked, raped and murdered a series of young women in and near Toronto. In his chilling new collection, *The Scarborough*, Lista explores one of the couple's most notorious crimes, the abduction and murder of fifteen-year-old Kristen French.

In one poem, Lista tells us his age during Bernardo's rampage, but rigorously denies any passion that might have gone into voicing the concept of monster as an adult poet. His bait and switch—"I remember the terror of my mother and I didn't understand what it was," Lista tells us about his twelve-year-old self—is a spoiler that readers will never be comfortable with. The thing is, he knows about the terror now, and has for some time. Had Lista been an angry American poet and not the perceivedly fanciful, Ralph Lauren ad, Griffin gala guest who once put on airs about his perspectives in the world of poems in conservative Canada—had he owned the sinister elements he was secretly championing, had he told the *Village Voice*, "It's about Paul Bernardo!" instead of telling *The Puritan*, "It's not about Paul Bernardo!"—the book might have been easier to condemn, admire, or get upset about. Think O. J. Simpson's book, *If I Did It*, through the lens of competent poetry. But Canada would never publish a book like that. And maybe that's okay.

Originally published in *subTerrain*

THE WOLVES OF BLOOR STREET ($100)

Why in the world aren't more Canadian women running alongside the arrogant wolves of Bloor Street and beyond? Stacey May Fowles is busy, I realize, working on a slew of new editorial projects—none of which, however, is a collection of her excellent literary criticism (most of which, if not all, is about women-authored literature). Stacey's team could hire an intern to go through her contributions to assist in creating a more balanced pie chart. I'm wondering where the female equivalent in book form is to the byline ego of the male poetry reviewer who reviews just as much for his own glory as for the cause of book culture.

There have been recent books by women authors that have dealt with writing and life, such as Amber Dawn's excellent *How Poetry Saved My Life*, a memoir about sex work, sexuality, and how writing became her salvation. Catherine Owen's *The Other 23 & a Half Hours* is a survey crash course in surviving, thriving, and fighting in the Canadian publishing scene. These outings are a type of non-fiction examination of the life of a writer, tearing down the dry fourth wall of Canadian publishing, but with an air of community and generally marketed in a different manner than arrogant male entitlement crusades such as *The Pigheaded Soul* by Jason Guriel, a collection of barbed reviews that set out to be entertaining for readers. In his review of the book, Phillip Marchand (whom Jason cites as an influence) suggests that he was startled by Guriel's intent of entertaining people with literary criticism, as "poetry itself seems remarkably impervious to the concept of entertainment—certainly many poets would be startled to hear their art described in such terms."

I can think of at least three hundred Canadian poets (both male and female) who consider themselves to be entertaining. But what I don't understand is how male literary critics seem hell-bent on sounding a bit—if not completely—pompous, didactic, and cruel, as if they were in fact sadistic lawmakers. Is that entertainment? Being forced to see things under the sweaty gun of a barrage of mansplaining? Michael Lista's *Strike Anywhere*, whose introduction and press release seem to be fantasizing about the author being publicly hanged for his crimes against Canadian poetry, is a collection of reviews and essays that memorialize a particular career in literary criticism. It's well written, but the entire fact that it was compiled reinforces publishing entitlement and continues the time-honoured tradition of gender inequality in publishing. The lack of women publishing these books is a binary failure which has been brought to our attention for many publishing seasons.

Erin Wunker, chair of CWILA (Canadian Women in the Literary Arts), has some insight into why women aren't collecting their literary criticism in book form, and possibly more importantly, why some publishers don't seem bothered by this.

> I think *some* publishers notice the dearth of non-fiction and lit crit by women (and I'd add women of colour, people of colour, trans and queer people to that list). But, on the whole, I'd say the big presses haven't done enough to wonder why women and WOC and POC aren't submitting those manuscripts.

While some publishers are dabbling in the world of essays and changing their mandates to include work by women, people of colour, queer people, trans people, and differently-abled people, the dark side of the freelance writer's life in Canada is still rampant. "The toxic masculinity of some areas of Canadian publishing, the whiteness of many areas of Canadian publishing are the two central reasons those manuscripts aren't getting submitted," Wunker suggests. "The work is getting written, I am sure of it, but when you publish into a toxic public space you're opening yourself up for more aggression, and when the publishing industry is so beleaguered that it can't pay writers a living wage for books, why bother?"

Can we change this toxic environment and simply appreciate well-written pieces about publishing, about books, about writers without being assholes, holding grudges, or celebrating hatred and bullying? Who can help out? Why can't academic institutions, who make countless dollars on the hopes and dreams of aspiring poets, publicists, journalists, book editors, and beyond, and who claim to be moulding the future of Canadian publishing, get some contemporary voices from both genders into the curriculum? And I don't just mean a photocopied article. If you want to teach literary journalism and cite examples of contemporary voices in this area, why not actually source out those in the field? Emily M. Keeler, Stevie Howell, Amanda Jernigan, Anita Lahey, Zoe Whittall, Sina Queyras, and dozens more could easily be taught in schools alongside the Mad Men of Canadian letters.

Men can't assume they live in a publishing playground where they win all the prizes, publish all the books, write all the reviews about their male friends' books, and intimidate (either online, in person, or both) women who do the exact same job. Corporations have zero tolerance for this behaviour, so why shouldn't our industry adopt a similar policy? Because the toxicity is seemingly unmitigated and unchanging. When she was asked to speak at the Literary Press Group of Canada's mid-winter meeting last year about the lack of women-authored non-fiction manuscripts, Wunker found that a few publishers were speaking up on the issue and were "really vocal about wanting them but not being able to secure them. I think *that*—the why of why aren't women and women of colour submitting these kinds of texts—is the real heart of the issue."

Originally published in *subTerrain*

WHO KILLED THE THIRD PERSON? ($100)

He stood in front of his computer and wept, as there was not a single world remaining to conquer. No world would allow him to conquer it. He smelled the peanut butter. He saw the bread of his domain and wept—hating his breath, he prayed for death. "Man," Nathaniel G. Moore wrote, "third person sucks!"

In 2005, my first novel was an unmitigated flop, despite garnering a lot of rigged/real media attention. Now, as "I" investigate the rigor mortis of third person at the alleged hands of the first person and voices everywhere in between, I am reminded of Kevin Chong's appraisal of my cherry-plundering debut. Wrote Chong back in *Broken Pencil* issue 31: "It's too bad that much of Moore's debut is told in a bland third-person narrative that goes behind the scenes but lacks flair for characterization. When the narrative does come alive, it's normally in the voice of Robert Towell, whose pronouncements can be outlandishly megalomaniacal or anomalously highbrow."

It is estimated that by the year 2012, fewer than three Canadian writers will start a novel in third person. That's from sentence one, draft one, and word one. As is always the case with *Broken Pencil* research pieces, my investigation carries me across the vast land of Canadian literature, and to no one's surprise, the answers, when they do in fact come through, are unanimously written in first person. Toronto agent and former Gutter Press publisher Sam Hiyate says he asks most of his writers to re-write their books in first person, if in fact they have written in third. "There are two main factors," Hiyate says. "Market conditions and trends, both are connected.

"In the commercial marketplace and literary marketplace, the psychological stakes for a character are paramount these days, and readers want a strong character with a strong story." Hiyate says first person is the best way to reach this desired effect. "We identify more readily with the first person, we are spoiled and have built a stronger connection" with this perspective. Hiyate also claims that the resurrection of the memoir (even when it's faked) in mainstream culture has brought first person into a global market trend that won't soon dissipate. "When we want to know that someone did something, third person seems untrue. We always knew that fiction was a lie that told a greater truth, and we want to be closer to it."

I can't speak for every writer on earth, but when I write, I creep up so close to the characters I break through the veil, the veneer, the aluminum siding that separates me from them. "Obviously experiences and ideas for characters come out of real life, but there's a transformative thing that happens, hopefully," said *New York Times*–bestselling author Ibi Kaslik in a previous interview. "Like acting, you can inhabit characters, see the world from different perspectives. I like to give characters strong occupations: in *Skinny*, Giselle is a med student, so there's also a third voice, a medical-textbook voice, that narrates the action."

Is the complex way in which one accesses a third-person character/story arc so different on a cognitive level that writing in first person becomes an essential style choice, like fashion itself? "We're living in the First-Person Present Age," says Toronto writer Spencer Gordon. "Writers don't seem to want the excess baggage of a big, baggy, third-person story or novel. The standard compulsions of the third-person author seem outdated, less cheeky and immediate than the prattle of a typical first-person present narrator." With blogs, LiveJournals, and MySpace forums, one would think more writers would strive to push against the grain, but he finds the opposite to be true. In his view, first person is the surest route to accessible, marketable prose.

Andrea MacPherson, mainstream novelist/indie poet, creative writing instructor, and rival literary-journal editor, agrees. "It seems everything I read is now in first person, from first novels to novels from established authors," she says. "I wonder if it's the immediacy, or the ease with which one can immerse themselves into a character in the first person?" MacPherson wrote her first novel, *When She Was Electric*, using multiple perspectives, but every piece of fiction she's written since has used the third person exclusively. "I prefer it for many reasons but find myself wondering if I'm of a dying breed. I also teach creative writing, and more often than not students use the first person without much pre-planning or reason. Is it that we are drawn to the idea of confession, to the feeling of a whisper in our ear that the first person allows?"

"Everything can make a comeback," says Eva Moran, author of *Porny Stories*. "As I am writing this there are probably 100 creative writing students embracing the third person, just to be rebellious." Daniel Allen Cox, the author of *Shuck*, thinks the reason for the overuse of first person could be that writers of CanLit fiction are just sick of pretending they're writing about anything other than themselves. "The awkward teen at the party puking up butterflies, the dark Sith poisoning her friends so she can stage a dramatic hospital rescue: we confess, these characters are really us."

Jared Young, editor of the always fun and bitingly edgy *Lies with Occasional Truth*, did a quick count of the recent submissions he had received, and an overwhelming majority were first person. "Apparently we are seeing less third person," he says.

> Weak writers seem to use first person because they think it's becoming the norm or they don't know how to approach a story any other way. At least we're not seeing second person. That would make me want to punch someone in the eye. As Gradey Alexander once said: "When people write about what they know, they install themselves in the story with devastating first-person results. It comes down to laziness. Pure and utter laziness.'"

Beloved *Pulpy and Midge* author Jessica Westhead has her own confession about the first person. "Lately I have been seduced by the first-person siren song, because for some reason this point of view lets me write meaner people, which is exciting since I usually go for characters on the nicer end of the spectrum."

While "I" can't prove anything, it would seem that third person will never really die, but will always morph into something else. That we are only truly sentimental, energetic, and enthusiastic from the voice of a first-person narrator may be the result of years of media manipulation or a clairvoyant desire to have others immediately identify with our linguistic intent. I would suggest continuing this investigation, and long after this article has been enjoyed by our loyal readers, that we open a national discussion on this very topic and find out who killed, or who is killing, the third person. Is it you?

Originally published in *Broken Pencil*

FULLY LOADED ($125)

> Sometimes a word is important enough to you that you must keep using it, whether other people find it loaded or not.
>
> —Sara Tilley

> In writing fiction, I balk at using the word *beautiful* to describe someone's looks. Well, now I do.
>
> —Johnny Pigeau

We use them all the time: Loaded words. Sometimes we just cut and paste fragments, and they're there. Adjectives, nouns, even proper names.

How about *delicate* or *drastic*? Or *FEEL*.

We take them from songs, the news, television, and quotidian routines in pedestrian culture, or from our list of standards and practices that float in the deluge or rise from our brain dregs. Rework them? Cut them out or include them? We hack away or gloss over loaded words as we race to a sentence's finish line, in the subconscious word flow, only to read them later in horror or with concern. Word preference is entirely subjective, but that doesn't mean the words we choose to use aren't loaded or don't appear that way to others. As Associated Press missives continue to be the standards by which we read texts, as we continue to accrue new sayings and expressions, as we continue to comment on each other's social media statuses day in, day out, the temptation to use quick-fix, knee-jerk words also swells. What are we doing with language?

I feared that my discussion of this subject would make writers worry that the words they had used in their forthcoming books had already been used elsewhere, or possibly stood to be judged for their lackluster meanings. That nothing could be further from the truth became apparent when Trillium Book Award–nominated fiction writer Ken Sparling sent back this comment, which I will pass along verbatim:

> All words are loaded in the sense that we all have some unique investment in every word we use—they are loaded with what we bring to them, loaded because we bring to them something no one else brings to them: our history with that word, our unique encounters with that word in all that we have read. Good writing creates a space where the reader can bring her or his own invested meaning to the word, and the best writing allows us to bring our own unique understandings into that space the writer creates and then come out the other side of that space feeling like we've experienced the word anew, so the next time we find this word in someone's writing, we have a newly forged investment to bring to the work. It isn't that this or that given word is loaded. It's the pleasure that we can bring to another person by offering up a word in a context that honours what that other person brings to the word and doesn't try to definitively restrict how they come away from reading the words we present to them.

While Sparling's approach and reaction is philosophical, exacting, and reader-meets-author oriented, destroying my entire chaos theory, I did want a specific example of a loaded word to hold up to the crowd and see what they thought. Jenny Sampirisi, author of *Croak* (Coach House Books, 2011), says a loaded word for her is *daggers*.

"Because daggers show up in writing, yet who's ever seen one? I think things get described as daggers because it's an easy way to show danger. The word itself sounds like "danger," but the shorthand comes off as archaic and forced."

FULLY LOADED ($125)

Toronto playwright, poet, and critic R. M. Vaughan says loaded words can take on all forms and appear in between literary acts. "Years ago, I was doing a reading with bill bissett and I said to him, 'Should I go first or should you go first?' and he got very serious (in his particular way) and told me that *should* was the single most evil word in the English language because it is both bossy and people who overuse it often think they know the future, or what is right or wrong." Since the encounter, Vaughan says he balks at the word *should* and has grown a phobia around it, going to any lengths to avoid using it. "I also try not to use it in conversation, but I don't think as fast as I should prefer."

For poet and novelist Mike Blouin (*Wore Down Trust*), loaded-word syndrome is subtler and more laid back. "I try to hunt and eliminate the word *and* for its usually superfluous quality. And that's all I've got. See what I mean?"

"A loaded word is a word that can cause harm in some way, or that is perceived capable of causing harm. My mind turns first to racist terms when I think of loaded words—while just composites of vowels and consonants like all other words, these particular terms have weight, and they can really cause damage, depending on who uses them, in what context, and for what reason," says East Coast novelist and playwright Sara Tilley (*The Skin Room*). "I was just reading Carson McCullers' last book, *Clock Without Hands*, and in it she is very free with a particular racist term that most people these days would consider to be quite loaded, especially when used by a white author." Tilley points out that the book focuses on a specific time in the Southern US, so the parlance she found in the book was "appropriate and even necessary to use."

The concept of a loaded word, however, is perhaps something more subjective than anything else. Writers can choose any word in the universe to describe a person, place, or thing, project or concept, but we have no control over how said word will be perceived. As Tilley explains by sharing a story about a past theatre-grant rejection, "a word can be perfectly safe to you and loaded to other people."

Tilley recalls being told that the jury had rejected her project because her pitch used the word *feminist*, which was too political. "When I changed the mandate to say 'women's theatre,' I started getting grant funding again.

(I have since decided to stick to my guns and use my 'loaded' feminist mandate and let the juries decide if they can 'man' up!)"

I wanted to include some formative insight into my decision to write about loaded words, but felt that if I started off with my usual pontification, the piece would seem manipulative, self-serving, and rant-like. So I will tuck the rant into the end here.

There was a catalyst for this essay's topic. It was a talk with an artist friend in Toronto whom I refer to as CSR (chief social rival), to crib a term from *Arrested Development*. He suggested that the title of my (possibly) forthcoming novel was in fact a "loaded word." I balked, wondering if the rest of the living world would feel the same way. Then, in a moment of Zen, I was reminded of George Costanza when he was workshopping a comeback for an upcoming meeting. He was convinced "Jerk Store" was the perfect joke to go with, and Jerry and Elaine began providing ample doubt of the joke's impact. George refused to alter his joke, insisting "Jerk Store" was the perfect comeback, firing off, "I'm not gonna dumb it down for some bonehead mass audience!"

I also believe that given the volume of appropriated and associate text we digest in a given week, it's quite easy for us as humans to rely on default terminology—that we are perhaps, at times, inherently lazy. The loaded-word awareness campaign is new, something to chatter about and discuss whilst working on bits of dialogue, a press release, or even the title of your next underwater sea-monster erotic thriller.

Originally published in *Open Book Toronto*

SO YOU THINK YOU CAN DANCE WRITE? ($100)

> How does a writer choreograph the movement of letters within the flow and syntax of a sentence? How could a choreographer translate these glyphic movements from the page to the stage? Think about the metre (scansion) of a line, and how this rhythm could translate into the rhythm of movement. How can a choreographer look at the flow of a sentence for its linguistic visual or sonic material rather than (or in addition to) its semantic content?
>
> —a. rawlings, "Mark My Words: Text and Movement," 2012

A few years ago, for an extended period of time, I had a collaborative artistic relationship with Toronto-based artist Geoffrey Pugen. We worked on a couple of Bravo!FACT shorts together, one of which I co-wrote and one of which I performed in and wrote the voice-over for. (This short film, *Fictional Dance Party*, appears in the early parts of *Wrong Bar*, and the voice-over is also in the novel verbatim. The novel's cover features Toronto dancer Andrya Duff.)

For many of these Bravo!FACT projects, we had to incorporate something called a "dance component" into the narrative and do a lot of script rewrites and cutaways to legs in the air and posturing. Our last collaboration, *Sahara Sahara*, involved vigilante girls attempting to subvert the then-hot gas-war crisis. We got a grant from the NFB to blow up a car. I did a lot of the cold calling to inquire about equipment we would need down the road for this to happen. (I ended up not being on set for the shoot as I was furiously working on some line breaks for a poetry manuscript for Jason Camlot, my editor at the time.)

The experiences of having one's script edited versus writing a page that winds up in a novel are fundamentally different; with script edits, the actors can suddenly be performing something other than what you had originally intended. The consequence is visual. It's a startling and engrossing experience.

In *Wrong Bar*, the action culminates at a dance party gone to hell. I wanted to do my best to describe how these people appeared both to the reader and the protagonist and to each other. How do you write dance? Dancespeak is something that choreographers come up with, much the same way poets write about their manuscripts during grant-feeding season. One can't help but notice the similarities of tone in a description of a dance and a poetry-copy blurb.

Notwithstanding, my investigation's focus here is on the actual moments of dance that characters experience in a poem or fiction piece and how the author deals with these scenes. Do you skip ahead until the dancing is over? The song ends? Do you just indicate that time has passed and the dancing is over? That the characters are now in a cab, in bed, vomiting outside the club, or in the washroom?

Sara Tilley, the author of *Skin Room*, says that the difficulties of writing characters who are dancing is evident from the get-go: dance is, by its nature, a non-verbal thing:

> To try and describe people dancing is difficult, and to try and convey the sensations of dance on the page is, one might think, impossible to do accurately. I suppose that when I write about dance I try and describe what it feels like from the inside out, so it's less about accurately describing what dance looks like, as trying to get to what it feels like. What does it feel like to marry yourself to music and allow the body to move? It is one of the simplest and yet the most vulnerable actions that we allow ourselves in public space.

Tilley points out that she no stranger to writing about the act of dancing. There are dance sequences in both of her previous novels and the manuscript she is currently working on. "I guess I am attracted to the energy surrounding social dancing, the tension between everyday life and 'dance life,' where there is the possibility to transform oneself and to feel part of a larger community simply because you are linked by music. Have I written about dance well? That is for others to judge!"

When asked about dance in her poetry collection, *Croak*, Book*hug editor, novelist, poet, and teacher Jenny Samprisi says:

> There is something both disturbing and appealing about the spectacle of a character physically directed in language. In *Croak*, the Frogirls are, in a way, humiliated through dance— that is, if we're defining humiliation here as a loss of agency, while being simultaneously exposed. The dance scenes in the book are usually dictated by the Narrators, who are directing the action using non-human antecedents such as cartoons, animals, and puppets. The dancers are asked to dance as "other," which is mostly awkward. So, dance in the book is vulnerable. It's yet another way for the character to fail to perform as expected. The primary point of failure being the potential to fail in language, in the ownership or recovery of voice, but I think that applies to the body as well, so, enter the dance.

Montreal's Daniel Allen Cox, author of *Basement of Wolves*, says the dual trajectories of a piece of writing correlate with our experience as humans or characters in the act of dancing. "There are always at least two stories in a piece of writing. They can tell different truths. So too with dancing. The face can contradict what the arms are saying, and it adds meaning. There is no difference between writing and dancing. It is all balance." Cox ends our short conversation with a citation from *The Muppets Take Manhattan*: "Hey, I tell you what is. Big city, hmm? Live, work, huh? But not city only. Only peoples. Peoples is peoples. No is buildings. Is tomatoes, huh? Is peoples, is dancing, is music, is potatoes. So, peoples is peoples. Okay?"

Something to consider, for sure. So perhaps somewhere down the road, the publishing sect can get on the dance-trend bandwagon. We could have an anthology of the best dance writing in fiction and poetry in Canada; best dance scene in a short story; best dance poem; seminars and workshops on how to improve the lacklustre dance scene in your novel—taught, of course, by both authors and dance instructors; industry experts willing to take the time to nurture and shape writers' vulnerable dance scenes into something beyond the quotidian language one would think to use for such a moment: *shake, writhe, twist, contort, grind,* etc.

Writing dance scenes is time-consuming because you have to describe the physical movements while getting inside the character's head as well. And what happens when the song changes? The best thing to do, I think, would be to shoot some iPhone video footage of a night out dancing and try to sit down and write a few minutes of said footage, preferably in between song changes. So, until a master's program in dance literature opens up, I wish you good luck in the writing of dance in your next poem or short story.

Originally published in *Open Book Toronto*

PART TWO:
HYPE, HUSTLE, HELVETICA

Don't follow my path to extinction.

—Allen Ginsberg

HEATHER BIRRELL: *MAD HOPE* ($100)

I got the idea to inform the reader of the exact moment in which I began my thoughts about Heather Birrell's work after seeing Los Angeles artist Kerry Tribe's show at the Power Plant, which included the Canadian premiere of *There Will Be _____* (2012), a film on the Greystone Mansion in Beverly Hills. Every few minutes the date appears (the same date, February 16, 1920) with a new vignette or imagined moment. I liked this interruption and semi-didactic lineage, much like a page break, poem title, or story title that we find in the common poem or short story. From Power Plant's site: Tribe's work uses actors in '20s costume to perform diverging accounts of the events leading up to the murder. All of the dialogue is appropriated from scenes of feature films that have been shot at the mansion. Although these lines are restaged and taken out of their original narrative context, Tribe's work evokes a sense of familiarity or déjà vu.

In a very real way, fiction—regardless of its original intent or inspiration, original focus or gait—is a restoration of a semi-imagined state, a barely-recollected, never-experienced life. A moment of assumed acuity.

MONDAY, APRIL 16, 2012, 2:21 P.M.

I just got off the phone with an author. The main part of the conversation was about the possible subject of her column for a new magazine I'm developing. I suggested the term "post-genre" as her focus. As a former books editor, I have seen my fair share of press releases and publisher-created mini-interviews with authors, in which they share their insights into the process by which they created their final vision—be it poem, novel, memoir—and I thought that it would be nice to see some different approaches to book discussion, approaches that transcended normative—let's say even predictable—trajectories.

For years at launches we have heard those standard FAQs: "Is it fiction?" or "What do you write about?" I always feel that as artists, the fact that we have created our work and that it has reached a finality and been presented for all time invites the public to accept, inquire, and discern on their own time. But industry standards insist that authors weigh in on their own creations. So, like a boxer days after a gruelling fight—or like a lover days after a gruelling fight—one must try to be objective while defining one's own craft. I'm never surprised by the impassioned answers this vein of questioning elicits. Here is the question as originally posed to Heather, and here is her response.

SUNDAY, APRIL 15TH, 2012, 8:45 P.M.

Nathaniel G. Moore: How do you know when a story is over?

Heather Birrell: I actually have a pretty good idea of the ending of a story when I begin, although this idea may change as I write. I usually have an image or impression I'd like to convey to the reader, and I write towards this. It's good to have this "goal" floating out there ahead of me, but it's by no means always the way the story ends up.

NGM: In the song "Headlines" that national treasure and former Degrassi icon Drake sings, "The real is on the rise / fuck them other guys" (it's a personal mantra). Do you think with books like *How Should A Person Be?* and other autofiction titles we are moving towards a deeper reflection of ourselves? I guess what I'm asking is how do you approach the cliché "write what you know"? How much of you is in these stories?

HB: Hmm. The stories in *Mad Hope* are fiction. I hope the stories feel authentic and real, but they are not meant to be read as autobiography. The "concerns" (for want of a better term) of the collection are all mine—issues I have been busy with—and I suppose some of the characters could be considered my people—mothers, teachers, social work-y types—but many of them are clearly not me—a woman whose mother was killed in an airplane crash, a male high school teacher who fled Ceaușescu's Romania. But I would also like to argue that even those characters whose circumstances perhaps closely match my own are NOT me. The distinction between fiction and non-fiction here seems in the realm of intention. As soon as I decide a detail will be part of a "story," it becomes very clearly separate from me and my life, and I manipulate it as if it no longer belongs to me.

MONDAY, APRIL 16TH, 2012, 2:32 P.M.

After just re-reading the first story from *Mad Hope*, I was taken back to those strange moments in time where parks and woods and ravines were to die for. Where things went down, where dogs and strangers seemed larger and scarier. Where we grew up faster. I liked how tight and focused this opening story was, but I was never 100 percent certain if there was a moral to it. If a lesson existed in the hemline, let's say. It was an inviting story, one that seemed focused on placing characters in an exact moment and in circumstances awaiting casual fate. I don't ask Heather about this story because I don't want to be denied my own vision of it. Perhaps others will ask her what it was really about. I like that opening story and it still kicks around in my head.

2:40 P.M.

Scanning reviews of Heather's first book on her website. I remember Ibi Kaslik reviewing it for *Matrix Magazine* like it was yesterday. But first I read the Annabel Lyon review (from *The National Post*):

> My favourite beach read so far this summer has been Toronto writer Heather Birrell's short story collection, *I know you are*

but what am I? Birrell's writing is full of tastes and colours and zingers like "the slow red sun" that "bursts into the white light of southern hospitality. 'Y'all,' says the sun, and really means it. 'Y'all!'"

6:01 P.M.

For those of you in the know, it's been six wilderness years since Heather's debut collection of short fiction, *I know you are but what am I?*, was released to a slew of positive reviews and accruing buzz. This was coupled with other attention-worthy asides, such as being shortlisted for National and Western Magazine Awards, being excerpted in *The New Quarterly*, and winning the Journey Prize and the Edna Staebler Award for creative non-fiction.

Some things I learned about Heather's reading tastes and about putting her books together: Heather lists Deborah Eisenberg, Anne Enright, Annabel Lyon, Ian McEwan, and David Mitchell as current favourites and Kim Jernigan at *The New Quarterly* and Alana Wilcox at Coach House Books ("she prompted some great re-writes and came up with a structure for the stories that really resonated with me") as invaluable supporters of her stories over the years. "The story writer's road can be a rocky and lonely one—and although there is satisfaction in finishing a story (versus the longer haul of the novel), there is also often a sense of 'now what?' at its completion. And even once a collection is assembled, the fight to get it published in its entirety can be a harrowing one."

6:15 P.M.

The second story in *Mad Hope*, "My Friend Taisie," is a tagalong for the hustle and bustle of registering someone for their wedding, sharing visions of domestic virtue and the triumphs of introducing an adopted child into a new family order. This is sort of like listening to "Fast Love" on George Michael's 1996 masterpiece, *Older*, after listening to "Jesus to a Child." The song and this story are both spoken in a lucid, accessible, matter-of-fact, "listen, this is what it's all about, okay, trust me" manner that breeds interest and enjoyment. The story is breezy, full of chatter, and it gains momentum:

> Once joyful and quick to laugh, Taisie is now prone to bouts of humourless intensity when her attention is not flitting like a debutante between topics. It's the hormones, I know, but it can make things a drag or a crapshoot.

8:45 P.M.

NGM: What was your response to the YOSS (Year of the Short Story) campaign and how do you feel (if anything) about the genre in Canada?

HB: I think the YOSS manifesto put into words a lot of frustration myself and others have felt in trying to get our stories out into the world. I love reading and writing short stories, but I feel like I've been trained by certain naysayers to apologize for my passion. And the funny thing is that whenever I do, most readers deny that any prejudice against or even lack of interest in the form exists. As for the genre in Canada, my stepfather-in-law, who lives in the Scottish Hebrides, recently remarked that being a great story writer in Canada is like being a great football (soccer) player in Brazil. So we've got a rep! We should embrace it!

10:28 P.M.

When the newly forming family in "My Friend Taisie" returns home from a baby shower registry at a department store, the adults discuss further expansion:

> On the way home Anton falls asleep in the car, propped up against an overturned, second-hand bassinet.
> "Maybe we need a pet," says Taisie, changing lanes. "Now that we're like a family. A dog?"

"Fish, maybe," I say. "It's good to start small. We had two fish when I was little. Names: Rhubarb and Custard."

"Why?"

"We had no idea at the time—just heard the names on a British TV program and thought they sounded exotic. But our cat understood."

The scene moves briskly: a domestic lane change that turns into a quest for pets. "A book is a part of speech," Yann Martel says on the book on tape I'm listening to simultaneously (*Beatrice and Virgil*).

I had just looked up the Irving Layton–Leonard Cohen quote about preserving the self. It's in that film *Ladies and Gentlemen, Mr. Leonard Cohen*, in which Layton says that what concerns Cohen is preserving the self. That is what Thomas is doing: preserving the self as he recalls it to Taisie. Not because it's the truth, not because it's a verdict, but because it is how he remembers the story he's told his whole life, perhaps as a performance about the fish and his cat. The acceptance of the name choices. It's part of him.

TUESDAY, APRIL 17TH, 2012, 7:46 A.M.

I woke up about ten minutes ago with a splitting headache. I want to remove all the doors and people from my house. I check my email and Heather hasn't gotten back to me on the next round of questions.

8:52 A.M.

Reading *Mad Hope* while listening to Michael Jackson's "Black or White."

9:00 A.M.

Just finished rereading "My Friend Taisie" and the narrator Thomas's self-description of his own profile: "less like a shadow than a spy."

5:16 P.M.

Back from a publicity meeting/research jam at the Toronto Public Library. Bought a new shirt for the Teen-Choice-Awards-grand-finale-Griffin-Teen-Poetry thing (also known as Poetry In Voice).

WEDNESDAY, APRIL 18, 2012, 7:51 A.M.

Still recovering from Poetry In Voice. People kept asking me if I liked it. What is the right answer? I hate children and I hate poetry? Or I really think they are special kids?

In context, the night was entertaining. I felt, however, that it should have been hosted by a 16-year-old, not a 30-something man. The teens were dedicated and passionate. The room was teeming with poets and people who make money off of poetry. I asked someone in the row ahead of me for gum and she gave me a dagger stare. I think she was a cheerleader or possibly a (Toronto publishing house) intern.

Heather hasn't responded to my second round of questions, so I'm going to do some more reflections on the text.

8:28 A.M.

Heather emailed me about 30 minutes ago and will be getting answers back to me today. All right. Excited. Watching *New Order Story* on YouTube, but several of the 14 clips are missing. I have asked Heather questions about raising a family and writing and if there is a relationship between the two; plus I asked her about magazines and their editorial focus, whether they tend to showcase genres rather than individual authors, or if there is even a pattern. Sometimes I think there is.

11:31 A.M.

I get the sense that mortality is the key to the narrative-empathy machine in the story "My Friend Taisie." From the onset we learn Joe is deceased, and from there a discussion of mortality is woven into the piece; how arbitrary death is, reminding me of my friend who came with me last night to Poetry In Voice and how her day started with a clean-up crew removing a jumper from the asphalt where they landed. A suicide. And earlier in the week, a Ph.D. candidate I know just got a gig at the Centre for Addiction and Mental Health and was going to one of her patients' funeral in Hamilton. An accidental overdose. How many deaths go on in a single living person's workweek? How many do we witness or experience a connection to in some way?

1:28 P.M.

I got invited to a national treasure's house tonight for dinner. I am going to bring *Let's Pretend We Never Met* and some *Savage* postcards. Plus cucumbers and tomatoes. She is the third person I've called a national treasure this week (along with Camilla Gibb and R. M. Vaughan. Oh, and Drake, above). I don't throw this term around. I told Karen I'm working on this column but should be done soon. Right now, I'm listening to the soundtrack to *This Is It!*

In the short story "No One Really Wants to Listen," Heather writes about the found culture—or simulated found culture—of online advice posts or advice columns. After reading snippets from various moms about their experiences, with topics such as getting horny whilst pregnant, losing your sense of smell, or changing your identity, "Wings" writes to one mother in the forum: "Whoa! Pregnancy has made you all goth, eh? Which is funny because before I got knocked up I used to listen to a lot of punk and old-school angry hip-hop. I loved that shit. Especially NWA. Then, it was so weird, as soon as those hormones got pumping, I was flicking the dial to easy listening. You know who I can't get enough of now? Faith Hill!"

We then travel with the narrator in a childhood recollection. "When I was a child, my father packed us all into a van and we headed down to Florida, through Ontario, Ohio, then all those friendly waitress states with the fat people and big brass belt buckles." I think about the genre of the short story again. The collection is a great thing because it's like 12 miniature novels, really. I mean, you need the same structure—a sense that these characters lived before and after the framework.

Drake was right: the real *is* on the rise. Let's see if Heather has gotten back to me.

1:40 P.M.

Not to get too Kenneth Goldsmith, but I'm reading this on the back of *Mad Hope* now:

> This is a beautiful book: funny, whip-smart, compassionate and gorgeously written. Heather Birrell belongs in the short story pantheon with Alice Munro, Lisa Moore and Zsuzsi Gartner.
>
> —Annabel Lyon

In addition to her launch this Tuesday, April 24, 2012, at the Dakota Tavern in Toronto, Heather is reading with Carrie Snyder in Toronto on May 16. What a cool pairing. Nice work, Evan and Kate (Toronto's pre-eminent book-PR warlocks). I told Evan last night that this new article concept of mine—in which I include a timeline to chart my reaction to a book and my interview with the author—could be likened to something of Goldsmith's. It's intense, but I find that immediate reactions to whatever is going on are refreshing in that they're unguarded and, I hope, for the most part coherent.

My roommate, Astonished Mike, is blending something. He is always blending. Two days ago it was nuts. Today I think it's finishing nails. He does this at least four times a day. My other roommate and I are creating "Ban the Blender" signs in covert meetings in Christie Pits. I want Astonished Mike to use his blender in the backyard like a good boy.

2:02 P.M.

What I like about Heather's book is that it is "post-anecdotal," if I may (I do create book-buzz words. "Post-retail" is my new lexical tagline for the book industry). What? What do I mean? I mean so many books are carved from the crude matter of real life, which is great, but then these morsels are drawn out for one and a half pages and are told in perspectives that read as if they've just been cut and pasted into dialogue. We lose the sense that the book has been written, because it sounds as if it's talking to us without letting us think. I'm guilty of that in some of my cruder works, but the point here is that where a moment could have been exploited and overblown, Heather takes control. The stingray moment is a prime example.

2:11 P.M.

It's refreshing to see a dedication to detail and blending at work. A story about a stingray and a dad and daughter is told from the daughter's point of view rather than from the dad's. The daughter's narration is subtle and humble. Plus, she says "brambly thicket" in a passage. So a moment between father and daughter about the perils of stingray culture becomes an opening into the narrator's psyche. We learn as she tells us how she learned.

5:16 P.M.

Reading over Heather's answers. I asked her what her favourite classical myth is.
    HB: It's Persephone's story, partly because of Eavan Boland's beautiful treatment of it in her poem "The Pomegranate." Here's the beginning:

> The only legend I have ever loved is
> the story of a daughter lost in hell.
> And found and rescued there.
> Love and blackmail are the gist of it.

6:54 P.M.

My questions touch on motherhood, what Heather will read next, and the business of recording stories and putting them online. I asked her what she thought of the archival act.

HB: I hadn't really thought of it other than with gratitude—for the opportunity of having my work communicated in a way other than on the page. I'm especially pleased with "Trouble at Pow Crash Creek," a story that Miette recorded on her Bedtime Story Podcast (miettecast.com). Pleased and proud but also somewhat abashed because she makes the story sound so darn good—so mellifluous and professional it's hard to believe I wrote it.

7:51 P.M.

Raising two daughters (three and a half and eight months) takes up almost all of Heather's time, and time for a writer is a precious thing, perhaps something we non-parents take for granted. Of course, the experience influences her writing, as does everything that happens in one's life.

HB: I'm still mired in those hands-on, boobs-out early years. I'm tired; I have no time; we're out of bananas and pull-ups again? And: I'm tired; I have no time; the world is more beautiful, joy and sadness more acute, because I get to care for my children and watch them grow. And: a fierceness and focus, a more ready dismissal of the trivial and banal, a different form of engagement with the world and my creative work.

Heather hasn't decided yet what she'll read at her upcoming launch at the Dakota Tavern, but is excited to see how the work is received. "I think maybe a section of 'Geraldine and Jerome,' which is a story about two very different people who strike up a conversation and forge an unlikely bond in the waiting room of a breast cancer clinic. It sounds bleak, but it's not, or it is, but the bleakness is leavened by humour!"

Originally published in *Open Book Toronto*

JEN SOOKFONG LEE: IDAHO REVISITED ($0)

Jen Sookfong Lee's *Gentlemen of the Shade: My Own Private Idaho* (ECW Press, 2017) is the latest entry in ECW's Pop Classics series. As a highschool senior in 1991, the Vancouver author saw photos of River Phoenix and Keanu Reeves in *Interview* magazine and was so drawn to the images that she skipped school with a friend to see *My Own Private Idaho*. (About a year later, on the other side of the country, I grabbed the VHS from a local rental place in Toronto and had the awkward misfortune of watching Gus Van Sant's iconic hustler film with my father and brother). Teenage viewers coming of age in the sexual twilight zone of high school found catharsis in the characters of Mike and Scott and the rest of their dramatic, drug-obsessed gang, and we felt kinship with their search for temporary comfort in the chaos of life.

I recently had a chance to talk to Lee about her new book, yelling at parties, and the cultural roots of fandom. For fans of Lee's work, she has a book of essays forthcoming called *Superfan* about pop culture and her own life, honing in on the author's obsessions with such icons as Princess Di, Anne of Green Gables, and the Kardashians as springboards to discussing family, grief, female rage and its power, and trying to avoid falling into the stereotype of being a "good Asian girl." *The Conjoined*, Lee's most recent novel, is a blend of literary fiction with mystery novel and opens with the shocking discovery of two dead bodies in a freezer. The story moves from Strathcona in the present to Vancouver's Chinatown in the 1980s and Lions Bay in the 1950s. In her review of *The Conjoined* for the *Georgia Straight*, Tara Henley wrote, "Inspired by a grisly news story Lee once came across, the narrative follows Jessica Campbell, a Lotusland social worker who's grieving the death of her saintlike mother."

While petty theft and drug addiction are the biggest crimes taking place in Gus Van Sant's *My Own Private Idaho*, I find it telling that Lee's concern with the lives of young people in her community (the missing girls) is similar to Van Sant's fascination with the downtrodden youth of America's Pacific Northwest.

Nathaniel G. Moore: Reading *Gentlemen of the Shade* feels like reading someone's diary, in a way; it's genuine and intellectual, but it's not difficult or dense—like a great conversation at a party. When you started writing this book, how did those initial hours of creation go down?

Jen Sookfong Lee: Those first hours were very stream-of-consciousness, in a way. I had written an outline when I pitched the book to ECW and, for the most part, I stuck to it during the writing process. However, so much of the content within the chapters was really meditations on all the emotions and thoughts *My Own Private Idaho* provoked in me. I have always had a very intimate connection to that film that wasn't easily articulated or intellectualized, so I knew *Gentlemen of the Shade* couldn't read like an academic treatise. Nor did I want it to!

It's funny you should say that about a party conversation. My interest in cultural criticism started while I was drunkenly yelling my theories on how any cultural phenomenon is connected to a zeitgeist or revolution. I'm really glad I finally put some of that into a book! Makes me less tiresome at the bar.

NGM: In your book, you touch on River Phoenix's early life, specifically the possibility he was sexually abused and how it informed the character of Mike. Even though Gus Van Sant wrote the lines, River's personal life came through in his performance. I feel as though Phoenix's life and death were a huge part of our adolescence, which perhaps we as Gen Xers haven't fully come to terms with, on some level.

JSL: River Phoenix (and, by extension, Mike) is a fascinating figure for many of us, I think. His death didn't have the same reach as Kurt Cobain's, largely because he was an actor who purposely obfuscated his real self and, of course, privacy was still possible in the 1990s. Kurt Cobain, on the other hand, was in the business of selling his personality as a musician, whether he liked it or not. However, River was a blank canvas on which we could project our alternative dreams. He was visibly alternative enough that he appealed to those of us who felt marginalized, but he was also a cipher, and many of our forming thoughts on individuality and making space when no space was afforded to us seemed to be projected on to him. Will we ever fully process his life and death? I doubt it. His filmography is too thin for that and has been overshadowed by his brother Joaquin's work and life.

NGM: I'd describe *Gentlemen of the Shade* as a type of informed, spiritual nostalgia. I had a better word than *nostalgia* when I was in my car this morning.

JSL: For sure *Gentlemen of the Shade* trades on nostalgia. I didn't try otherwise! My goal for the book was to really examine the intense nostalgia I had for the film and that time and try to figure out why it all came together as it did for me and a bunch of people I knew who identified as social misfits. I'm a firm believer that our love for cultural moments always has its roots in bigger phenomena. You can call it zeitgeist or whatever you want, but no intense fandom exists in isolation. There are reasons rooted in cultural politics that explain why Beyoncé speaks to so many people, for example.

NGM: Do you think people born around when the film came out, who are now coming of age, will find this film? What do you think they will think of it? What have younger readers thought of your book?

JSL: You know, I have some friends who are younger than I am, who saw the film for the first time because of my book (which is a lovely thing for friends to do). For them, I think it feels like a historical piece, which makes me feel so old, but there it is. What I think struck them is the way gender and sexuality were treated but also the aesthetics of film from the 1990s. I do think that people who are interested in LGBTQ films and issues have seen *My Own Private Idaho*. It is part of that canon, after all. Honestly, I meet so many people of all ages and communities who love that movie, so I think it remains a classic that gets viewed to this day. I'm biased though!

Originally appeared in *Maisonneuve*

CAMILLA GIBB: THE EXTERNAL WORLD ($50)

Camilla Gibb was born in London, England, and grew up in Toronto. She is the author of three novels, numerous short stories, articles, and reviews, and the winner of the City of Toronto Book Award in 2000 and the CBC Canadian Literary Award for short fiction in 2001. Camilla's new novel is *Sweetness in the Belly* (Doubleday, 2005). Her debut novel, *Mouthing the Words*, was first published by Pedlar Press in 1999. Her second novel was *The Petty Details of So-and-so's Life* (Doubleday, 2002).

Nathaniel G. Moore: Can you tell us a bit about your education, background, upbringing?

Camilla Gibb: I was born in England but moved to Toronto when I was very young and was raised by a single and very hardworking mother. Neither of my parents went to university and there was never any expectation that I would, so in many ways I had to chart my own course. I went to U of T to study anthropology—I was curious about the world and the myriad ways in which we live in it—and became particularly interested in the Middle East. I spent a year of my undergrad at university in Cairo, and that led to me looking at Muslim practices in Africa—particularly the Sudan and Ethiopia—as a Ph.D. student at Oxford. I spent 1994–95 conducting research in Ethiopia and wrote a big, boring, dry, dispassionate thesis which earned me my Ph.D. but left me feeling rather hollow. I started writing fiction to fill some of that hollow, though continued working as an academic until my first book had been published abroad and I had some alternative income. Then I packed it all in—left academia in 2000 and decided this was it. I wanted to write to the exclusion of all other things.

NGM: Who are some of your influences, and if you were to suggest a reading list for the summer, or if you have one, what would be on it?

CG: My influences have shifted as I have grown as a writer. Early on I was drawn by language and emotion, not by plot—the lyricism of early Jeannette Winterson, the poetry of Dionne Brand and Nicole Brossard, the piercing angst of Sylvia Plath, Anne Sexton, and Dorothy Allison and, just for some relief, the raw cheekiness of certain British female writers like Kate Atkinson and Esther Freud.

Now? I read about the external world more, I enjoy good plot, I value the work of male writers much more than I did early on, and I enjoy a great deal of work in translation—people like William Boyd, Haruki Murakami, and Oscar Hijuelos. But specific influences? In the writing of *Sweetness in the Belly*, Kapuscinski was huge. As was the *Qur'an*. There's also a bit of Paul Bowles and Reza Bahareni. And the next book? A bit of Saramago, a bit of sci-fi Atwood, and a bit of Camus.

Summer reading: Orhan Pamuk's *Snow*, D. C. B. Pierre's *Vernon God Little*, Allan Hollinghurst's *The Line of Beauty*, Coetzee's *Elizabeth Costello*, Ishiguru's latest.

NGM: Are you looking forward to your upcoming stint as Writer-in-Residence at the University of Toronto in 2006? What do you expect to be up to after that?

CG: It's like a homecoming for me. Having left academia, it's enormously satisfying to return in this new incarnation. I'll be running a fiction workshop with about 12 students, which is the part I'm most looking forward to.

NGM: Your work has been translated into 14 languages. Do you ever get fan mail from other countries, and how does this impact you in terms of motivation, inspiration?

CG: I do get mail from people in other countries on occasion—I particularly did with the first book, which was quite raw and seemed to strike something quite raw in others that they then felt they wanted or needed to share. I'm always very moved by that. I suppose, as a writer, you hope to get at some emotional truth, and it's very validating when you get feedback that suggests that truth is important and universal.

NGM: What motivated you to concentrate on Ethiopia? And when did you decide this was a novel and not non-fiction? Did you ever feel like it could have been non-fiction, like a travel memoir?

CG: Part of what depressed me about my thesis was that I felt all the humanity had been expunged in the name of bigger theoretical statements. All the colour and texture and flavour of the place was missing. As were the people and their stories—the things that moved me while I lived there for a year with a local family.

I knew I wanted to "revisit" Ethiopia, but I didn't know the form this would take. I could have adopted a child from Ethiopia, or started an NGO; I thought and still think of doing both; but being a fiction writer, I suppose I did the thing that was most natural to me and wrote a novel. If it was going to be text, it was going to be a novel.

NGM: When you are knee-deep in a writing project, what is the writing process like for you?

CG: There's the euphoric initial flood of ideas, where the fingers won't keep up and the story is unfolding on the page and dragging you along with it, but that eventually yields to the slow and methodical work of editing and rewriting and persisting through the confusion and frustration. I am impossible to communicate with in the initial instance—lost to the story—and then engaged in something much more routine, which I view as the "job" part.

NGM: Was the white Muslim nurse protagonist Lilly drawn from any particular experience or interaction?

CG: I've never met anyone with a story like Lilly's. I knew that because I'd encountered Ethiopia as an outsider my main character would do the same, though I made her a Muslim, which I am not.

NGM: Because I want to create a possible web interference by mentioning a popular novel, and perhaps some random Dan Brown fan will happen upon our conversation, have you read *The Da Vinci Code*?

CG: HAH! I'm afraid not. I don't think I could bear it. I will, however, admit to reading *HELLO* magazine (although there isn't enough text in it to actually call it "reading") and *InStyle*. I've read one popular novel in the last twenty years—one of the Precious Ramotswe books by Alexander McCall Smith, because I was curious as to how this old white guy could portray a Botswanan lady detective. I found it charming, but one was plenty enough.

NGM: How does a writer's relationship to the text change once their book is published and promoted? Or does it? Are you thinking about this book a lot? Working on a new project? Or am I completely off?

CG: You care about your book in a vaguely parental way—you want it to do well on its own in the world because it is no longer living in your house. Certain characters stay with you, I think. In each book there's been one, and I continue to think about those characters and, however ridiculous it sounds, hope they're ok. It's Yusuf in *Sweetness*—he's just beginning to emerge, and I feel very protective of him.

While they stay with you, you move on to the next book. I did begin something last fall and am now trying to carve out some time to work on it. I'm not quite ready yet, but it's waiting for me.

NGM: Define *otherness*—you've used this word in previous interviews. To achieve otherness, we need to create at least two cultures, two dynamics... Can you expand on your idea of the term?

CG: I think where otherness becomes the stuff of hatred and violence is often between people where the smallest, rather than the biggest, differences exist. Hutus and Tutsis, for example. I'm interested in the way differences are artificially constructed to serve certain political agendas or social aims.

Race, ethnicity, nationality, and anything "normative"—all these things are socially constructed and potentially destructive because they can be manipulated and used to exclude others and discriminate.

NGM: Do you think Canadian writers need to go outside of Canada to achieve something that is actually about something? I mean, at the Tim Horton's chain #3253, we are not going to experience the missing years of Ethiopia's Mengistu regime, or stumble upon tales of asylum seekers or refugees roaming contemporary first-world cities.

CG: But there might be a guy sitting in Tim Horton's, taking a coffee break from driving a taxi, who has exactly these stories to tell. In fact, not *might be*, I'm sure there is.

Originally appeared in *The Danforth Review*

SHEILA HETI: HOW SHOULD A NOVELIST WRITE? ($100)

> You said to me after he told you that he had made out with me, you told Alexei: You should try fucking her. Lend me to Alexei then, to whichever one of your friends. I will fuck them like I'm fucking you and think of you all the while—your body, and the greatness of you that makes me do such things—fuck your friends while you're not home, or watching. And I will lick it up—whatever trails you leave and wherever you leave them. You just call me. I'll be there with my whole mop of hair to clean it up.
>
> —*How Should a Person Be?*

Last fall, Michael Turner released his first book in nearly a decade: *8 × 10*, a fiction, or novel, devoid of character names, city location, or general sense of time and place. The promo copies for the work alluded to this heavily during the early parts of the book's exposure to media and readers. But did it really matter? Was it a gimmick? No. It was a truth about the book that seemed emblematic of Turner's artistic beliefs around the time of *8 × 10*'s creation. As I interviewed him, I recall him answering my question about the book's construction and whether it could have been pulled apart and rendered threadbare from a large unravel, from a book with too much crammed in at first. Turner wrote, "To the question of whether this book could have been written clothed, then stripped naked later—it wouldn't have worked. *8 × 10* owes more to multiplication than subtraction."

So far, a little bit of fuss has been made about the fact that Toronto writer Sheila Heti's novel *How Should a Person Be?*, released by House of Anansi in 2014, is about a woman writer named Sheila, struggling to complete a play she's been commissioned to write. Hey wait! That's the author's name! I don't see how it's particularly interesting to dwell on. This detail is a basic approach to discussing the book, quotidian, pedestrian and part of what I call grim ritual. (I mean, didn't Pasha Malla have a story in *The Withdrawal Method* whose protagonist was named Pasha? Your honour, let's move on...)

Back to the book: I was much more excited about how readable the work was; how it focuses on a compelling philosophy, a socio-human quest if you will, one which the protagonist attempts to fulfill. At times the sexual lyricism of *How Should a Person Be?* is reminiscent of Henry Miller (as previously noted in Sheila's recent interview with Lee Henderson, author of *The Man Game*) and creates a rhythmic hypnotism that gives a provocative and conflicting view of a character's overall and all-encompassing desires: a desire for self-preservation and interests in playing out sexual subordination and in questioning everything that motivates everyone around them. These are the secret/fun bits of the book, the primal howling that goes on just down the street. There are artists and art parties, discussions about the creative economy, the creative landscape, and the obstacles that creative types face in a world that seems proud of its anti-intellectualism.

Heti's novel also shows examples of how people *have* been. Whether or not they exist in the story to show how a person *should* be is up for debate. Take the inclusion of expat Toronto painter Eli Langer, who brewed up some national controversy nearly twenty years ago when his paintings and drawings at Mercer Union Gallery received a negative review in the *Globe and Mail* on December 14, 1993. Two days later, police seized thirty-five drawings, five paintings, and a slide collection from the gallery. A warrant was issued and the art seized. Langer and Sharon Brooks of Mercer Union were charged with possession of child pornography. Langer (who is currently represented by Toronto's Paul Petro Contemporary Art) makes two minor appearances in the book; his work itself is described in detail and seems to haunt (at least for a moment) the narrator's reality and psychic space. This intricacy is just one of the many fascinating nuances the book encompasses, and it helps reinforce the humanness Heti's writing is capable of delivering.

When asked about Langer, Heti said:

> I have always found painters so much more interesting than writers. Margaux [Williamson, a painter and Heti's close friend] and I had this ongoing argument, where she thought writers led the culture and I thought painters did. Telling you this now, I see that the truth is probably that neither writers nor painters lead the culture. But that's what I'm interested in—the artist as someone who stands at the centre of culture and does the work that art is meant to do, which involves showing the culture the things it has forgotten to see. But to answer your question, I do think artists and writers are potentially great teachers for each other, because while both are looking at the same world, how you work with materials affects how you understand that world. Right now, I think probably computer programmers—those whose work involves a series of IF THEN and IF NOT, THEN codes—kind of steer the way we see the culture. But it would be nice to hear from the painters a little more.

How Should a Person Be? covers a lot of different types of human thinking and human processing. Perhaps that is its strength. The novel never tries to tread into other "experimental" channels. Its humour and palpability rely on the reader's own ability to question the motivations and emotional truths behind the daily routines we endure and continue to tread through in our Sisyphean quests to get by, live, love, like, eat, fuck, and express ourselves. *How Should a Person Be?* is straightforward, about a specific social code or order, trying to figure out how this code works, or if there even is a code. The novel never tries to tell a story that is not there.

Taking a cue from the book itself, which at times plays out in interview format, I thought I would ask Sheila a few more questions. I think it worked, as Sheila gave me some behind-the-scenes details as to how the book was conceived, and insight into what was going on in the world around her when her two previous books were released:

> I didn't start a book. I started thinking. I was thinking about why I couldn't read any novels—and about why it felt so dreary to write one. I was thinking about what would it mean to write a book that wasn't primarily concerned with style—the style of the sentences, that is. I was thinking about whether I was a good person or not, and wondering why I felt like I had no soul. I didn't know where I should live or how I should make money.

Heti says she carried these questions around with her on cue cards.

> And I carried around quotations I liked, and I read the few books I could stomach, and bought a tape recorder and started taping all my friends and transcribing us to help me understand who we were. Very gradually all this work became a book, which I'm very happy about. I love books.

I mention to Heti something she obviously already knows: she debuted in the beginning of the decade to considerable fanfare (*The Middle Stories*), followed up in the middle of the decade with her debut novel (*Ticknor*), and has closed the decade with this, her third book. I asked her about that time stretch.

> Ten years is a long time in a person's life, and also in the life of a culture. I think the publication of a book and its reception are very tied to what is going on in the world at the moment. *The Middle Stories*, before it was released in the States in early 2002, had a bunch of stories removed because "the events of 9/11" made the editor feel that certain stories would not touch the audience in the right way. I never found out exactly what that meant, but it seemed to the editor like a different book before and after that September. Do you remember, at the time, that irony was declared dead? So a lot of things weren't permitted for a time. Then, around when *Ticknor* came out, George Bush was re-elected President of the United States,

and suddenly no one wanted to read fiction, only non-fiction. If you looked in the *New York Times,* almost no fiction was being reviewed. Also, I had created a figure who was neurotic and could not leave his head; meanwhile the whole world had its eyes trained on a man who could not even enter his head. The common element to all three publications was that what was happening in the world seemed to matter. That was instructive. We all think of art—or at least I used to think of art—as some eternal object that could transcend time, but if a book comes out at a time that has nothing to do with the book, it's not really as meaningful an object.

How Should A Person Be? is stripped of postmodern tricks and self-imposed (self-referential) narrative structures that other writers seem trapped by. Though a lot of the promotional material does focus on the fact that the protagonist is named Sheila, I was curious as to how the author found the "voice" in her work. Did she consciously think she was writing about herself, or was that just the book's voice, or a bit of both?

It's a good question. I wrote the Prologue in about six- or seventeen minutes, straight through. It was one of those rare moments of inspiration. It wasn't the first thing I wrote—it came about a year-and-a-half into my work on it. A few months later, I gave it to Margaux to read as we sat in an airplane that was idling on the tarmac, and she was really excited about it. Then we had to deplane and it was another seven hours before the plane's wings were de-iced and we could get back on. Those seven hours, we wandered around the airport and talked about the Prologue. She said it was the best thing I had ever written, which made me happy. Then I sent it to my friend Mark Greif, who sent me a very intense email that showed that he understood what I was doing. Finally, he said, "Now you just have to carry on like that for 300 pages." I wanted to punch the wall.

Heti says the voice in the Prologue came to her in a similar fashion to the voice she used in *Ticknor*, but it isn't her actual voice, simply the voice of a character that had something to do with her. "I feel like the character of Sheila in the book is partly me, but with parts of me removed, and the culture poured into those empty spaces." She is thrilled with the book's positioning, straddling somewhere between fiction and non-. "I think non-fiction is wonderful, for it talks directly about the world we all experience—or at least, that is non-fiction's conceit. I hope the book also has some relation to self-help books. Self-help books are as close as books come to theatre, and I love that one is supposed to act differently after reading a self-help book. It's so direct!" However, Heti points out that the limitation of non-fiction is a block for her. "Why I'm not interested in straight non-fiction, is because journalism can't play like fiction can, it can't make things up."

While Heti is fully aware that some people will think it's a work of non-fiction or memoir, she feels that what people think of her is not the same thing as who she actually is, so it doesn't really matter:

> This is a necessary development, I think, not just for me, but for many of us. We have representations of ourselves online, and in order to maintain your sanity, you have to know that those representations, and what people think of you based on those representations, is something radically different from you. If you don't, you get all sorts of suicides. Online bullying wouldn't work as well if we understood our personas to be radically detached from our beings. It was writing this book—and my work with Margaux—that taught me this. I felt very nervous about representation before, as did she.

How Should a Person Be? deals with obsession and purpose and a quest of self, a quest to belong and to find a life. It also attacks superficial structures like club culture and pokes fun at the experience of reading a book versus the experience of having sex. In doing so, it ties into the idea of what a woman is in the modern world:

I was definitely interested in the experience of being a woman today. I would love for this book to be considered part of a century-old—and longer—conversation about feminism. It seems to me that having to contend with half-naked women all over the place changes how one feels as a woman in the world. It changes what it feels like to be a woman when there is such an abundance of porn. I have nothing against porn, but it has a tremendous effect on who we are. It changes men, I think, to see models of dominance in porn; to see the cultural ideal of a man as having a harem. I overheard a conversation on the bus yesterday between two men in their late thirties: working-class men talking about women. One man, clearly in love with his girlfriend, asked the other man, who also was newly in a relationship, "Are you going to move in together?" He was really eager and excited to know. The second man said, "No no, I like to take it slow." The first man, almost sounding humiliated and contrite and as if putting on an act, agreed, "Cheryl and I are taking it slow too, you can't move in too soon. Life is short, and you can't take it so seriously—especially when it comes to women." But it was so clear that this man was a romantic and wanted to move in with his girl and take it all very seriously. That kind of romantic, hopeful tenderness—where can men find models for that in this culture? I don't care what people take away from the book. There's lots in the book, I think, stuff about how to protect what we love from our own impulse to destroy it.

Originally published in *Open Book Toronto*

ZSUZSI GARTNER: THE CRAFTY WICK ($125)

Over the last couple of years, one of my closest friends in the writing community and I have been meeting up, and, on occasion, have talked fandom for certain styles of fiction. He often professes that no one in Canada writes in an elongated sentence structure, the kind of writing that luxuriates in a profound and occasionally maniacal system of thought. I was reminded of these discussions while reading Zsuzsi Gartner's latest book, *Better Living Through Plastic Explosives*, possibly the best-designed book in the history of Canadian publishing. Whether this will lead to a revolution in how prose is delivered and absorbed remains to be seen.

Gartner was born in Winnipeg and now lives in Vancouver. In 1999, her first collection of short fiction, *All the Anxious Girls on Earth*, was published. In 2009, she edited *Darwin's Bastards*, an all-star anthology of speculative fiction, which led to a parade of innovative and entertaining launches. The *Globe and Mail* praised it, saying, "Canadians who read this book will be proud to see that their imaginative landscape is as wildly bizarre—and honest to the truth—as ever," and challenged readers to look past the apocalyptic tones for virtue.

The stories in *Better Living Through Plastic Explosives* appear to be carved from emotional starting points, where characters are fully formed and in the midst of vignettes of confrontation or interpretation. I asked Gartner if she had ever heard about the "old future." It's a term they applied to George Lucas for his first stab at the *Star Wars* trilogy: an aesthetic that is futuristic but is beaten up, established, and raw.

"I love the term 'old future'! I'm reading a lot of steampunk stuff right now and it seems to apply to that as well, although that wasn't something I was conscious of while writing the stories in *Better Living...*" Gartner tells me in rapid-fire syntax (special effects via email).

I continued to assault the keyboard with queries, like a Dr.-Pepper-strung-out-high-school-arcade pimp: How do you feel about your characters: did you beat them up enough before final-drafting them and putting them out on exhibit? How drastically do your stories change from early drafts to their final resting place in the virtues of domestic voyeurism and lucid hilarity?

"My characters come to me already 'beaten up' (or pre-distressed?), and then I don't start writing really until I understand most of the story I want to tell (in the form of notes in notebook, and on index cards, and in my head)," Gartner explained.

> I usually have my starting point and I write my endings early on, so much of the struggle during the actual writing process is getting from A to Z. Because I usually start each writing day going through what I have from beginning to end and adding and layering and filling in incomplete scenes, I don't so much have "drafts" as multitudinous layers, so by the end there is a (hopefully) satisfying palimpsest (or, as you say: "their final resting place in the virtues of domestic voyeurism and lucid hilarity"! that's a keeper for me).

Lately I have been examining the short story, and it is, in my opinion, a vulnerable and possibly endangered species, yet authors such as Jessica Westhead, Sarah Selecky, Carolyn Black, Matthew Trafford, and Hal Niedzviecki are demonstrating that not everyone is "working on their novel." I asked Gartner to comment:

> I really don't think it's endangered so much as undervalued by publishers (and marketing departments), who treat it as a warm-up act to a novel and demand a two-book deal from authors with the second book being a novel (which the bulk of the advance goes to). I want to make it absolutely clear though that neither Patrick Crean, who published my first

collection when he was at Key Porter, nor Nicole Winstanley at Penguin with *Better Living…*, demanded a two-book deal. They respected and valued the story collections in and of themselves, for which I am very grateful. If only booksellers and awards lists and Heather Reisman would follow suit, the readers and customers would follow.

Gartner points out with poise that Jessica Westhead's first book was in fact a novel (*Pulpy and Midge*), and her latest book is a story collection. She reminds me that Sarah Selecky "is uniquely and strongly dedicated to the short story," while Matthew Trafford is, "I believe, now working on a novel, and Hal Niedzviecki has published novels" (*The Program* and *Ditch*). She surmises: "That said, I have no genre prejudices. My next book may be a YA steampunk novel, a book of non-fiction, or another story collection—or all of the above!"[2]

This of course brings us from the teetering wall of the present literary landscape to the soft, doughy horizon of the future. What powder keg of literary acumen does Gartner have in store for us down the road? "Ah, I've already spilled part of the beans above. As for daily routine, I currently don't have one, as I've just come off a full month of being under the weather, teaching in Banff, and travelling in and out of town doing various book-launch events. When I am writing, I have to get at it first thing in the morning and am not allowed to check email or Internet at all or answer the phone until three hours have gone by or I've written at least 500 words. I have to be my own bad cop; otherwise the mental energy of the day gets squandered."

Originally published in *Open Book Toronto*

---

2   Her next book was the novel (her first) *The Beguiling*, published in fall 2020.

CHUCK PALAHNIUK: MIGRATION PATTERNS IN 21ST-CENTURY BIG-BOX RETAIL ($100)

The events described are unlikely and preposterous, though possibly not untrue. Sort of like Pirates of the Caribbean 3.

>Indigo Eglinton, Store #278
>Tuesday, May 22, 2007
>1 p.m. – 12 a.m.
>Toronto, Canada

This is my ex-manager, all nineteen years of her, at noon: "I've been told Chuck's doing a soft signing for his hardcore fans, but he'll be in the staff room all afternoon signing paperbacks."

"His books?" I ask.

"Yes, his books." And my ex-manager scurries off to an office to check her Facebook.

I don't follow. I'm still in litigation with MySpace and can't open a Facebook account.

In 2005 Chuck Palahniuk came to this same Indigo to read from and celebrate the Canadian release of *Haunted*. Rumours started floating that he was dosing the Yonge & Eglinton population with roofies, though no charges were ever brought up because the Y & E population itself is considerably dull and thoughtless to begin with.

This migration pattern repeats itself. We are in *Rant* country, and the Random House vipers are here too, snaking around the shelves and scented gift items in biblical numbers.

On the way to the washroom, I brush past Chuck, and since I've been "channelling" George Michael (*Quill & Quire*, May 2007), it seems a fitting location to begin my *TDR* interview with the man who penned *Fight Club* and *Choke*.

"Chuck, your new book is written in the form of an oral history with a multitude of perspectives. Was this something you had planned on from the get-go?"

"Why don't you mind your own goddamn business!" Chuck replies. He's dressed in black pants and a white dress shirt, very Tyler Durden.

I tell him he is being unreasonable and compliment his ability to imitate the typically thoughtless and irritating Y & E Indigo customer. I then explain how he also fits in this area fashion-wise, as *Funhouse Magazine* has recently featured this horror show of a neighbourhood in an article called "The Worst Dressed Neighbourhoods in the History of Cloth."

I continue with the interview from outside the closed men's-bathroom door. "Would you please just open up, for your fans if not for me!" He doesn't answer. I wait for what seems like an hour but is more honestly about three minutes, then decide to bother the people in HMV and buy all the copies of *Fight Club* to peddle outside, even though Indigo signage clearly states no memorabilia, mobiles, or xylophones. For some reason I also buy *The Goonies* and *Seed of Chucky*.

A half an hour later, Chuck is back in the staff room soft-signing his heart out while his "hardcore fans" are lined up in the hundreds, most of them celebrating Teen Pregnancy Week here at Indigo, dressed in bloody bridal attire. They snake all the way into the kids' section. Some have plastic vomit and broken ashtrays with them. Most have copies of *Survivor* and *Choke* in their grubby little paws.

"Is Chuck your favourite author in Canada? I mean today?" I ask one pimply prince.

"Yes. Even when he's not here, he's my favourite."

"You make me want to kill myself," I reply.

"But how can that be? I just met you."

I turn to his friend. "And what about you, what is *your* favourite Chuck book?"

"*Choke*."

"Indeed."

Chuck Palahniuk is a big deal in Canada. They've even named an underground parking lot after him in Pickering, mainly because it resembles the underground parking lot in *Fight Club*, but that's beside the point. It seems like the people of this country like it when he's here, perhaps more than any other author in North America. I mean, he's bigger than candles today, and that's saying a lot here at Indigo.

Using my Indigo immunity, I call an emergency meeting with my ex-manager and some cash supervisors. I explain how rude Chuck was in the hallway, and how apathetic he sounded through the closed men's washroom door. "He's not willing to do business with me, and that's bad business for *The Danforth Review*. I think as a result of this, we have to teach him a lesson. This country isn't his ATM, his place to come and snack, impregnate our cashiers, eat organic trail mix from our hair-dryered-out skulls. We should swerve tonight's reading. We should swerve his whole goddamn life!" I yell.

"What are you saying, Nathaniel?"

"Okay, Betty, or Sandra, go print up a CER (Customer Experience Representative) contract, get him to sign it saying it's a release for Indigo to publish his photos online or something."

"Then what?" my ex-manager says to me she says. *Then what?*

I say, "Then we knock him out and put him in a big bag, throw him in the safe with the other people we keep around, then when he comes to in the morning, fit him with a vest and put him on cash, opening shift, till number three."

"We can't do that. Listen, let me talk to Chuck, see if he's willing to do the *TDR* interview," my ex-manager says. I think it's Betty. But she grabs me by the wrist. "Go put on your sweaty red dress!"

I shake my head in confusion and turn my attention away from Betty and continue. "He's left us no choice," I continue. "Look, we have to keep him in the store, it'll be good for business, and we have to do this on our terms. Heather would want this too, you know it, it's not fair that she's in the Bahamas!"

"There's going to be a lot of heat on you, Nathaniel, can you handle it?" Betty says, watching me slip out of my civilian clothing and into my alleged red dress.

"You're talking to the man who was ranked 7th in I-Rewards sales last spring in all of Ontario. Sure I can handle it. I have so far. I just think we have to set an example. We can joke about catering to our horribly-dressed customers, carrying them around the store on our backs, reading the books for them, and doing their children's homework, but they're laughing at us harder than we laugh at them when they leave the store. They're getting away with murder, behaviour-wise. At least this way, they'll think twice before talking back to us or complaining that we took away the beds and the couches. Like they don't have furniture at home! Fuck them, fuck them and their Cotton Ginny scowls."

So we decide that we'll all beat Chuck down after the last fan has pimple-popped his way down the Bruce-Mau-designed stairwell (which I used to spit-shine with my sad cheerleader tears every Friday night).

A few of my vest-wearing associates warm to the plan when they hear Chuck berating a young philosophy grad named Des (who is not even two weeks into the vest) about the "piss-poor" bottled water, that he wouldn't even let his goldfish drink the stuff.

"That's it," I said to the group. We were seven. "We go in, take him down with sharpened gift cards and scentless third-world candles, and put him in this big denim bag."

"Where did you get this large bag from, Nathaniel?" Harry asked.

"Wouldn't you like to know, Harry. We don't have time to discuss this by committee." I'm waiting for him to yell I AM NOT A COMMITTEE! but I remember that he hasn't seen *The Empire Strikes Back* 1,324 times.

Des joins us 40 seconds later, so now we are eight. "I can't wait," Des says. "I mean, yesterday it was that Goth boy asking me out, today it's Chuck…"

"Des!" I shout. "We don't have time for your fucking drama. I know you're new, but this is serious stuff and it's more effective if I remain the singular narrative God. You're all sprawly."

Des blinks in accordance, apologetic and a bit ashamed, as we all begin our attack.

"He's not bleeding, he's likely dehydrated," I yell.

The eight of us are enough to get ol' Chuckster into the denim bag and down the lazy-customer elevator. I throw in some stale chocolates and three bottles of microwaved (1:02) Indigo Clear water and we close up the bag, tossing it into the safe in the cash office.

Mike Fuhr from Random House is standing in the middle of Bruce's stairwell and is livid. "Let me handle this," I say, noticing my ex-manager sniffing the armpits of her stretchy red dress.

"Where is Chuck?" Mike asks me. Mike and I go way back. If it isn't a nod at Book Expo once a year, then it's a toast with champagne and strawberries at Random House headquarters celebrating another Giller nomination or a polite e-mail praising my violent bowling theatrics on YouTube.

"Chuck is resting in our hospitality suite," I assure him. "He has phase-seven carpal in both of his hands though, and it's spreading to his lower intestine."

"Is he going to be all right?"

"Yes, we've given him 300 cc's of FCC. Mike, have I ever let you down?"

The next morning, I visit my old store before a conference call with my psychiatrists, my personal trainer, and an LPG sales rep in Halifax.

I see Chuck Palahniuk (sporting a Sponge Bob band-aid on the bridge of his nose) at the cash in a vest ringing in a stack of Dan Brown books. Chuck's customer is hyper, like a puppy ripping newsprint with his feet.

"He's so good," the customer insists, pointing to the books.

I can't resist. "She's not talking about you, Chuck!" I yell from the edge of the counter, even though I know that my yelling is in clear violation of the Indigo Sales Prevention Act of 2006. Good thing I have immunity.

"I just loved *The Da Vinci Code*." The customer's eyes light up, wanting validation for this prehistoric and most desperate of retail gestures.

"Yes, he's very popular," Chuck finally says, giving in to her consumer vanity, his lip still fat from being sucker-punched by Des and choked out in Betty's armpits.

As I leave, a small tear goldfishes at my right tear duct, and I hear Chuck whimper out a question to the cashier next to him.

"When is my first break?"

Yeah, choke on it, Chuck. This is your *new* life, and it's ending one Dan Brown gift receipt at a time.

Originally published in *The Danforth Review*

DEREK MCCORMACK: TO BE GAY AND GET FUCKED UP ($125)

Author Note: Derek McCormack and I have been friendly since around 2003. Always polite, sweet, and charming, Derek is one of the things about Toronto I miss the most. Artistically, there couldn't be an author more opposite to my style. He's brief, succinct, and humorous in a way I'll never be. Someone once came up to me after Derek had read and said, "He makes your stuff look like the Girl Scouts." In this double book profile, conducted years apart but combined for the purpose of this book, McCormack examines his literary thread count and oh so much more...

In Derek McCormack's panicked new novel, a reporter from *Vampire Vogue* remarks, "We wear clothes... We're not werewolves." Sigh. McCormack has done it again. But he'll be the last to admit it. His new novel *The Show That Smells* (ECW Press) is already garnering positive attention and a lot of his friends (and enemies) are calling it his best yet. The copy reads like an experimental film of the Ed Wood variety: "Starring a host of Hollywood's brightest stars, including Coco Chanel, Lon Chaney, and the Carter Family, *The Show That Smells* is a thrilling tale of HILLBILLIES, HIGH FASHION, AND HORROR!"

I caught up with Mr. McCormack to discuss his new literary offering. (In one such encounter, on a sunny Monday morning, I encountered the author as I limped along Queen West, having been "bitten" on the heel by a vampiric construction caution sign in a fit of publishing irony.)

It's been five years since McCormack launched *The Haunted Hillbilly*. When it came time to start work on his new novel, the author had to map out a completely different premise. "It starred Jimmie Rodgers—I knew from before finishing *The Haunted Hillbilly* that I wanted to write a novel about Jimmie Rodgers—but it had a completely different premise." The author worked on it for a year, then began to chart another course. "They both blew. I abandoned them in favour of the current premise, which blows less, I pray."

I bring up a previous interview with John Degen, who asked why McCormack's sentences were so short and why "do you run away from a description you've only just started." I offer him four possible answers:

a) I am the same writer I was in 2003.
b) I didn't really think about it or remember the question being asked.
c) Maybe I have shortened my sentences more.
d) Most things make me want to cry.

McCormack chooses d.

The Show that Smells is scheduled for publication in the US as well as Canada, but McCormack is wary of one aspect of the tour, suggesting that his new novel is a very difficult one to read aloud. "There's tons of repetition in it; I have read from it a few times and within minutes the audience always gets angry. That said, I'm excited to tour." McCormack has a steady following in the States, and for his previous book tour with *The Haunted Hillbilly*, he read at City Lights Books in San Francisco with Dennis Cooper, Benjamin Weissman, and Martha Kinney. "Kevin Killian introduced us. It was a dream."

Nathaniel G. Moore: Do you know that *The Show That Smells* is going to be taught at University next year? How does that make you feel? Like Eminem?

Derek McCormack: No, like Auntie Em!

NGM: But, Derek, you must have realized that people will actually read your book, and that they haven't had anything new from you in five years. So?

DM: I want my book to make men love me. Would you like to know which men in particular? I will name names.

NGM: In that same interview with John Degan, which is quite good, you said, "I describe exactly what I mean to describe. Or maybe I describe exactly what interests me." So what interested you the most about this book?

DM: I wanted to write a Lon Chaney film. Lon Chaney, Sr., I should say—my friend Joe Meno prefers Lon Chaney, Jr., to Lon Chaney, Sr., which is so weird. And wrong. When I was a kid, I loved reading about Lon Chaney. I never got to see his movies. They were never shown on TV. This was before video. Tod Browning, too—I dreamed of seeing his stuff. I wanted to see *Freaks*. When I was in Grade 8 I wrote a screenplay for *Freaks*—my imagining of what the movie was like. I still have it. Twelve pages, including cover page. I am almost forty now and I am doing the same damned thing.

NGM: I still do things I did in Grade 8. It gets me nowhere, but I'm good at it. Um, what is your favourite Joe Meno book? I enjoy the detective one a lot.

DM: *The Boy Detective Fails*—that's my fave, too. There is a gay brother in it named Derek. I think he is based on a character in a Belle & Sebastian song. That is my sneaking suspicion.

NGM: If you could live in any era what era would it be? And why?

DM: I wouldn't want to live in any other era. I mean, I wouldn't want to live as myself in any other era. I am a pretty aggravating person—I don't imagine that would change century to century. If I could be somebody else, though...

NGM: Okay, so if you could be someone else, then?

DM: I would do anything to be a handsome man.

NGM: So, your obsession with Jimmie Rodgers. Is this what you meant when you said in an interview that you think you write fan fiction?

DM: Absolutely. I'm not content to just write about the historical figures I admire—I have to rewrite their lives and grant myself a starring role.

NGM: That's hot. You could get a mixer to repeat the words for you, Alexis O'Hara style. Or you could get a DJ to tour with you. Or just learn some new software. It might sell more books.

DM: I certainly couldn't sell any fewer books.

[SEVERAL YEARS LATER]

The Well-Dressed Wound is Derek McCormack's first novel since 2008's *The Show That Smells*. Or *Smelled*, since it's been a few years now. The new novel comes on the heels of a stressful period in the author's life, as McCormack was diagnosed with a rare form of cancer in 2011 that took a series of massive surgeries to cut out of him. His recovery took years—it's still in process, really, but it was more dramatic in the early days. "I could not walk. I could not eat. I could not concentrate long enough to watch a sitcom and understand what was going on. I wanted to write but I couldn't sit up or type." So, slowly, McCormack began writing in his head. "The book was written in my messed-up head, and so I wrote as concisely and cleanly as I could. A line, and then another line. After I had a couple of lines in a row that I could live with, I wrote them out. I've always been concise, but this book makes my old books look logorrheic!"

In brief, *The Well-Dressed Wound* is a play-script séance: a fashion show by the dead for the living taking place during the heat of the Civil War. The story is set in a theater in P. T. Barnum's American Museum on Broadway and features Abraham and Mary Todd Lincoln participating in a staged spiritualistic rite. McCormack's work, according to his publisher Semiotext(e), "evokes the evil-twin muses of transgressive literature, Kathy Acker and Pierre Guyotat."

With inept humour, I inquire as to whether McCormack's new book started out as a biography of the Lincoln family. "I can't say I ever considered writing a biography of the Lincolns," he replies, telling me, in his own way, that in the course of his life so far, he has read his fair share of books about the Lincolns, about the Civil War, and about American life in the Civil War. "I did consider writing a biography of Stephen Foster—the end of his life was awful. As was the middle. And the beginning. The stories of him as a bum on the Bowery as the Civil War began—they fascinate me. So do the stories of his supposed gayness. So do the stories of his diaries being bowdlerized."

In the end, McCormack felt his creative forces would be better served if he could find a way to insert himself into "this big blankness that is the history of Stephen Foster." While the author confirms that he didn't write a biography of Foster, the late father of American music does have a starring role in the book. "He has a rectal prolapse in Act 3!"

McCormack identifies Stephen Foster as the first country musician—his songs were massively popular, and he constructed a romantic myth of a South that never really existed. But perhaps most intriguing to the author was the true life behind the music. "He was a fuck-up. And he was gay. In my books, that's the fate of all country singers—to be gay and get fucked up!" But McCormack says he didn't really listen to Foster's music while writing the book. "The songs are sickeningly sweet and racist as hell."

McCormack's work has always tended to magnetize towards old music. "I am drawn to old music. No—I'm drawn to old country music. No—I'm drawn to old country musicians, less for their musical accomplishments than for their clothes. I love the culture of old country music—so in *The Haunted Hillbilly* I wrote about Hank Williams, and in *The Show That Smells* I wrote about Jimmie Rodgers."

Almost everybody in his new book is dead—but Martin Margiela is alive. "The thing about Margiela though is that he's famously elusive—there are no official interviews with him, no official photographs. When he left his own house he disappeared completely. He was a ghost. He is a ghost. I love him and always wanted to write about his work." That's a decision that feels perfectly normal in *The Well-Dressed Wound*, which features many long-gone figures (the Lincolns, Stephen Foster, P. T. Barnum) conducting a séance.

Whom do they conjure? Margiela, who is modern, but about whom almost nothing is known. "He's a blank in the way that Stephen Foster is—but time blanked out Foster, whereas Margiela's blanked out himself."

NGM: I looked at some of these sentences longer than I would for a normal book. And I don't mean to be rude by this question. I've read plenty of non-normal books, like *Anne of Green Gables*. My point is, some sentences, like, "Confetti's an anachronism," mesmerized me like a really good ad campaign in some antique issue of *Rolling Stone*. What is your whittling process like? I mean to say, how do you pare down and refine and tenderize these sentences, so to speak?

DM: You're not being rude! I do use a lot of declarative sentences. I make a lot of declarations about stuff that nobody gives a shit about—confetti is this, sequins are that. Why? I give a shit about those things. And I do like the process of distilling my sentences down to almost nothing.

Originally published in *Open Book Toronto* and *Verbicide*

JULIE BOOKER & JESSICA WESTHEAD: *UP UP UP* + *AND ALSO SHARKS* ($125)

We knew this would happen. The middle of poetry month and a slew of hot fiction titles get released. It happened two years ago, though a few weeks earlier, but you know, the same month. It was April 1st, 2009, a glorious spring evening, when Stuart Ross launched his eventual ReLit champion title, *Buying Cigarettes for the Dog* (hey, that's short fiction!), at Clinton's to a jam-packed audience and cunningly reminded the stir-crazy crowd that it was in fact the beginning of poetry month. And the spectators, of course, went wild.

So here we are, staring into poetry's lovely, vulnerable soul, admiring the sexy line breaks and in the distance hearing the catcalls from crowds yelling, "Check out his long dash yo, damn!" and *Bang! Crash! Boom!* Some much-hyped Canadian short fiction be storming da beach, as they say—nowhere. But that's okay, poetry-maniacs. Because all of the agents, editors, publishers, bloggers, and bookish super-fans have given fair warning to the community that this was all going down in mid-April—brothers and sisters.

This month at Conflict of Interest, we decided to focus on two very special guests who are about to launch new collections of short fiction. So get out your BlackBerrys, calendars, and other note-taking equipment: the info follows my friendly interrogation. So. "Who are these mystery authors?" you ask. "Mystery!?" I reply. "Don't confuse things!" I say, and continue to baffle you all for a few more seconds until it is revealed, with a large dose of glee, that we'll be chatting with Julie Booker, author of *Up Up Up* (House of Anansi Press), and Jessica Westhead, author of *And Also Sharks*

(Cormorant Books), on these very pages. That's right, two collections of short fiction, both of which are, as we speak, accruing local buzz. Why, it's hard to go anywhere in our beloved lit trenches and not hear about these two.

It is perhaps fitting that Julie Booker's collection deals with small investigations and portraits of the human condition in all its clutter, mischief, desire, and emotional roulette. She explains that the stories one finds in the pages of *Up Up Up* are culled from a decade's worth of material. "I don't plan on taking that long with my second book," Booker confesses. I inquire about one of the author's stories in particular, "Scratch," and see if I'm right about its purpose, or if, as is the case sometimes, I'm completely off my futon. I offer the premise that the story appears to deal with the power of discovering language in unusual places: graffiti. In the age of electronic excess, how do these cave-like inscriptions define our culture? Are they the beginnings of minor detours into larger stories for our own lives? I ask Julie if she agrees. "I think graffiti's kind of like YouTube; it's an accessible, inclusive medium of expression. The imagined 'who' behind graffiti is definitely a gateway to story. I think Rob Ford's clean up Toronto campaign is short-sighted by including wall art with tagging and other forms of graffiti."

Both Westhead and Booker have embraced the magazine market in Canada. A quick tour of the endnotes/acknowledgements in their collections reveals shout-outs to various journals and magazines that had previously showcased their stories. Recently poet Michael Lista wrote a piece in the *National Post* about the fate of literary magazines in Canada and suggested perhaps it was time for a new model of reality. "Lista may be right when he says there's more supply than demand," Booker muses, "but literary magazines are part of the structure that promotes emerging writers and helps establish this country's identity. It's the way up the Canadian ladder: get published in some literary journals, win some literary contests, and your name starts to circulate."

During our conversation, I touched on the importance of social issues (domestic violence, body image, etc.) in Booker's work, and asked if there was ever a time when she wanted to make a statement about something in particular, but for whatever reason, it didn't fit in the story. "If I set out to make a statement it would make for a very bad story," Booker explains.

> I write about those things because it's how I control the stuff that overwhelms me about this world. Many of my characters never get what they want. By containing my angst in a complete arc and sending it off into the world, somehow, I manage to take care of that one thing, that one issue, that's gnawing at me. If I can nail a feeling in a story, then I'm saying to someone up there: See? I'm paying attention. I don't need bad stuff to happen.

Jessica Westhead is no stranger to the Toronto literary scene, having spent over ten years making cameos at local zine and small-press fairs, reading series, and other noble outreach programs. Westhead's debut novel, *Pulpy & Midge*, was released in the fall of 2007 by Coach House Books. The book is a local and beloved tale of office neurosis and barbed vocational politics. Westhead takes a moment to dissect the different processes for preparing her novel and her forthcoming short fiction collection:

> I've published one novel, *Pulpy & Midge*, with the amazing Coach House Books, and I'm still very proud of that book. I do feel more excited about *And Also Sharks*, though, because the writing is darker. I think I felt I owed it to readers to give *Pulpy & Midge* a happy ending, because they had invested all that time reading all those pages—how could I possibly leave them feeling sad? I didn't feel any such obligation when writing the stories, though. Plus, for me, writing short stories is way more fun than writing a novel. Not to say writing short stories is easy—it's not—but I personally found the process of writing a novel much more laborious than writing short stories.

Adding to the pleasure, Westhead says, is the sense that after each story is complete you can celebrate, whereas with a novel you have to stick through and revise things "draft after draft."

With its well-crafted humanist focus and the usual Westhead confluence of charm, timing, suspense, and hilarity, *And Also Sharks* could end up vying for sleeper-hit-of-the-season status by the time we're all in flip-flops. I was curious about the collection—since it's been a few years since *Pulpy & Midge* was published—and just how old some of these stories were, or for that matter, how young. "The oldest story in *And Also Sharks* is 'Some Wife,'" Westhead confesses. "I wrote the earliest draft of this one in December 2002, and a version of this story also appears in what was technically my debut story collection—a three-story chapbook published by Greenboathouse Books in 2006, called *Those Girls*. The youngest story in the collection is 'Community,' which I first started writing in June 2010."

Soon, the topic of the Year of the Short Story (YOSS for those in vogue) cropped up. Since one of Westhead's long-time conspirators and compatriots is Sarah Selecky, I thought I'd get some insight into the manifesto from someone close to the camp. "I think when both Sarah Selecky's *This Cake Is for the Party* and Alexander MacLeod's *Light Lifting* were shortlisted for the Giller last year, people started to take extra notice of short fiction in general." There have always been devoted short story readers, but in the YOSS, we're hoping to reach more of them. "I've heard some people complain that short stories 'end too soon'—a reader will get to know the characters in a story, and then they're gone. I think it's a good thing to leave people wanting more—it's way better than overstaying your welcome."

When asked the marvellously entertaining question, "Which of your own characters would you most like to meet and why?" Westhead balks at first, then narrows down her choices to two varying characters, not any specific culprit. "It's a toss-up between Graham, the supporting co-worker character in 'Some Wife,' and Shelley, the protagonist in 'Coconut.' Shelley is totally unaware that her world view is bizarrely skewed, so it would be fun to follow her around for a day and see what she gets up to. And I'd love to go for beers with Graham because he just cracks me up."

Being entertained by one's characters shows a deeper understanding of the craft as well as a passion that goes beyond navel gazing and the superficiality that can sometimes be found when people discuss their work or "creative process." So if this insight is any indication of what we have to look forward to from Westhead's latest book, it will indeed be refreshing.

Originally published in *Open Book Toronto*

VIVEK SHRAYA: THE EARNEST EXPRESSION OF SELF ($125)

It's no small feat in the age of multinationals, big houses doing good numbers with e-book sales, and celebrity memoirs to self-publish a book that garners both the respect of one's peers *and* general and lasting interest. It's also no small feat to have this same book be a 2011 Lambda Literary Award finalist. Recently re-released, Vivek Shraya's *God Loves Hair* is a DIY masterpiece in the age of Walmart top 10 book clubs.

Shraya began writing *God Loves Hair* in January 2009, when she found herself inspired to write a story she herself had not yet read, "particularly in the queer literature genre," she explains. *God Loves Hair* is a pared-down series of vignette-styled fictions, carved from the crude matter of Shraya's own life to reveal the intimate interactions and personalities of a South Asian Hindu family and what it's like to grow up with immigrant parents. Adding to the enchanted post-nostalgia tone the book offers is enigmatic and hyper-coloured artwork by Juliana Neufeld. Artwork like this, Shraya says, was also something she herself missed in her own experience. "These are illustrations I didn't see in books growing up, featuring brown skin and a general Indian aesthetic."

Shraya, an accomplished musician whose recent film, *Seeking Single White Male*, was screened at festivals throughout 2011, says the focus on writing was a welcome change from music, which up until recently had been an all-encompassing artistic outlet. "What started off like blog entries eventually evolved into short stories, especially with the encouragement of friends who believed that there was more for me to uncover and tell."

Reduced to a simmer, *God Loves Hair* is a coming-of-age tale told in a confluence of visually stunning artwork and exacting prose that delivers. The book is packaged as one of those cozy children's book reads from the 1980s (*Henry the Explorer*, *The Snowy Day*, or *Where the Wild Things Are*) that address issues of gender identity, economy, race, and sexuality, but it's harnessed more in the earnest expression of self than a typical murky kitchen-sink drama. Shraya's turns of phrase are poetic and intense, as in the scene where the narrator covets the cut of his mother's wardrobe. "It too is small and tight, with a life of its own," she writes.

Or take the majestic scene at 12, after the narrator tells their parents they are just "earth parents," while Sai Baba (Divine Mother and Father) is their true caregiver. As he waits for Him "in the sweltering south Indian heat," he internalizes his desire for a connection:

> Who does God love? Maybe if I was white, maybe if I was a girl, maybe if I was younger, maybe if I was older, maybe if I was prettier, maybe if I was troubled, maybe if I was more kind, maybe if I fasted, maybe if I recite the Gayathri mantra 108 times, maybe if I didn't lie to the woman selling flowers yesterday...

Whether being called a pervert (for playfully making a snake out of his hands near a cousin while watching a playoff hockey game), encountering homophobia in early teen erotica, getting Bollywood crushes, staring at a gym teacher's "bubble butt," or searching for the perfect starter sports-team cap to blend in with male counterparts to blow off essential social steam, Shraya's story transcends the boundaries of genre and categorical obsessions many book lovers enjoy debating over the water cooler.

"As a queer person of colour," Shraya explains, "my main intention was to bring visibility to an experience we don't often see or hear." With the support of writer friends and loved ones, and using the successful sales model she found lucrative in promoting music, Shraya's book is already in its second printing. She says the biggest sales boost came from a university who began using the text in gender/sexuality courses, while steady sales continue online.

Ultimately, Shraya found that the more spiritual stories were the hardest to write because they were often the most personal stories to share. "Sometimes we find safety or comfort in the most unlikely spaces," she says. "As a queer kid looking for signs of normalcy, I really identified with the male Hindu gods whose masculinities were infused, not diminished, by their dancing, singing, long hair, etc. What has surprised me is that these stories are the ones that readers often connect to the most, versus the more broadly themed stories."

Shraya is still keeping busy, having just released a new EP entitled *1:1* this past fall and recently released the second edition of *God Loves Hair* with Positive Space Ryerson and RyePride, which includes additional material from the 2010 edition. She is at work on a new book.

Originally published on *Rabble.ca*

IBI KASLIK: DEMYSTIFYING CLICHÉS ABOUT ANOREXIA ($50)

Ibi Kaslik is a writer, journalist, and teacher. She graduated with her master's degree in creative writing from Concordia University, and her short stories and articles have appeared in literary magazines such as *Matrix* and *Geist*. *Skinny* is her debut novel (Harper Collins Canada, 2004). She dreams of one day owning her very own banjo.

Nathaniel G. Moore: Where did the concept for *Skinny* come from?

Ibi Kaslik: I wrote the first versions of *Skinny* in a creative writing novella class, and it eventually became my thesis project. It is indeed cut from myself. As a topic that I experienced directly in my personal life and social group, I never saw eating disorders represented in media discourse in the way it played itself out in life. Somehow Kate Moss, *The Karen Carpenter Story*, and *Afterschool Special*s never cut it for me. Eating disorders and distorted body issues seemed, to me at least, to be about something more significant than the media influence on young women and had less to do with the formulaic pop-psychology pursuit of blaming it on overbearing parents. In one sense, yes, anorexics are products of their upbringing: in *Skinny* the anorexic character, Giselle, is a twenty-two-year-old med student who grapples with her dead father's rejection and the high standards her immigrant parents have set for her. Yet many people coming from ambitious and overachieving families are not anorexic.

One of my aims with *Skinny* was to demystify clichés about anorexia, one of them being that anorexics are these vestal virgins who fear sexuality. Growing up, having an eating disorder was almost a common rite of passage, like experimentation with drugs and alcohol. In a society so obsessed with food and youth consumption, kids, especially girls, are likely to succumb to one of the aforementioned modes of experimentation, and for most people it's a phase. My interest was to follow a character, Giselle, who never outgrew the anorexic stage, and made rejecting food, and the values of abstinence and purity, a way of life. I also wanted to glorify the notion of perfection implicit in anorexia that some theories about the disorder dismiss so rapidly, for at the heart of it is a sort of idealism and romanticism, the desire to arrest change and resist the carnal world. Evolutionary psychologists are now saying anorexia was a way for tribes to survive long periods of famine and nomadic life, and that women leaders starved themselves to enable their tribes to survive, so I don't think I'm too far off on this tip of martyrdom.

At the same time I wanted to juxtapose Giselle's sombre and cerebral approach to another view of the body as manifested in Holly, Giselle's younger sister, the second narrator in *Skinny*. Holly's a junior-high athlete who pushes her body to physical extremes, but she does so in the glorification of her body's capacity, not in its destruction. I guess I always had two voices of women who pushed their bodies to extremes in my head and never really saw anything like that reflected in society. That, and I had just finished reading *As I Lay Dying* by Faulkner. Good mentors and editors are also critical in shaping the mess of voices and ghosts in one's head.

NGM: With a seeming dearth of amicable paths for certain publishers to get their books into giant stores without being compromised financially, are you happy you have avoided a lot of the LPG pitfalls/the frightening mess that a lot of small presses have to fight for to stay afloat?

IK: Of course, but there are many thriving presses out there still whose books are selling and being read. We read them, right, people?

NGM: And how has it been working with a large publisher?

IK: As I mentioned earlier, having support of your work, great editorship, and a good community of artists around you is necessary. Basic ass-in-chair work philosophy also helps. It's been a long haul for me. I started this book six years ago, have gone from grad school to the publisher with it, and while I'm well aware that I live a charmed life having the opportunity to work with a major publisher, I've done my time like anyone; this is the book I wrote in my early twenties and I am now thirty. You really make a choice as a writer, like any artist, to commit to being alone for long periods of time to work, or daydream, or stall. Orwell wrote that anyone who writes a novel is vain, selfish, and lazy, and at the bottom of their desire to write is a mystery, and I tend to concur.

NGM: When you write dialogue, do you hear two voices or one? Do you hear both voices or just one? Then do you imagine the other voice?

IK: So many voices talking! A product of postmodernist attention span, writing for newspapers, watching TV.

NGM: Can you talk about creative control and the cover art? Did you take that bite out of the popsicle?

IK: I like that the book has an iconic symbol, a popsicle. I sort of thought there'd be a body but I'm glad there isn't, in the end. Anorexia and bulimia have been portrayed as cool diseases in the fashion world. (Even Ben Stiller jokes about them in his film *Zoolander*.) For those who have suffered with the ailment, or who have been affected by someone who has suffered from the aforementioned, how does the narrator's purpose change beyond carrying the story, when these issues are so human and relevant to modern culture? Without being annoying, I think the book examines those very questions but through a personal framework of experience and history. Make the personal universal, I guess, is what we're striving for here, with all these words.

NGM: How do you think it affects the tone of a book, versus a comedy? Do you think books are a more serious platform for dealing with issues? Do you think the power of voice, for example, can convey truths that other media can't because they require less audience or reader attention?

IK: With the visual, you can't have a voice, and obviously the physical is displayed in film media, while writing draws on individuality, character, and detail; there's a humanity with words you can't transmit the same way in other arts; the internalized caprices and quirks of people have to be described and the character's face has to be imagined.

Originally published in *The Danforth Review*

SONJA AHLERS: GREETINGS FROM LAKE COWICHAN ($50)

Sonja Ahlers is art and books and more. Her nostalgia is personal and inviting to all; her artistic concoctions realize a crucial celebration to create and find deeper meaning from the drab confines of our symbolic world. She is the author of two graphic novels: *Temper, Temper* (Insomniac Press, 1998) and *Fatal Distraction* (Insomniac Press, 2004). Her work is a blend of the artist book and the zine. Her goal is to continue to refine her style, falling somewhere between Beatrix Potter tales, Gary Larson's *Far Side*, and public service announcements. She lives in Vancouver, BC, where she has access to the Internet.

Nathaniel G. Moore: As a "mighty mild seventies child,"[3] did you eat TV dinners? What did you think of them? Did you find them oppressive?

Sonja Ahlers: I wasn't allowed to eat junk food at my parents' house, but we (me and my brother Cubby) would go to our grandparents' and do whatever we wanted. I remember having a TV dinner and settling in for an episode of *CHiPs* on a Saturday night, pre–remote control—I went to turn up the volume and in some *CHiPs*-induced trance went back to my footstool perch—forgetting that I had placed my hot TV dinner there. I ended up sitting on it. For some reason, this is a memory I think of OFTEN. As for taste, they were definitely gross. Aluminum. But I liked the compartments. The peach cobbler was especially gross. I have a sense memory of all of the tastes. Like the mashed potatoes taste. All weird. Everything in my life is compartmentalized. (Pls note: I hardly ate any TV dinners—I just have a good memory.)

---

3   A lyric from the song "Combat Baby" by Metric

NGM: Tell us how it all started. Where did you kindergarten, school, summer, what is your background, etc.?

SA: I grew up between Victoria, BC, and a place called Lake Cowichan... Victoria is a beautiful little paradise... Lake Cowichan was this fucked-up weird logging town. I grew to hate both places. I have since made some kind of peace with Victoria. LC is a total ghost town now. I have really bad memories of being there. As for school in general—I had certain learning disabilities but was also considered "gifted." My whole life has been a mass of contradiction. I am a self-taught artist... (whatever that means). I have also had good mentors.

NGM: How would you describe your work? Do you find it therapeutic?

SA: I don't know how to describe my work—but YES it is totally therapeutic... in fact, that is what it mostly is. But as I (ahem) mature—I am more interested in skilled craft—rather than emotionally-based rantings and such—but we shall see what happens.

I think I am turning into one of those people who need to live on a small island. I think you have to be independently wealthy to afford that luxury. So I guess one of my main inspirations is music. A friend was saying my work is pretty rock 'n' roll. I guess it conjures up or references that energy. That is the spirit that is there. I think that is a cool thing, to be making book stuff and poetry and images and having it be rock 'n' roll. I miss making music. I keep saying I don't, but I think I do. I think it might help out with anger management.

When I had that old band forever (Kiki Bridges), I think I funnelled all my *Temper, Temper* anger and disappointment and all the shit that came up with that book into music. It was really hard for me to stand behind that book because it was so, so personal and I had no clue of how to handle such a situation, so I basically mostly turned my back on it and pretended like it wasn't really out there. It made it easier to deal with negative criticism or ANY feedback.

NGM: What are some of your inspirations?

SA: I'm listening to the new Mary Timony, *Ex Hex*. I am a li'l obsessed with her music. Anyone feel free to send me a mix CD—I'll send something back as a thank you. I like the new Sleater-Kinney... Corin Tucker's voice is an inspiration... and uh I really like Queens of The Stone Age, which disgusts my boyfriend, who is a total musician. I can't even sing around him without going out of tune because I am so self-conscious around his musical genius. And I used to have a band for seven years! We opened for Modest Mouse, who was one of my favourites back then, in the late '90s...their *Lonesome Crowded West* album had an impact. His lyrics on all that earlier material blew my mind.

My life is pretty boring. I kind of like it that way. I don't like loud noises and sirens and most people in cars. They drive like maniacs in this city. One thing that made me happy today was watching this Rad Dude zooming down Commercial Drive on his bike, and naturally a driver pulls out in Rad Dude's way to make HIS left turn and Rad Dude is going straight for the truck with this awesome flipped-up bird. I started laughing out loud. I almost applauded. That was a big inspiration.

Further inspiration: movies like Robert Altman's *Three Women*, starring Shelley Duvall and Sissy Spacek. I love that movie—it's even better w/ the director's commentary. I like haunted movies too, like *Picnic at Hanging Rock*. And I love *Over the Edge* and *Foxes*. I like a lot of stuff from the seventies. Music from then. I like some boogie rock and earnest early-'80s power-ballad rock like Streetheart or Harlequin. But then I usually only like one song on an album. My tastes span a few decades and they are definitely weird all together. I just went to Niagara Falls for the first time. That was magical. I like nature. I went with Ian/Pas de Chance. Pas de Chance is very influential.

He just made me a copy of *Christiane F.*, the soundtrack. It is David Bowie. I was obsessed with the ad in the paper for that movie as a 9-year-old kid. I would stare at the picture of the girl, but I wasn't allowed to see it b/c of the rating. I find it unusual that a kid that age would be obsessed w/ a junkie movie. But I don't do things like that. I am currently a goody-goody.

NGM: Please tell me, what is the highbrow zine?

SA: To be totally honest with you, I have never felt comfortable with the word *zine*...but in answer to your question...I'd say something that employs art.

NGM: Tell me about your mother.

SA: Her name is Louise Bernadette Frances Jordens. She is very quiet, like a mouse. She was one of those "babe moms"...she had me when she was young. When I was a teenager we fought like vicious cats... usually about clothes. She has an amazing collection of clothes that I would help myself to... we get along fine now. She's changed over time. We both have. She used to take ballet. As did I. We lived in an old-fashioned house.

NGM: Tell us how Insomniac Press came to publish your first book, *Temper, Temper*.

SA: Back in 1994, I started making little books. The first one was called *A Wandering Eye* (because I was born with one—as well as other birth defects). I couldn't stop making them. I pored thru all my journals and made notes—typing them onto index cards. I had a tall stack of cards. I started to reduce those and incorporate images. I was doing some crazy poetry at that time—with interesting wordplay. I was in love with beautiful words. I do not write like that anymore, so it is easy for me to step way back and see how it was... a lot of it hasn't been shown. So I made those little books for free on the photocopier at my friend's work, which was the Parliament buildings in Victoria, BC... Susan Farmer helped me out a lot. She would help w/ the production because I have semi-dyslexia. She also helped edit *Fatal Distraction* and we had that band. I would send out these little books far away to people I admired and wanted to connect with... writers, musicians, artists, other people making (ahem) zines.

NGM: But how did *Temper, Temper* come to be realized? It was your first book. Remember? 1998? Hello.

SA: I am an introvert/extrovert. I lived most of those years through my post office box. I had a million pen pals and had a hard time socializing in person. So the books—I barely showed them to people around me... it was too close. I didn't want them knowing such personal information. It was easier far away. I had a lot of walls built up for protection... so one of those people I sent books to was Lynn Crosbie. She was great. She put me in a feminist anthology she was editing called *Click* and I got paid really well. Shortly after that, Insomniac Press came along. Lynn edited *Temper, Temper*. I sent them a massive shirt box full of material. She pieced it together. It all happened very fast.

NGM: Can we talk about the term *spoken word* and not get into a fist fight? How do you feel about the classification of art? Is it good for the economy? Anyone?

SA: Spoken word. I am a big fan of this new "alternative" stand-up comedy. I admire people who work that way. I'm fascinated by people who can stand ALONE on a stage and entertain...monologue. It is so very brave. I've been super influenced by comedians—Lucille Ball, Carol Burnett, Gilda Radner, Amy Sedaris...SCTV...comedy and tragedy. My specialties. These questions are quite broad...uh...as for art—some of it is good for the economy. GOOD ART helps people survive. But of course there is a lot of bad art out there, and I try to be discerning. There is this amazing quote by Kathleen Hanna from a *Punk Planet* interview she did just after Bikini Kill broke up...I don't have it handy but to paraphrase—she's talking about how making art is a job—just not a "sucky job"—and that artists should be honoured and supported because what they are doing is totally valid and necessary for our society. She also speaks about how most artists are considered to be slackers...and how lame that is. I work really hard, but my grandfather's generation considers me to be a deadbeat...or at least that is my projection. I know he thought I was a degenerate ten years ago. I wasn't working a Real Job at all. All I did was make art. I was possessed. I had no money, but I was so happy making art. I treated it like my job.

NGM: How do you tour a book like *Fatal Distraction*?

SA: I haven't done a lot of hardcore touring & a lot of that has to do with being busy. I usually have a few projects on the go, like visual-art gallery obligation stuff, and I make bunnies to support myself...I sell a few different wares to support myself. I do freelance graphic work sometimes...a lot of this kind of stuff I just mentioned is seasonal. My goal is to narrow my focus. For *Fatal Distraction*, I did an installation for the book launch. That proved quite successful/rewarding...a lot of people saw the show because it was at this popular space called Antisocial in Vancouver. Their openings are total parties. There is a famous story for me of attending my own art opening for 15 minutes...I don't like art openings very much. So yes, I also did a slideshow reading at Canzine. That was hilarious. And I did a little mini-leg of Jim Munroe's Perpetual Motion Roadshow for *FD*...last spring I toured with Emily Pohl-Weary and Tamara Faith-Berger...imagine two writers and an artist-type person going down the West Coast in a nice rental car...it was very punk rock. I think we did 10 shows in nine days...readings. I have stories.

ALSO I think of creative spaces to put my book in—I find my book gets lost in bookstores, so I try to think of places they can be showcased. I also do window displays or get friends who work in bookstores to make shelf-talkers and stuff like that...so yeah. The slideshow readings. I would like to do more of a multi-media thing with my books. I hear music and I see visuals. I'd like to present my work more like that. It's more entertaining for people and less taxing on me...so if there is anyone out there who wants to help me do that—bring it on! Anyways, I'd like to hit a few more major cities by doing some installations. We'll see. *Fatal Distraction* took me five years to make, so I am willing to promote it for a while longer...these things are about Life's Work. However, I am getting anxious to start the new book.

Originally published in *The Danforth Review*

RANDALL MAGGS: THE SAWCHUK SESSIONS ($125)

When Martin Brodeur eclipsed Patrick Roy's all-time win record last month, Internet search engines were ablaze and debate grew to rabid levels for hockey geeks young and old. Some lasted into the midnight hour, defending their airtight theses as to why Roy, Brodeur, Sawchuk, Plante, Hall, or Dryden was the greatest of all time. Personally, and I've stood by this since 1991 for different reasons, I think the three greatest goaltenders are Plante, Sawchuk, and Hall. No one dominated and played so well at such a high level from the 1950s through the 1960s than those three men. I was obsessed with Plante: he was a diva; he was neurotic; he knitted toques to calm himself, faked illnesses, and was loathed by his coach. He refused to stay in certain hotels because of his asthma. He was experimental, egomaniacal, and cocky. He, much like Sawchuk, was a winner; but still, I always found the latter a threat to my idol Plante.

When I read Randall Maggs' book I saw a different side to Sawchuk, someone who always seems to be called the greatest over Plante, someone I didn't want to like. But Maggs made me at least understand the man as someone more than just the goaltender who always had my hero's number when it came to the record book. So when I arrive at Toronto's Hockey Hall of Fame in early 2008 for the launch of Maggs' *Night Work: The Sawchuk Poems*, at first glance I think I'm at an induction ceremony at some posh New York NHL head-office corporate event. With a slew of well-dressed literati and sports journalists and a fantastic spread, it's a special way of launching an epic novel-like poetry book about Terry Sawchuk. Even the Stanley Cup is a few metres away from the podium. There's a short film adapted from the book being put on by Judith Keenan at Book Shorts and, in general, the evening resembles nothing you would imagine (if ever you did) finding at a lowly Canadian poetry launch.

When I meet up with Maggs a few months after this event, we delve into the gritty world of the 1950s NHL. For some reason I know everything about these men. I should. In the early 1990s I was obsessed with 1950s hockey. I was all over this period. I even wrote one of Sawchuk's contemporaries, Glenn Hall, a letter, and he sent me back an autographed postcard. I would go to trade shows and get more and more autographs, watching the shrinking hockey stars holding pens, waiting to sign shirts, jerseys, cards, and books. These were real gentlemen, gangsters who appeared to have survived a war. One casualty, however, was Terry Sawchuk.

*

Nathaniel G. Moore: How do you feel this book works for the poetry fan and the hockey fan? How did you come to put this book together?

Randall Maggs: My hope was that the more open-minded hockey fans might overcome their indifference to poetry. I think there were things inside me that got shocked out. I was out west to do a reading and driving past a small town, two or three houses, and I see the name *Floral* up on the one grain elevator. That kind of shocked me back to my own upbringing in the West. Floral was where Gordie Howe was from and probably the best-known hometown of any player in the country up to that point. That was in the nineties, and I'd really gotten away from the game after 1967. I watched a bit when my brother went up with Chicago in the seventies. But that name up there, after all that time, that got a lot of things going through my head.

NGM: Did you grow up with the game?

RM: My dad and I would listen to the games on the radio. My father disliked the Montreal Canadiens, to the point where after the game, if the Habs won, he'd disappear into the barn not to be seen 'til the next morning. He got so caught up in it.

*

RANDALL MAGGS: THE SAWCHUK SESSIONS ($125)

Maggs says that, in Canada, poets are "much better off financially than fiction writers," because poets don't have any illusions that they might live off their writing, and so they seek out some additional job or profession to pay the bills. He describes how the public attitude about poetry changes from place to place. For example, Maggs states, Newfoundland is very receptive to the arts compared to Western Canada, where he's from.

When it came to putting the book together, Maggs says he never lacked confidence: "I don't know why, I wasn't thinking of myself… I was just writing poems about something I wanted to write poems about."

His family and friends would often come and read pieces from the work-in-progress, wondering when in fact it would be complete. "My son is a classical pianist and he said to me, 'Dad, why are you turning this book into poetry? Why don't you write a novel?' And my brother is a hockey player and [he] said the same thing."

Maggs recounts how, every once in a while, he'd send his brother a poem and say, "You know, I'm getting closer to having this book done." One day, after a moment of silence on the phone, his brother exclaimed, "You mean the whole fucking book is poetry?"

*

NGM: Writing about hockey, and putting it into the genre of poetry, was there any hesitation? Did you think you were doing a disservice at all—I mean, isn't there a stigma attached to poetry?

RM: I think this book kind of drew people in, I don't think they're hostile to it. You can have a certain hostility to poetry like Shakespeare just from high school, and then you never see it again.

NGM: Why do you think people are so anti-poetry?

RM: It's not that they hate poetry, they just don't even think about it. I think the whole spirit of the age is a short attention span. It's like classical music: people aren't willing to put time into something. This kind of draws them in and it's relatively accessible because the language I settled on had to be something that worked with the subject. But I wasn't trying to write stuff that people would read—that wasn't on my mind at all.

NGM: Does it upset you at all?

RM: I'm not hostile about the situation. We have been a pioneer community where the arts were not well regarded; now we've moved into a technological era. Somehow we've missed the period where we've had the opportunity to develop an appreciation of the arts.

ONE YEAR LATER (APRIL 2009)

NGM: What's new? It's been almost a year since we've spoken. Any new developments? —Beyond the recent Winterset Award win, which I'll ask you about shortly.

RM: Ron Hynes, the great Newfoundland singer and songwriter, has written a Sawchuk song in response to the book! Steve Brunt emailed me recently to tell me that he and his crowd had gone to hear Ron sing at some Toronto club and Ron talked about the Sawchuk book and sang his song, which was eight minutes long. Got a message from Ron a couple of weeks ago that he was really pleased with it and has given me a co-write and wants me to join SOCAN so I that I would get a share of the play money. I guess I'm sort of answering your first question here. The book does seem to be getting a second wind or even better, "getting traction" (to use an expression of the present Leafs coach). Dave Stubbs, the excellent *Gazette* sports columnist who has an extensive knowledge of sports literature, said once that it was in his top three with Andy O'Brien's *Scrubs on Skates* and Dryden's *The Game*. If it turns out to have the longevity of those two books, I'd be delighted. It's also being used in several university courses, and that's a promising development.

NGM: Anything else?

RM: What I have enjoyed most in the last year, though I had no thought of any of this when I was writing the book, is having found that many hockey people have gotten into the book even though they were initially wary of the poetry; and that many arts-oriented people have come to have a little greater understanding of the game itself. Heartening to find so many open-minded people.

Stubbs is a Brodeur fan, and I gave him a copy of the book last spring. I used to watch the TSN highlights and the New Jersey game just to see the first goal scored on Brodeur... and the hallowed shutout record intact. I feel differently now. Brodeur will break the record and good luck to him. He's an entirely admirable person and a great goaltender. My god, when you think about what he has done in international play for Canada...yes, good luck to him. As to who's the best—impossible to say, really, as the game has changed so much; the gear, the defensive play. I'd say you can only judge who's best in his own age, and Terry has sufficient competition with his own contemporaries.

NGM: People from the home team, Newfoundland, really seem to love the book. What do you make of the fanfare?

RM: The local people that I talked to, the Newfoundlanders, have loved it, and I've made a bit of fuss about them in reading locally. My brother, the hockey player, was skeptical at first (as was my son the classical pianist). But he loves it now and keeps a copy on the bar at his Chrystola Inn, which is in Colorado at the base of Pike's Peak. He called me last week, as Corb Lund (and the Hurtin' Albertans) were playing there and Corb wanted a copy. He loves the game, it seems, and I see he's released a version of Stompin' Tom's old hockey song.

NGM: Beyond those you spoke to while compiling the book, have any NHLers contacted you about the book? Have you followed up with anyone you talked to during your creative process?

RM: I really haven't gotten back to the pros yet. It's only now I'm getting breathing space, and I'll certainly call Bill White, Ralph Backstrom, Glenn Hall, Johnny Bower, and Ken Dryden, all guys who were a big help to me. Of course, the Hall of Fame people Phil Pritchard and Craig Campbell remain my close friends and big supporters. Phil sent Craig up to Orillia with the Vezina when I read at the Leacock festival last summer. What's that kind of friendship and support worth? Phil's working on a Canadian embassy visit to Washington among his many other planned ventures.

NGM: If you could read or show one poem to Terry, what would it be?

RM: The one poem for Terry. Hmm. Remember, he hated the limelight. And he was a westerner. There's that poem based on an incident where the reporter wants to make a fuss over his protecting... was it Toppazzini's face in the crease with his trapper? Terry'd probably say the same or worse to me. But if I could send him one piece, maybe it would be "Things in Our Day," where he might secretly enjoy the unheroic portrait of himself and, I'm sure, the players' respect for him that Bergman, wonderful guy, really conveyed to me.

NGM: Congratulations on the Winterset Award. What was that experience like?

RM: I did mention in an interview down here on that subject that having to suffer through the March Music festivals with my kids over the years made me very skeptical about mixing the arts and competition. Nonetheless, the recognition certainly does give me great pleasure. I think too that the jury showed their courage and openness in giving the award to a book that deals with a subject such as mine. I know the arts world well enough to be pretty certain that this would not have been a popular decision with the more "rigorous" faction in that world.

Originally published in *Open Book Toronto*

LYNN CROSBIE: FORGOT ABOUT LYNN: 72 HOURS WITH *LIFE IS ABOUT LOSING EVERYTHING* ($125)

THURSDAY, APRIL 26, 6:16 P.M.

Okay, first the City of Compton thing. When I initially met Lynn in 2008, I asked her where she lived, and she wrote me back: "Parkdale, City of Compton." I knew then that everyone else on the planet was made in an Easy-Bake Oven, and that she was my alien sister sent back in time to save me from Horace-quoting line-breaking chumps at the poetry soup kitchen, who were talking about yearning and their lifelong dreams of getting published in *Qwerty*. (I have yet to fulfill this dream. It's a fine magazine, and I was just making a point about our desire to be published versus our desire to be more interesting while in the poetry soup line.)

    The thing is, I've been talking to Lynn about this interview for 100 days, probably more. Maybe 200 days. I don't even know how I know her or why she speaks to me. Or if we even speak to each other. It's always intense, amusing, poetic, and full of wonder. It's how she puts together words (whether Anansi publishes them or not); it's the way she waits for you to stop talking (or in my case, if you don't stop 'cos you are nervous, she finds a way into your beam of language and dissolves your first person into something else) and amplifies things. Makes them more real.

    In the world of surrealist books of poetry and fiction with titles like *My Leg Is Made of Bacon* and *I'm Going to Jump Inside A Balloon How 'Bout You?* Lynn Crosbie is about a real as it gets. Written in self-imposed exile, *Life Is About Losing Everything* is literally hundreds of short stories—or what a black-and-white-chain-smoking French theorist would call "vignettes"—that chronicle Lynn's periphery of pain, anxiety, love, debauchery, memory, desire, reinvention, domestic virtue, and self-scandal. Meanwhile, other Toronto authors in their 30s and 40s write about the make-believe or half-recalled memories of teen-fresh sex or sing songs (*cough*, Metric) about teen-vampire values ("I'm All Yours" from *Eclipse* and their new single "Youth Without Youth." Even Metric's market-seeking tagline on Twitter is "We're in The Prime of Your Youth," which is perhaps a not-so-subtle awareness that Emily and Jimmy are, in fact, singing for people born when *Jurassic Park* was coming out on VHS). Don't get me wrong, I like Metric's brand and their CanCon sensibility. I'm just making a point about focus groups in the arts. Plus they are also Parkdale artists-in-residence. And I have the world record for most Emily Haines references since 2004 that I have to add to as well.

Despite not having been a teen in over 20 years, Lynn's portrait of the human artist/addict as an aging, love-seeking human is honest, brave, heartfelt, and relatable to anyone who feels their exact age. When you read *Life is About Losing Everything*, you can't hide from her thoughts. From what she wants you to know and feel.

I called Lynn on the phone about a month ago to set up our interview. I don't really have a phone so I called her from Jet Fuel Coffee Shop, where I had gone after a gallery show at the Power Plant. Picking up, the first thing she said after "Bell Phone" was how this whole moment reminded her of *Back to The Future*. Suddenly I saw myself as an orange-vest-wearing Michael J. Fox scouring the phonebook in 1955, looking up Doc Brown's phone number. So I told Lynn that Ronald Reagan was the president and she laughed. I couldn't really hear very well because the café was loud and the espresso machine was attached to an amplifier, which was then attached to the pay phone—or so it seemed.

What I'm saying is, you don't really need me to interview or get a sound bite from Lynn Crosbie. You just need to read her book. It's taken her a long time to write it because it took her a long time to live it. Here are some thoughts I have on her other books, a collage, if you will, of things that are all Lynn Crosbie–related.

FRIDAY, APRIL 27, 8:17 A.M.

Listened to the song "I Need A Doctor" for about 30 minutes to get into the mood. The music video features a lot of Dr. Dre's deceased friends and past glories. Why is hip-hop so emotional? I find it overwhelming sometimes. They really love each other; maybe that's why the music sells so well. It's not fiction, is it? I mean, this all really happened. Easy E died of AIDS, Tupac was shot, there were fights with rival labels. Dre's 20-year-old son died of a heroine and morphine OD in 2009.

12:18 P.M.

"I have this recurring dream. Lynn Crosbie has become Governor General. Canada is finally a fascinating and dangerous and glamorous and terrifyingly intelligent place to live. The next motherfucker who wakes me up during this dream is getting a football kick in the nutsack. I swear." —R. M. Vaughan on Lynn in an email response to a request for a quote that I sent out this morning.

2:16 P.M.

Reread the pink handout that I made for Lynn's class when I read and talked at them on Feb. 28. (My roommate Astonished Mike found the sheet in the bathroom and later commented that it sounded "judgmental." I don't know what terrifies me more, that he occasionally reads my garbage or that he feels qualified to critique my approach to performance lectures.)

> Feb. 28: Terrify and alienate children of tomorrow at Lynn Crosbie's poetry class while fellow authors look on in abject horror. Also, you should all be grateful you have such a terrific teacher. She's NWA to my Eminem. But please don't grow up to be just like me. Go study a tape of NWA. And remember, only you can prevent bad Canadian poetry.

SATURDAY, APRIL 28, 5:53 A.M.

Poetry is about history and life and reimagining worlds we knew and didn't know. It's a folded note in the most boring class of all time. I take *VillainElle* out of the library every few months. The Jack the Ripper poems are my favourites. At the Anansi poetry bash I tell Michael Lista that I learned about Ted Bundy's appreciation of socks from Lynn's poetry.

I can't sleep and have a head cold and I'm sneezing and it's annoying. I mess around on Photoshop with fan-art aesthetics and obsessive West-Coast rap visuals, fusing Compton and Parkdale in homage to Dr. Dre and Lynn Crosbie.

6:22 A.M.

One of the stories in Lynn's book is based on a story by Daniel Jones, her friend who died 20 years ago. They launched books together in the early 1990s, and she lent him a whip, which he used on stage. The first time I spoke with Lynn in 2008, we talked about Daniel Jones and Ian Curtis. When I think of that moment, it's like how I would have envisioned interviewing someone for *Q Magazine* in a garden near some dead castle in the UK, and the photographer leaves and we're covered in a new wind and we're left in the late autumn frenzy and Lynn is talking about Ian Curtis like he had just died. I think Lynn knows what life feels like more than anyone else. And she tells us.

6:33 A.M.

Lynn's new book reminds me of how one critic called Leonard Cohen's *Death of a Ladies' Man* Cohen's third novel, that its intensity perhaps transcended the genre it was lumped into. But we don't need to mess with genre at this point in the article. (Strangely enough, a year or so later, the ReLit Award would give Crosbie the award for best novel.)

Let me just say then, in many ways, the 100 or so stories that make up *Life Is About Losing Everything* are a personal inventory, a time bomb that thankfully exploded and repaired. Well, let's hope, mostly repaired. And while many will opt to read the latest briefcase-toting-lawyer-boat-chase-summer-blockbuster-trash novel or something Kate Winslet recommended on Twitter, I have a good feeling about Lynn's book finding sensible homes in the dysfunctional Feng Shui of readers new and old.

Originally published in *Open Book Toronto*

MICHAEL TURNER: EVERYTHING I HAVE GOES INTO EVERYTHING I DO ($100)

No, sadly, the title of this piece is not an announcement that Michael Turner and Bryan Adams are working on a new version of Academy Award–nominated song "(Everything I Do) I Do It For You."

Michael Turner was one of the first small-press authors I truly thought was cool. He was well-groomed in television interviews (yes, back when authors regularly appeared on cable television), in a bed with a sheet over his possibly naked body, with a host right next to him. He wrote about sex and seemed like he was poised to be the next Douglas Coupland.

In 2003, I spoke with Richard Nash, then the publisher of Brooklyn-based Soft Skull Press, and he couldn't stop gushing about Turner's novel. "It came to us from his agent Hilary McMahon at Westwood Creative. I'd not heard of his other work, though Martha Sharpe from House of Anansi just sent me a copy of her two *Hard Core Logo* tie-in books."

When Nash got in touch with Toronto agent Hilary McMahon, he asked her if she had any author suggestions, and she sent him *The Pornographer's Poem*. "I just couldn't believe it. It's certainly one of the best novels I've ever read. Period. And here it was, being offered to me to publish! I showed it to my Marketing Director, Tennessee Jones. Tennessee's reaction was that it was the best depiction of adolescent sexuality he had ever read. If I, a conventional straight guy, and Tennessee both had that reaction (he's a tough critic), we knew we had to do it."

By the time I had finished *The Pornographer's Poem*, a perverse coming-of-age novel never overwhelmed with postmodern parlour tricks, there was talk of a movie. House of Film in Toronto kept renewing the film rights. The novel was published in the states. The film... never happened. And Michael Turner, like the rest of CanLit, aged, switched from dial-up to cable, became vegan, quit smoking, gave up MySpace, and the world became the Internet; acuity in identity, status, the subjective, and the anecdotal became the norm. This intensity was mimicked in fiction and poetry.

In his first book in nearly a decade, Michael Turner is back with the pared-down *8 × 10*, a book that tells a story about the lives of eight people—and the lives they come in contact with—exposed over ten events each. With stealth precision, *8 × 10* is instant, engaging and direct: a book without character or city names, a book without race, religion, or nominal indicators, a book devoid of Turner's usual bag of tricks (script or screenplay breaking up prose), a book in which the character's actions—not their identity—moves the story to its dramatic core.

Michael Turner is the author of several books, including *Hard Core Logo*, which was made into a feature film by Bruce McDonald and for which Turner received a Genie Award for his contribution to the movie's soundtrack. His 2000 book, *The Pornographer's Poem*, won that year's BC Book Prize's Ethel Wilson Award for Fiction. What follows is an interview with the Vancouver author about what went into creating *8 × 10*.

Nathaniel G. Moore: *8 × 10* is considerably mute in terms of naming characters and locations. Was there ever an overdeveloped name and location-heavy version of the manuscript, or did it just work out in this very unique, sparse way?

Michael Turner: The first eight people we meet are engaged with those who appear at the subjective centre of the next eight events. As we move through the totality of these events, the potential for people to appear out of sequence increases—to the point where they abstract, become all people. This is what is best about keeping names, places, races, and dates out of it: the development of a subjectivity based on pattern and recurrence; the structures that govern our lives, determine our bodies.

We live at a moment when the dominant mode of production (full tilt since the 18th century) is inverting. The world that had poverty and homelessness as symptoms of structural problems (dismissed as pimples, stuff we'll grow out of through legislation, revolution)—that world has turned, and these structures have suddenly stepped from the fog and are staring us in the face.

8 × 10 is an attempt to make portraits of such structures, to turn them into people. What is happening in Vancouver is not unlike what is happening in Johannesburg. The second invasion of Iraq showed us that the rich in Baghdad are not unlike the rich in Las Vegas.

Wherever this book is read, I would like its setting to be wherever the reader is reading it—be it Melbourne or Karachi, Oslo or Tel Aviv. To the question of whether this book could have been written clothed, then stripped naked later—it wouldn't have worked. *8 × 10* owes more to multiplication than subtraction.

NGM: It's been ten years since you've published anything in CanLit. Some of your past works have included working in music, poetry, and the screenplay. Some of the lives in your new book include a poet and a musician. How much of yourself do you think went into *8 × 10*?

MT: Everything. Everything I have goes into everything I do.

NGM: Do you think that we, as a society, are too spatially, nominally aware? Was the removal of location, race, and identity a statement on its own about our current over-identified world?

MT: The Enlightenment brought with it a desire to name, classify, and map. Once something's named, there's a death—from which we begin again (a point of departure? imperialism?), or the lid gets slammed on the pot (Hiroshima?).

The world is no longer enchanted. Many of the younger people I come in contact with—those who aren't obsessed with money—are affecting the strangest behaviours, and in some ways, I think this is in response to the unenchanted world.

The condition these people aspire to is a kind of autism, a world of innate and unquestioned genius, where no one is accountable and everyone has their own names for things and is anxious to see those names endure. There is no critique, only anger, diffidence and, as a last resort, the fetal position. For them, irony's the enemy, because it is perceived to be mean-spirited, useless when it comes to healing or making money. I despair both ends, and I refuse to call what's left the middle.

Originally published in *Open Book Toronto*

PART THREE: THE HARD SELL

KINGPIN OF FEAR: LOATHSOME SECRETS OF AN ADOLESCENT BOWLING STAR IN THE DYING DAYS OF THE NINETIES ($0)

> I am a limitless series of natural disasters and all of these disasters have been unnaturally repressed.
>
> —Kathy Acker, *Pussy, King of the Pirates*, 1996

It was my greatest friendship of the 1990s and it ended in colossal obscurity; any words describing its finality wouldn't be believed, created in 1996 from the dust of Slurpee Gods at 7-11 and the Boy Factory, the strange loft where we all would meet and smoke and exist in an elixir of fantasy and gritty realism. Couldn't get to Toronto to witness the bowling trial that spring? Don't sweat it! Now you can own a piece of history with this exclusive T-shirt and poster of the biggest trial, plus a commemorative mugshot. Limited to twenty. Legal aid advised. What do you mean we're all out? The story, that's it? Okay then.

As I write this now, in the dying days of 2020, few readers know I wrote an entire book about professional bowling. The book, *Bowlbrawl* (Conundrum Press, 2005), was complete gibberish—an abject, nearly ESL musing on staged bowling antics, culled from the pomposity of my own imagined alter ego, Robert Towell. Acclaimed author Kevin Chong took time out of his busy schedule that year to review it, saying, "Too bad that much of [it] is told in a bland third-person narrative that goes behind the scenes but lacks much narrative tension or flair for characterization. When the narrative does come alive, it's normally in the voice of Robert Towell, whose pronouncements can be outlandishly megalomaniacal or anomalously highbrow."

In a piece in the *Globe and Mail* on my publisher at the time, a journalist wrote about the book being "listed in the Conundrum catalogue as 'biography/sports/humour,' not a friendly combination for the Indigo shelver." Despite all this, as well as testifying in interviews that it was all true, I was sentenced as "novelist" by its mere existence in the years that followed. But this is by no means a celebration, a retrospective, or grotesque tour notes from that experience. That ordeal is well documented in the concrete pixilation mixers known as YouTube and Internet Explorer. What I want to write about here is my second and final adolescence, my failure as a writer, and the four years in which I first went sober (1996-2000), a timeline concurrent with the most unbelievable time in my shredded life.

I can only imagine how depraved, horrific, and deranged things would have been for that four-year stretch had my friends and I been on drugs and/or drinking. The fact was that for the latter half of the '90s I aligned myself with a gang of sober thugs, misfits, stay-at-home welfarians, single-mom scratch-lotto artisans, deadbeat dads on the lam, latchkey felons and their GenX girlfriends, the odd broken-down construction worker—each and every one of them fuelled solely on caffeine and nicotine. I'm already feeling the hyperbole blot my retinas some twenty-years later. We were like the cast of *Friends*, only we worked for free, and we couldn't escape one another. It all started one epically humid global warming of a day in June 1996...

I had just washed up on the shores of another failed attempt at stabilization (read: employment, housing, romantic sustenance, a decent number of cats) when I fell in with a group of ex-cons, teenager rehabbers, and other court-appointed contemporaries. This was mid-1996, and while my presence in their lives was not court appointed, their appearances at a certain number of regular Anonymous meetings across the city were. Soon I found myself taken in by the charity of these individuals and their chain-smoking, coffee-guzzling ways. And so, because we were late-teens/early-twenties folks deprived of the fallbacks of drinking and drugs, we found ourselves searching for social settings in which participation would not result in an appearance on the evening news. While I ran with a misfit list of nineties extras (ok, roll call: Jenna Venom, Barrie Martin, Jordan Binner, Greg

LeBelle, Dale Godfrey, Gabe Rayburn, Billie-Joe Davis, Denise Bathos, Debra Kabab, Leigh Dennings, Glenn Ralph, John Taylor, and so on), my sole true friend from the era had the mythic-but-real first name of Dragan. (It's as if the universe wanted this story to be even more far-fetched than it actually is).

I met Dragan Momchilo Stajanovich when I was twenty-three. He was eighteen, and we were dating two women who were roommates. Over the next year we began to create a roster, league, and propaganda both real and imagined supporting a make-believe bowling league called World Championship Bowling. Dragan was the no-good champion, having won it all in September. For many months we would taunt each other on VHS-recorded interviews, until a rematch took place in late 1997. Thrown into the mix was the thirty-something, two-hundred-and-thirty-pound ex-con Greg LeBelle. I met Greg at the hospital one sunny morning when I was having some tests done for a minor concern. Dragan had come along too, and soon we found ourselves laughing with this strange friendly giant with whom we had nothing in common. He looked like a wrestler, while Dragan and I were scrawny and youthful.

But behind the scenes is where the story truly took place. All in all, we only went bowling half a dozen times. But the strange outsider quality that Dragan and I basked in consumed hours, spanned miles and years. It seemed like everywhere we went our presence agitated. Once, after we gave a homeless man a cigarette, the hapless individual found himself drowning in one of our strange conversations, until he turned around and shouted, "WOULD YOU TWO SHUT UP!" We would get kicked out of cabs for talking about fears that our known associates (read: court-appointed friends) were really sex aliens sent back in time to destroy us. We were doing anything we could not to grow up and become responsible adults. (The fact that we are now both fathers isn't all that astonishing, but at the time our preoccupations left many wondering if we'd ever amount to anything beyond the humble Tim Hortons clowns we portrayed in real life.)

Dragan and I were Beavis and Butthead to Greg's strange gargoyle-like presentation. It was odd to see Dragan and me, who appeared to be (and were) very young, walking the streets of downtown Toronto with such a specimen. Greg grew up just north of Saint Andrews in New Brunswick with his twin brother Richard. They were born on September 18, 1963. "Until the age of 16, all my stories about my life started with *we*," he said, reminiscing. "We would catch bats using burdocks. And I liked meat and Richard was a vegetarian, so at dinner I'd spit on my meat and he on his peas so we wouldn't lose our favourite bits of our food."

In the summer of 1999, I was out with Greg Lebelle, who, like most of our band of recovering egomaniacs, had relapsed. He got blackout drunk in the club district and picked a fight with a scrawny construction worker he alleged reminded him of Dragan, with whom Greg was in a scripted storyline feud within our semi-pro, semi-fictional bowling league. To make a long story short, Greg handed me his street meat (read: hot dog, $3 in 1999 prices) and entered into a one-punch fight with the young man, who had come at the both of us with a two-by-four. By the time I had him against a wall, trying to protect him from getting the shit kicked out of him by my Frankenstein monster, there were three cop cars at the intersection and Greg was being arrested.

Two months later I meet with the accused and his government-appointed defence lawyer to go over my statement. The lawyer suggests altering my language. I'm asked to go over the scenario multiple times. When the court date arrives in April 2000, our bowling league is all but over. Greg is still our recognized champion, and we joke that he should bring his trophy to court. The sad truth is that the story Greg wants everyone to believe is that he was so stressed from his job as a street counsellor that he *had* to start drinking again, and the line between real and fantasy collided. He thought that he was face to face with his bowling nemesis, but real-life friend, Dragan. "That's disturbing," Dragan told me over the phone. Our friendship with Greg would never be the same again. Once happy members of his band of merry men, we had now truly lost our way with this entire bowling experiment.

I can hear the Michael J. Fox voice-over for the final scene of the ten-part Canadian-funded made-for-TV special: "There was only one road back home from the Bowlerama—the Thorncliffe 81 bus, just a burnt-out bump across the Leaside bridge to the snug confines of Dewhurst Avenue, just off the Danforth, straight into the multifibre finality of a hand-me-down duvet, where sleep awaited us, free from the cruel obscurity of our sporting fantasies and fallacies...just another jock in the locker room for the clinically insane..."

The trial date is set, and I'm to be called to testify as a witness. When I arrive at the courthouse on April 6, 2000, in a nice suit, Greg is there with his share of supporters, including a twenty-year-old exotic dancer/mom and some of his, not her, coworkers from the harm-reduction street service centre he has been working at for the last two years. They are there as character witnesses. I'm there in the capacity of an actual witness, which I liken to a crime reporter.

The trial started at 10:00 a.m.; by 10:15 I was asked to leave the courtroom since I was the only witness for the defence. The sad truth is, I missed the entire trial save for my ten minutes on the stand. By 3 p.m., I hadn't spoken to anyone and was not informed until after my testimony that Greg had told the court that the whole incident revolved around him being so drunk he thought the guy he hit was his bowling nemesis Dragan. Not a word of a lie. Well, in my opinion, he *was* lying, but he did say it in court. I didn't know that was what his defence was relying on though. So I took the stand, lucid and clear, describing what happened in the one-sided fight, not really talking about bowling at all. The judge was interested in how I knew Greg and whether or not I was in a recovery program with him. I said I was not, but that we often hung out with people in recovery.

At this point in my life I appear youthful, not yet jaded by the perennial rejection from publishers and magazines that will come in the decades that follow. I am well-rested and well-groomed, and the judge immediately asks my age, as if I'm buying firearms or a quart of vodka. "I'm twenty-six," I say. Everyone wants to know my relation to the nearly forty-year-old ex-con with the knife scars along his neck, shaved head, and outward appearance of a gargoyle who stepped down off some medieval architecture for a cigarette break. The Crown asks what Greg's mood was like, and we get into semantics about the difference between "angry" and "upset." Then I'm asked the question that wraps the entire case up in minutes. "Did Mr. Lebelle hand you anything?" This question is the most loaded question I could possibly be asked. I'm under oath and I can't lie. "Yes, he handed me his hot dog." This evidence completes the picture of Greg's menace. The courtroom, including small children who are visiting on a field trip, now have the perfect image of their monster, temporarily abandoning his street meet to beat the crap out of an innocent TTC worker. They've got their criminal and as I leave the stand, Greg's face reveals a distant sadness I've not seen since.

My appearance in the chambers lasts no longer than a bad haircut, and I feel as young and irrelevant as an Alicia Silverstone miniskirt mall-heist project doomed for box-office glory. Soon, the verdict is read and the court empties, but I'm long gone. A call comes in a few minutes later, revealing that Greg was found guilty and will spend two months under house arrest.

Over the next few days, dial-up era emails came a-knocking. Friends of friends would pass on messages, voicemails from ex-roommates who knew us all: "I can't believe how far this has gone. Two police-related incidents in under a year. Wow." "A year ago I knew it would be a problem. You see, at first it was just some wrestling fun…a little wrasslin', a little bowling…no one would get hurt…no one would be the wiser. And now look. Two dead and the rest awaiting the crucifixion." "Here lie all bowlers who died for their sins." "The trial was a pig circus, he didn't have a chance…This is the story of the Hurricane. And it won't be over until Bobby changes his name…Nice answers though. I would've laughed for sure. You should change your name to Ashchan, or Bernee Parmalee." And there I sat, next to a box of bowling flyers and video cassettes, relaxing in a cheap suit and rotten dress shoes, shoes that probably belonged to some dead man, listening to the news trickle in, bound to a life of Internet horror.

Each September in the 1980s I had to write about my summer vacation. How I would love to submit my 1999 entry to all my former teachers, because I witnessed the oddest assault in the history of the universe. Greg Lebelle used himself as the message, himself as the archetype of a childhood-destroying ultimate potential. He himself watched, day in and day out, dozens of people twisted on booze and hard drugs, and he saw himself. "I was thinking of killing my parents when I was eight, cutting my wrists when I was thirteen. There was obviously something wrong with me," Greg told me once.

So how did the bowling trial impact Greg's life? Well, I'll tell you. Police and judges love to bully those who resemble bullies. The trial was a joke. Greg was articulate. I was articulate. The person who was assaulted came at Greg and me with a stick. The lawyer kept asking me if Greg handed me anything, like a hot dog. Apparently someone said he handed me his hot dog so he could go fight this guy. I should have eaten the hot dog. Was it evidence? Was it my hot dog? Why did they use this as a part of their cross examination?

Greg's first major interaction with the police had been in the mid-1980s in an Edmonton jail cell, and had resulted in him losing his testicle for the first time. A few kicks in the groin from a steel-toed boot separated his left testicle from the sack, and Greg found himself in the prison's infirmary, holding a cup of ice with his ball in it. They put it back together as best they could.

When Labelle was diagnosed with cancer in the mid-1990s, the cancer sprouted its fangs at the very same place that had been weakened years earlier. As a taxpayer, what "crime" merits your tax dollars? A one-punch fight or bringing to justice the military cop who stomped an eighteen-year-old prisoner's ball off? Which event should have had a trial?

For most of the late 1990s, day and night, Greg Lebelle was a hard-working Torontonian, and like most needed to kick back after the tear. As a harm-reduction specialist for street health in downtown Toronto, Greg spent all day talking with versions of his former and current self. Despite his personal lows, bankruptcy, the death of his brother, and his battle with cancer (the cancerous testicle was removed in 1996 and he went into remission), Greg was still fighting for the homeless and their rights. His letters in *Now* magazine were charged, intelligent, and urgent:

> I am disgusted and dismayed not only by what I've witnessed this afternoon, but by the process of accountability, which seems non-existent when trying to report police travesties to none other than the police themselves. At about 4:15 p.m. on Wednesday, April 10, while leaving Swiss Chalet on Yonge just south of Gerrard, I heard a 20ish black man screaming across the street. He was being handcuffed by 52-Division officers. Officer "D," who had the "suspect" handcuffed, was wrenching the man's right arm upwards behind his back, resulting in the young man's screams of anguish...

One evening in 2003, I was at a reading when Greg Lebelle staggered in and landed noisily beside me at the bar. He told me about a surgery he had just experienced a few hours earlier where they had removed five inches of colon rectally. "I don't want to be half a man," he said, "I don't want you to remember me like this." His dream at the time was to have children, and with his health always at risk, this dream became more painful each time I saw him. Later, during a walk, we saw a dog being beaten in the park, and Greg was reminded of a horrible incident involving a steel-toed boot and a former co-worker's small lapdog only weeks before. Something happens to people, something unknown, forgotten. To Greg, the weak's voices were just as loud and vulnerable, as basic or confused, as passionate or apathetic. He wanted the world to treat itself and its helpless so much better. He wanted the rich to share with the poor, and the police to act humanely. His utopia wouldn't be so bad, but it's just as selfish as any other kid's in the candy store. There's always someone with less. And someone with more.

We walked by the small farm in Cabbagetown. All the people there had moms and dads, came from somewhere else originally. "Over there last week an African man was murdered. He had a lot of property until his wife left him, took his things, and he ended up here. They called him Barefoot." People would stop Greg on the street to talk to him, to update him on how they were doing. "Do you know what is the hardest part about being a spiritual giant?" he asked me, chin dangled in cigarette smoke. "Having to be a spiritual giant."

On top of the Imperial Pub on Dundas Street we had a few drinks and smoked a joint.

The Bowling Trial finally resurfaced as a subject. "I lost." He lowered his head.

"I know," I said, thinking to myself, *I was there, two years ago, in my suit and tie...* "It could have been worse."

"So that guy worked for the TTC?" Greg asked me.

"Yeah," I said, feeling like Vince McMahon during countless showdowns with the law, defending his wrestlers, making calls to lawyers for bail and support. What had I created?

Greg put his drink down and looked down at his hand. "I thought he was just a punk."

It must have been bleak, constantly delving into one's demons to escape purgatory, which in itself is a sort of lovely hell. That night Labelle spoke softly about recognizing individuality and connecting individuals amongst the quality of chaos, which, he says, is so strong. Bowling became a sacred symbol; the alley was our Bethlehem, our sanctuary. Only in the belly of filth with its vintage second-hand smoke and continuous streams of entire families, born right here in lane seventeen, could we find peace. This is where the entertained ended up. When the movies ran dry, the sex numb, the dance bounce too painful to repeat—oh, the fucking bowling alley, let's go there, my dear one-and-only friend.

As we grew properly into adult roles, Dragan and I would meet a handful of times each year, referring to our hangouts as "Pay-Per-Views," based on a mutual expectation that something wild would inevitably go down which would boost our imaginary ratings—whether it was visiting a pothead barista friend's "Cottage du Horror" for a "pornographic family Christmas meet-and-greet" or the evening we spent wandering downtown, looking for an art show in the hopes of finding a beautiful art weirdo in a strapless tea dress carrying parts of a broken door, only to find ourselves under the Don Valley Parkway, being chased by security dogs, running towards the long-gone Irwin Toys sign, which seemed to be erected as a sort of licencing beacon to our own sense of nostalgia and childhood friendship playing out in our early-adulthood reality.

A note from a friend from the time reads: "Hopefully all is going well in Toronto and you haven't been floated out into Lake Ontario with cement shoes by a mean-spirited part-time phone sex worker employed by screaming Lord Jenna and her Ritalin powder-room friends."

Dragan's and my association with others in the system of court-ordered youth recovery eventually became tainted with the depressing statistics of their inevitable returns to abusing drugs and alcohol, though we tried to remain pure. Still, without a VCR to watch the films we enjoyed watching, we were sentenced to spend most of our days post-Greg wandering the streets with bags full of videocassettes in search of friends' VCRs (an antiquated form of media, popularized in the 1980s and completely extinct by the early 21st century) and bags of chips. So, we made up our own stories and sense of heroism. It was us, the Outsiders, versus the entire planet. *What's our storyline this weekend?* Whatever strange thing happens to us. We bump into: an ex-recovery associate on Yonge Street who doesn't have time to chat as she's on her way to doing her first stag party; or the five-foot-four construction worker in between wives, girlfriends, and custody battles, who we heard was sleeping in Greg's hallway closet with a woman of equal height and desperation; Greyhound hellhounds, bakers, ravers, candlestick makers...were these people really in front of us when we said they were?

Though we stopped "collaborating" with the late Greg Lebelle in 2000 (barring a few cameos), Dragan and I felt mythologically fettered to our monstrous bowling champion, social worker, and 29-time-assault-charged criminal action figure. It's tough—I think it's like a big mountain you're always photographed in front of and people are like, hey wow, you and that mountain!

The court transcripts have long been erased, despite my pleading with the Attorney General's office. I spoke with Dragan on the phone to finish up this piece. He reminded me, "You just have to remember that we were constantly running from him, towards the end, and all those people we once knew in recovery, who hung out with us. Well, when those folks all left him and we were all Greg had, he relapsed and became an addict again. That was what the whole trial was about. Everyone thinks we made it up. But it all really happened."

"That's true," I said.

Dragan added, "We could explain how you and I met each other without getting into weird conversations. You couldn't do that with Greg."

Dragan and I would talk on the phone a lot during the paranoid times in our lives. We needed second childhoods, I think, and found absolute immaturity in one another, which, in a "The Selfish Giant" kind of way, made us completely innocent. What was the point of moving forward in the late 1990s when all that awaited us was another dumb conversation about shoes or politics? The world was asleep! We wanted nothing to do with that. We both had family problems. So the Outsider thing was our way of having a family, even if it was only a few times a year for a couple of hours.

In a note from an old girlfriend, I see the architecture of my obsession with Greg Lebelle: "Why are you hanging out with Greg and recreating the rejection of your father?"

These days, Dragan and I check in, but we're busy dads. Greg Lebelle died from heart complications at the age of 50 in late 2013. No person ever before or since was as polarizing a figure in our lives, and that includes our fucked-up parents. After I sent him a draft of this essay, Dragan said, "That was beautifully said. I talk about you all the time as if you're living across the street and we sell lemonade on Saturdays. I always say you're my oldest, closest friend, even if we're miles apart." And with this I agree; it's the truth, the whole truth, and nothing but the truth. So help me Bowling.

HEART-KNOCKED LIFE ($275)

Steel Chair to the Head: The Pleasure and Pain of Professional Wrestling
edited by Nicholas Sammond
Duke University Press

Hitman: My Real Life in the Cartoon World of Wrestling
by Bret Hart
Random House Canada

Long has it been argued and bemoaned that pro wrestling is dumb, simple, and "fake." Thankfully, *Steel Chair to the Head* serves as a panacea to these popular allegations. The book serves fourteen arguments that swell over the simple fluff and shallow violence, prying deeper into the heart of the industry and its continuous thud and ritualistic timing.

Political upheaval, racism, homophobia, domestic and marital violence, sexism, ethical betrayal, mental health, physical handicaps, and the treatment of the elderly—there's no limit to the subjects pro wrestling takes on. Combing the earth for abject subject matter, professional wrestling gauges, examines, and exploits the entire morality meter on a weekly basis. All these aspects of the sweet science have been carefully cross-examined and hung out to dry in this no-holds-barred analysis.

Steel Chair to the Head provides an unparalleled look at wrestling's cultural interaction with history and the world. The contributors combine fanaticism with intelligent arguments. The "sport" is examined from a fan's point of view, exposing the psychology behind its continuing popularity.

As a performance genre, pro wrestling has enjoyed a steady economy and a steady line of controversy, begetting, like other sports, a series of real-life scandals and tragedies. Over the years it has had steroid scandals, tragic deaths, and countless reports of children hurting one another by emulating their heroes on television. For the most part, though, wrestling has been able to create more than it's destroyed. Its re-enactment of contemporary issues such as xenophobia (which seems to be the most consistent theme for the WWE over the years) is an appropriate testament to the theory that we are a society that never seems to learn from its mistakes.

The Nicholas Sammond–edited collection uses a variety of contributors to celebrate pro wrestling and counter the hypocritical stigma that it has garnered over the years. Perhaps no other industry is so heavily stereotyped, yet so influential and accurate in its reflection of the appetite of its audience. Take the 1980s tag team The Bushwhackers' homosociality exorcised by public performances of homophobia, or the dismal and outright racist way in which the Latino wrestlers (arguably more talented) are pushed down the card to make room for the larger white stars. Another interesting focus is the sexuality of pro wrestling. Did you know, for example, there is a plethora of women who write slash about their favorite big boys?

The Latino section—by Phillip Serrato—is particularly strong because it combines a history of the people as well as their nefarious dealings with mainstream wrestling culture, ultimately offering an example of just how real wrestling can be. It seems that racism in the workplace doesn't stop in the arena of sports entertainment. "Over the past twenty years, promoters have proven themselves predisposed to contain and debase their Latino performers," writes Serrato. It's a not-too-subtle examination of the real-life racism that occurs with backstage politics, where Latino wrestlers are reduced to sideshow status. Serrato makes a bold statement on the claim that what occurs in pro wrestling is a reflection of what transpires in our daily lives.

With careful examinations of wrestling as it happens in the ring, *Steel Chair to the Head* is a wrestling fan's best friend, and the anti-fan's worst enemy. The essayists include scholars in anthropology, psychology, film studies, communication studies, and sociology, one of whom even used to wrestle professionally. And as shocking and confrontational as the book is, it's just as inventive.

Steel Chair to the Head gives a sort of stigmatic closure to pro wrestling by elevating its criticism and delivering an intelligent sensitivity akin to that of books written about business or media culture. This fact-heavy anthology shows the brains behind the phenomenon that has disrupted our ever-unbalanced culture. A definite tool for a fan of media, wrestling fan or not.

*

In his poem "Death of a Ladies' Man," Leonard Cohen wrote: "I'll never see such arms again in wrestling or in love." It's a fitting poetic filter for examining the deeply emotional life of Calgary wrestling icon Bret "The Hitman" Hart via his memoir *Hitman: My Real Life in the Cartoon World of Wrestling*.

The sixth-born son of a family invested in "the business"—Stampede Wrestling was run by his late father, Stu Hart—Bret Hart originally balked at the idea of donning wrestling tights. The mere thought of his clothing touching his sister's leotards in the wash horrified him. Amid such comic recollections, Hart reveals his development into a universal wrestling hero. After a brief stint as an amateur city wrestling champion, he began working for Stampede Wrestling. By 1985, when the territory was sold to WWF (later WWE) owner Vince McMahon, Hart had landed a spot on the roster, where he would remain for the next 14 years.

The wrestling business proved as packed with melodrama as with blood-drenched plot lines. When a major steroid scandal hit the company in the early 1990s, Hart became the WWE's perennial world champion. In spite of his Hitman pseudonym, Hart was free from campy gimmickry; he was an emotionally vulnerable champion, an underdog with whom new fans could identify.

Nowhere is this more obvious than in an encounter during a 1993 trip to Israel, when a young fan dressed in "a crudely sewn pink and black replica of my ring outfit" paraded a sign that read, "NEW REL WORL SIMPION." Approached by Hart, the boy said, "I don't want to bother you. I just want to look at you. You are my hero." This kind of adoration was not unusual for Hart; he was an emblem of strength for the disenfranchised. Hart also recounts how an engineering student used his self-aggrandizing mantra to help survive in her broken home: "I remember looking in the mirror as a teenager and saying, 'Rosalie, you are the best there is, the best there was, and the best there ever will be, and don't let anyone tell you otherwise.'"

Wrestling, unlike other sports, has no off-season, and the hazards are numerous. It's a career without aftercare or unions, instead offering an accruing death count. Hart recalls the struggle to raise four children with his ex-wife Julie, a task irrevocably impeded by weeks on the road. *Hitman* is as much travelogue as autobiography, taking the reader on international gigs with wrestling's colourful fraternity, who resemble insecure playground bullies, juvenile pranksters, and masters of late-night excess. Some familiar figures from wrestling's past make impressions as genuinely caring men, such as a weeping Andre the Giant on his last day of work. Hart dutifully commemorates the passing of nearly 30 co-workers while providing insight into the creative process of putting together a believable wrestling spectacle.

In early 1997, Hart played the role of the pro-Canadian hero, which displeased US wrestling audiences. He would pontificate on Canada's universal health care, questioning American values and the USA's lack of heroes. Simultaneously, the WWE's product was growing raunchier, and Hart was used as a morality meter. In Hart's final WWE match, in November, 1997, Vince McMahon rang the bell early while Hart, then champion, was trapped in his own submission move, making it appear he had given up—a very different finish from what was planned. Hart's apoplectic sentiment is vivid in his recreation of his post-match confrontation with McMahon. He would never wrestle for the WWE again.

Disaster struck once more at a WWE pay-per-view event in May 1999. Owen Hart, the youngest of the Hart brothers, fell from the rafters while attempting a ring entrance and was killed almost instantly. Hart's tender reflections on his brother provide catharsis, at least for the reader, as he likens the brothers to charging stallions, "steam coming out of our nostrils in snorts." The painful familial tensions surrounding Owen's death were exacerbated by the touring WWE in Calgary, which "lit a fuse to the powder keg at Hart house." Hart's parents are described as proud but exhausted figureheads, drained from soothing the massive family in "an almost infinite circle of concern." There were, however, moments of levity. On a night out drinking with the boys, Hart recalls how respectful his peers were toward his father, and how, after a shot of Jack Daniels, his father's eyes lit up "like Dracula drinking holy water."

In 1999, while wrestling for Ted Turner's WCW, Hart, then 42, was seriously concussed in the ring and forced into retirement. A stroke in June 2002 left him temporarily immobile and hospitalized. It was in this abject state that he received a phone call from McMahon. Hart struggled to explain his desire to be remembered by his fans, and a partial mending between the two men began, culminating in a DVD retrospective of Hart's career released by the WWE in 2005. In an industry with a flimsy lifeline, Bret Hart survived a succession of grievous tragedies with his legacy intact. It is that combination of strife and strength that solidifies his spot as perhaps the last true wrestling hero.

Originally published on *Bookslut* and in the *Globe and Mail*

PARTS UNKNOWN: AN INTERVIEW WITH MICHAEL HOLMES ($50)

Michael Holmes is not on steroids. His writing doesn't put you to sleep with its suffocating grip. No, the author of *Watermelon Row* and *21 Hotels* is feeling just fine... and right now, in these very pages, *The Danforth Review* is calling him out! Ladies and gentlemen, from the hipster district of CanLit, will you please shut the hell up long enough for us to introduce, from Toronto, Canada, the centre of the universe, the reigning and defending author of *Parts Unknown*, Canada's Writer-in-Ring-Residence, Mr. Michael Holmes!

Nathaniel G. Moore: What was the first wrestling match you remember watching televised or live?

Michael Holmes: It's almost impossible to pinpoint where or when my fascination with pro wrestling began. I remember watching with my father when I was very young—I can still hear the canvas snapping, an inflexible Pop-O-Matic Trouble kind of sound, in a studio auditorium of the early 70s, as Jerry Blackwell, Nick Bockwinkle, or Mad Dog Vachon slammed some poor forgotten jobber. Superstar Billy Graham, Jesse Ventura, the Crusher, and a young Ric Flair: I remember them all, pre-WWF. In reality, my earliest memories are probably a Saturday and Sunday afternoon mix that misremembers four different territories: Vern Gagne's AWA out of Minnesota, Stu Hart's Stampede Wrestling, Grand Prix out of Montreal, and the Tunney's Maple Leaf Wrestling, broadcast on CHCH out of Hamilton, with Billy Red Lyons as the host.

NGM: I too recall CHCH wrestling with Billy Red Lyons on Saturday nights. Discovering a new language and witnessing seamless physical exhaustion seem to be two major results of watching wrestling. What does watching wrestling do to your brain, and if you were a wrestler, what would your gimmick be?

MH: Like many fans of the grappler's art, I'm an inveterate booker—for years now, after every Raw, Smackdown, and WWE PPV, and more recently after every NWA-TNA show, my imagination has played havoc with history and possibility, let loose amongst all those wildly improbable and deliciously limitless storylines. The narratives fire me up, and I admit I probably spend too much time trying to anticipate where the writers are going next. And yes, like so many fans, I bitch and moan (even if it's just with myself) about wasted opportunities and redundancies, about guys getting pushed while other, perhaps more deserving, talents are overlooked. In wrestling, the booker is a kind of God—the guy or committee responsible for all the big decisions—who wins and loses, who gets the title shot and who doesn't. So, watching wrestling, my brain becomes the owner/booker of all wrestling everywhere. Every week I write a new world for WWE—one better and more entertaining than what I watch on TV the following Monday and Thursday. Of course, I'm wrong. Every wrestling fan worth their salt believes they can "fix" wrestling, that they could make it better. Few have any idea how complicated the writing process gets, how many stresses and pitfalls the booker has to negotiate.

But if I was a wrestler? I think I'd develop a gimmick that was as carefree and hardcore as both Sandman and RVD, and as ruthlessly aggressive as Stone Cold Steve Austin, and then modify all three with Mick Foley's unlimited flexibility of character. It would definitely be a character as vicious on the mic as in the ring. You can't underestimate how important that is— the ability to cut a good promo takes you a hell of a lot further than the most impressive hat trick of gutwrench suplexes or the deadliest submission move. Great technical wrestlers, like Edmonton's Chris Benoit, are punished for not being as dominant in interview situations as they are in the ring. Again, it's exactly the same in the literary world. If you give good sound bite, you go over—Rolodexes everywhere are filled with the contact info for glib hacks.

NGM: For those at home who are reading this and realizing we are two grown men discussing millionaire fake sports heroes and that *The Danforth Review* is funded by Canada Council, can we appease them by perhaps alluding to the fact that most of their lives are scripted and fake? For example, the streetcars on Queen Street always stop at the same stops and always move east and west. We know how the ride will end. Poetry itself is staged as well, isn't it?

MH: Every government-subsidized theatrical performance—from Sophocles to that Lloyd Webber slapnuts—has a blood relative in pro wrestling. Jason Sherman and his plays get nominated for Doras and Chalmers awards—Edge and Christian have been 8-time tag champs, and Chris Jericho was the first undisputed heavyweight champion (in the English-speaking world, anyway) in almost a century. There's very little difference. The writing on Raw and Smackdown is often as good as the stuff that gets published here—not that that's anything to celebrate, it's just, as Stone Cold would say, the bottom line.

And yes, of course, good poetry is just as staged as wrestling. Always. Ultimately, what's "fake" about wrestling may in fact elevate it above most other "real" professional sporting events—more than a simplistic contest, it's art. Anyway, its physical challenges are very, very real.

NGM: The vernacular of pro wrestling is like a weird language one can suddenly engage in if one runs into a like-minded smart-fan or mark. And their names don't have to be Mark. What are some of your more favourite wrestling terms?

MH: Winnipeg's own Chris Jericho coined my favourite wrestling neologism, an all-purpose insult, *assclown*. Pretty much self-defining, but here it is in a sentence: Carmine Starnino is an assclown. Many things can earn you the assclown's mantle; in this case it's self-aggrandizing ad hominem attacks on other, more accomplished writers and thinkers; a Palaeozoic allegiance to the most parochial, chauvinistic tenets of high modernism; and the unmitigated gall to attack the poetics of Al Purdy as a way of making his bones when Al was gallantly living out his life's course.

As far as real, old-school insider wrestling lingo goes, I'm fond of *Kayfabe*. It's a term that refers to the protection of industry secrets, or inside info about the business, from the fans. The word itself originated in carnival slang, as a kind of pig-Latin for "be fake."

You mentioned *mark* and that's another fave. A mark is someone who believes that pro wrestling's gimmicks, angles, and matches are real. To *mark out*, though, is to be so into something that happens in a match or storyline, or with a character, that a fan *smart* or wise to the business responds as if they were a mark. I mark out all the time.

I'm also fond of the term *over*—which is wrestling lingo for popular, or for something that works with the fans. As far as *Parts Unknown* goes, however, the wrestling term most important to the poetry might be *work*. Work is both the ability to wrestle well, and the deception that underpins, that is essentially at the heart of, wrestling itself—it's the predetermined outcome that all matches and wrestlers strive towards. A wrestler, therefore, is a *worker*. So, in effect, is a poet.

NGM: The Canadian content in pro wrestling is one that many people won't know about until this very moment when we tell them. Can you go into some detail about ECW's (the press, Paul Heyman's former company) affinity with wrestling?

MH: Per capita, wrestling's biggest and best audiences in North America are Toronto and Montreal. The WWE folks know this (that's why two of the 20 Wrestlemanias—and two of the best attended—were held in Toronto). All those big American towns vying for those huge revenues, and a tenth of the events have happened here. Pound for pound, we've also produced some of the most beloved and loathed talents in the game: Killer Kowalski, Gene Kiniski, Whipper Billy Watson, Yvon Robert, Stu and Bret and Owen Hart, Archie "the Stomper" Gouldie, Abdullah the Butcher, Rowdy Roddy Piper, Chris Benoit—the list goes on and on.

ECW Press was one of the first in North America to realize the unexplored wealth of material wrestling had to offer. The truth is, until Mick Foley's *Have a Nice Day* became an unexpected *NY Times* bestseller, most book publishers dismissed the wrestling market, believing in the old, lowbrow prejudices: wrestling fans don't (can't) read. How wrong they were. They not only can and do read—they also have disposable income and, more importantly, buy books. And they're appreciative of good books, books that actually have historical relevance or are well written. Foley's memoirs are just that: well written.

ECW got into the ring early—partly because of my enthusiasm, partly because Jack David, our owner and publisher, is such a student of the publishing game. He saw, before almost anyone else in the industry, the wrest-

PARTS UNKNOWN: AN INTERVIEW WITH MICHAEL HOLMES ($50)

ling book market as something ECW could step into and make work. I knew I was into a good thing—in terms of my obsessions—the day I walked into the office to find Jack wearing a Goldberg T-shirt.

My favourite ECW wrestling title, to date, is probably Greg Oliver's *The Pro Wrestling Hall of Fame: The Canadians*. It's a phenomenal resource, an exhaustive look at Canada's contributions to the squared circle. *Wrestlecrap* (the story of the worst gimmicks of pro wrestling history), another recent book, has sold very well. As did our first wrestling title, *Slammin'*. Missy Hyatt's bio was our initial foray into books written by actual vets of the business.

NGM: Any new wrestling titles coming from ECW?

MH: We've got a memoir by Jimmy "The Mouth of the South" Hart that's coming later this year—it's a book I'm really excited about because it's given me the opportunity to work with a childhood hero. Yeah, I've marked out all over the place because of Jimmy.

NGM: Just to be ironical, were many ECW poetry collections or fiction books subsidized by non-fiction titles such as the Missy Hyatt book?

MH: This is tough to answer. Sorta. Kinda. But not really. I firmly believe that the success of our trade titles allows ECW to keep doing CanLit. Of course, like everyone else we're funded by the various government granting agencies to do our literary titles. But when distributors go bankrupt and you're on the brink of going out of business yourself, it's not the revenues from a bunch of short stories that's going to save the company. It's what you collect on *Wrestlecrap* that will put you back into the printers' good books and allow you to reprint a few hundred copies of Jennifer LoveGrove's wonderful debut collection of poetry, or give you the cash flow you need to properly promote the most important Canadian poetry title of the last decade, Gil Adamson's breathtaking sophomore effort *Ashland*.

Over the years ECW has tried to strike the right balance between literary and commercial efforts for both endeavours to flourish. I think we've been successful.

NGM: I enjoyed the piece in *Parts Unknown* on Trish Stratus. I've seen her so many times in the exact same way I never imagined she came from somewhere, like York University, of all places. There's a lot of detail in this book. How did you find these really great little insights into wrestlers' lives?

MH: When I was a kid just getting into punk rock in Brampton, there was no place to hang out—so the 8 or 10 of us with like minds and uniformly bad haircuts gravitated, naturally, to the mall's food court. One day a bunch of us saw one of our mohawked forefathers, maybe the first real punk in town, a guy by the name of Sean Gorman, walking through the mall happily talking with two very straitlaced older folks. I guess somebody shot him a funny look. He just shook his head, obviously disappointed in his minions. "Parents," he said. "Everybody's got two." It's still one of the most important lessons I've ever learned—we all come from somewhere, and there's always something to be learned from that place, those people, and those experiences. A big part of the challenge *Parts Unknown* sets for me has nothing to do with wrestling—it's imagining the aspects of these characters' lives that never make it into storylines, that never show up in the ring. Sure, some of it—like Trish Stratus attending York or the plane crash that nearly killed Ric Flair on my 9th birthday—is "true." Having Scotty Too Hotty read Coleridge, however, is my bad.

Ultimately, I wonder if folks will be surprised by the detail in this book. I've researched everything I've written, and I've probably done more work for this project than for anything else I've ever attempted. But then I remember: it's wrestling. Now, that's not a complaint, it's just a fact: CanLit folks who've got certain expectations for poetry aren't going to recognize the research. Fine. So what, who cares? What's more important to me, what I'm truly concerned with, and somewhat apprehensive about, is the quality of what I've done in the eyes of the wrestling fan. Is the research good enough to pass the test of someone who's watched every RAW, someone who cares more about Lanny Poffo's Frisbee quatrains than who was nominated for the Griffin or the GG? Is the poetry compelling enough to interest the wrestling fan who has had little or no experience—bless them—with CanLit?

NGM: *Wrestling With Shadows* (directed by Paul Jay) is the NFB-sponsored film about Bret Hart's struggle with the business as it boomed in the late 1990s. One of the themes of this film is the curious Canadian–American divide that gets to near–David-and-Goliath heights. Despite the subjective nature of the narration through Bret Hart's eyes, it would make a pretty good Canadian novel, don't you think?

MH: It's a great movie, rivaled only by *Beyond the Mat*, and it's great because it's more than just a wrestling flick, more than a documentary about Bret Hart the wrestler. I'm a nationalist, unabashedly; I'm damn proud, Don Cherry–like, of our in-ring heritage, but I'm not sure if the movie works as a Canadian-David-and-American-Goliath thing. It's more classically tragic. Almost Oedipal. I really think the film's importance lies in its exploration of Bret's relationship with his father, the legendary wrestler, trainer, and promoter Stu Hart. The ostensible "point" of the flick, Bret's problems with WWE owner Vince McMahon, and the whole story of the how he was screwed in front of his family and "country" at the Montreal Survivor Series, may actually be more interesting as an eerily true bit of metaphoric transference.

But Lord, yes, the Harts—they are the great Canadian novel. Stu and Bret, the senseless tragedy of Owen's death, the dungeon dojo in the Calgary mansion basement—walk-ons by characters as magical as Andre the Giant, Gorgeous George, the Dynamite Kid, and Terry Funk? Daughters that married the Anvil and Davey-Boy Smith? Stu doing the cooking and cleaning and Helen taking care of the wrestling promotion's books? The real stories are so good that if you put them in a novel, folks might actually find them too far-fetched.

NGM: I know he mentioned on *Off the Record* in 2001 that he wanted to write a big wrestling history book when he retired. Have you talked with Bret Hart about his next book?

MH: Bret's been hinting at publishing his memoirs for a couple of years now, and as far as I'm concerned, they're the Holy Grail of Canadian non-fiction. There's a contract with his name on it at ECW if he's serious—because any time he's ready, so are we.

Note: Hitman *sold for a reported six figures to Random House and was published in 2007, three years after this interview ran.*

Originally published in *The Danforth Review*

IT'S STILL REAL TO ME, DAMMIT ($0)

Parts Unknown: Wrestling, Gimmicks and Other Works
by Michael Holmes
Insomniac Press

For all its gimmicks, pyro, catchphrases, and gratuitously overacted performances, pro wrestling can be pinned down to a language so specific that the careful lens of poetry might be the only way it can be properly examined. Poet Michael Holmes has a desire to purge a lifelong dedication to the grappling arts, and while the book's subject may be written off as lowbrow, its construction doesn't fail to capture the imagination as each poem focuses—with wear-down detail and multi-camera perspectives—on a particular character or spot in wrestling history.

The Canadian focus Holmes has fostered in the collection is undeniable. Take Survivor Series 1997 in Montreal, the infamous site of the screw job where only a select few of the WWE's roster was in on the unscripted ending of Bret Hart's final match with the company. From "You Screwed Bret:" "They are mean, spiteful people and it's a barren, hateful place—it's always November and Montreal here." Or consider Toronto's Trish Stratus, the WWE's bubbly blonde diva, who in the poem "Stratusfaction (Can't Get No)" is described comically leaving campus to go to Wrestlemania XIV in Boston with "her York U knapsack packed with Miss Clairol and resolve."

Parts Unknown also comes with an exhaustive glossary of industry terms that complement the collection and act as detached footnotes. Words such as *heat, blade, job,* and *work* have entirely different meanings behind the scenes of wrestling. (For example, *job* means "a planned loss.")

In "Socko's Bök" (dedicated to Cowboy Bob Orton) Holmes is fettered to the singular-vowel construct in homage to Christian Bök's infamous *Eunoia*. "So hobo-low socko KO's Bök's boon, scoops O's form to toot woolly horns." The result is a lexical wrestling mobile culled from both nostalgia and frozen physical actions in the ring that also dips into the real-life risks the sport offers. In the abrasive "It's True, It's Damn True," the reader visits the hospitalised side of wrestling: "a flag of skin and ¾-inch flesh divot, profuse bleeding; 3-month course, intramuscular injection, (Rhabdoviridae); grave MRI results vertebra cracked, 2 discs pinning spinal cord, 4 pulled."

Holmes' finishing move seems to be quick-punch deliveries such as in "The Wrath of Kane," where, with one sentence, the poet manages to describe a wrestler's new look with a clever elixir of pop culture, eye fungus, and alcohol: "Now he's mixing Uncle Fester with a runny pink-eye chaser, feeling punchy." The poem ends with the macabre comedic slap, "a monster's first words are always Go to Hell." *Parts Unknown* may get slammed for being an unveiled defence of hyper-masculinity or even outright fanaticism, but Holmes is comfortable with being both poet and wrestling fan in this genre-infused overture.

Originally published in *Broken Pencil*

THE STEEL CAGE ($0)

"I hear voices in my head; they counsel me; they understand; they talk to me." So goes the theme song of current WWE champion Randy Orton. As he makes his way to the ring on *Monday Night Raw*, I feel cold and empty. The 11-time champion has fallen back into the good graces of his employers after a couple of years in the netherworld of the WWE's strict wellness policy for a handful of drug violations. It is wrestling, but I simply don't enjoy the product the way I did as a youth—any semblance of the old WWF has vanished considerably. During the embryonic stages of *Savage 1986–2011* (prior to its final edits), the novel suffered from inside wrestling lingo, paraphrased or shoplifted wrestling-script dialogue, hyperbolic pop culture–injected rants, and over-appropriation, tantamount to bookshelf poison.

Writing about wrestling is like battling in a steel cage while everyone else sits calmly knitting. Yet the genre's historical connection to the high and mighty of the culturally elite is well represented. Take Roland Barthes, who wrote: "In wrestling, nothing exists except in the absolute, there is no symbol, no allusion, everything is presented exhaustively, leaving nothing in the shade, each action discards all parasitic meanings and ceremonially offers to the public a pure and full signification, rounded like nature."

What I can say about the Jason Bourne level of intelligence I have been programmed with over the last 25 years as it relates to professional wrestling is that it's forced me to write outside of the biographical realm found in the mainstream wrestling books that are published annually. I don't have the access to wrestlers, living or dead, that other wrestling authors do. And furthermore, I'm not a wrestling biographer. I'm a marginalized small-press icon with an attitude problem who has to rely on lady luck more than ability.

THE STEEL CAGE ($0)

A source of inspiration that transcends normative guides to literary stardom in Canada has been *Steel Chair to The Head* (Duke University Press, 2005), edited by University of Toronto professor Nicholas Sammond. The socio-political agenda of pro wrestling, its misguided racial and gender portrayals and its exploitation of the middle class, is heavily documented with more exciting writing than any high-profile Randy Orton match.

In a chapter dedicated to Masculine Melodrama, Henry Jenkins III (who appeared in the Canadian NFB film *Wrestling With Shadows*) explains my childhood hero Randy Savage's appeal in terms of storyline arc: "The ongoing romance of Macho and Elizabeth bears all of the classic traces of the sentimental novel. The virginal Miss Elizabeth almost always dresses in lacy white, standing as the embodiment of womanly virtues... The Macho Man–Elizabeth romance is unusual in its heavy focus on domestic relations..."

What the book offered me as a creative thinker was a deeper insight into the structure of sports entertainment, its public reception from fans and the media, and how it all relates to what I eventually attempt to accomplish in *Savage 1986–2011* (gloriously illustrated by Vicki Nerino and Andrea Bennett).

For me, wrestling is an allegorical tool in the novel. For others, perhaps, it's perceived as the novel's entire subject and trajectory: a 300-page book about body slams, suplexes, and pile drivers. I'm so convinced of this I would have loved to publish a few joke prop books with a Jack Torrance type throughout: "All wrestling and no writing makes Nate a dull boy" on every page.

In America, acclaimed author Michael Muhammad Knight, who nearly equals me in age, has made a career out of performances and wrestling-inspired artistic outings. Ten years ago, the author claimed to have introduced himself to a member of the United Nation of Islam as "Ibrahim Hooper," Communications Director of the Council on American-Islamic Relations. The real Hooper threatened legal action, enticing Knight to publicly challenge the real-life Hooper to a wrestling match. On June 25, 2006, Knight staged a match against "Ibrahim Hooper" (played by a friend) at a punk show in Lexington, Massachusetts. (Two years later I did the same, except it was against a poet from Ottawa and we had no political integrity involved in the showdown whatsoever. I almost lost a tooth after rob mclennan hit me in the face with a frying pan and a steel folding chair).

In an interview Knight was asked about comparisons to Salinger and Hunter S. Thompson:

> Sometimes I think people are missing the real influence. I was not remotely influenced by Salinger in the way I was influenced by professional wrestling. The Hunter S. Thompson thing is one that comes up the most. It comes up naturally in this case because of the drug thing. But really, pro wrestling was the biggest influence on my writing. Like what I try to do with it, and how I approach it and how I feel about it... [Readers] see wrestling as some lowbrow stuff, but I'm a wrestler on the page. That's what I'm trying to do all the time.

Yet at the Toronto launch for *Savage 1986–2011* last month (hosted by Conan Tobias and Spencer Gordon at The Steady), through chance, we created an atmosphere that, according to guests, was an anomaly at book launches: people cheering and shouting and a room full of banter, gestures, and chaos. "I've never been to a reading or launch where this happens," one guest said. "It's a bit overwhelming."

Before the launch even happened, I purposefully played down any sort of explanation, telling the hosts to just go with it. We held a Randy Savage poetry challenge with prizes, and sure enough, five people signed up and delivered the goods. It was another way of articulating that anyone can write about any subject. I just happened to have been doing it quite a bit longer. The night worked though; the inclusiveness of the celebration went beyond my book into a sort of outreach program for writing and its subject matter, process, and more. Jenny Sampirisi remixed a classic poem, and two newcomers, Andy Ruffett and Mike Sauve, showed their wrestling-poetry chops with excellent poems specifically written for the evening's celebration.

Originally published in the *National Post*

PART FOUR: BLOOD IS THICKER

MONTAGE OF HECK: WRITE WHAT YOU FEAR YOU KNOW...*AND ARE*...AND HAVE BEEN *ALL ALONG* ($0)

1. TATOOINE CHILDHOOD

In Stephen King's *Doctor Sleep*, Danny Torrance is in AA, where he tells his recovery group that he drank hard to visit with his dead father. I can relate to that a bit. In the early stages, I wrote *Savage* while drinking a lot of white wine—though not my father's favourite drink, it was the closest to beer I could go (this was before cider was a thing, at least in my life). Later in the book, Danny thinks, "There came a time when you realised that moving on was pointless. That you took yourself with you wherever you went." This, of course, is a scientific fact as much as it is a passage from a bestselling horror novel. Now, to switch genre-references on you, although I was technically born at Women's College Hospital and my first home was on Mann Avenue in North Toronto, Leaside will always be my Tatooine.

For those who don't know it by name, Leaside is a North Toronto neighbourhood along Eglinton divided by South and North monikers, and has a cluster of public schools, some apartment complexes, lots of rebuilds, slightly if not disgustingly affluent residents, beautiful parks, and now (not back in the 80s) is known for its big-box retail amusement park at Laird and Eglington, a few panting bike pedals from my family home. At the time, we were an average-income family for this posh neighbourhood, living in a modest-sized home (two-bedroom, one-bathroom, smallish backyard), which included a half-finished basement where I would spend 1985–1994, its lone resident as I entered and exited my teenaged years.[4]

Early on in high school, bereft of consistent human interaction, I found myself writing in two distinct genres: autobiographical fantasy erotica and science fiction. This wasn't my sole focus, as other activities dominated my lonely landscape: road hockey with or without friends, filmmaking with or without friends, comic book drawing, bike riding, movie watching, paper route routing, and swimming lessons were all perennial activities.

Leaside is where I played out my childhood's contract with ageing toys, bike rides, and toboggan runs in Serena Gundy Park's bucolic wilderness, while at home I put my Han Solo action figure in a cup of water in my freezer to re-enact his carbon-freeze moment on Cloud City. Trips to Leo's Barbershop (before it burned down in 1990) made me look like a dweeb. There were stinky video arcades, the tennis club at Trace Mains Park near Leaside Library, rentals from Jumbo Video, The Yonge and Eglinton Centre, inedible snacks from Becker's.

An emblem of troubled, untalented youth, in my mid-to-late teens I was equivalent to a character River Phoenix might have played in one of his sad movies about being abandoned—maybe *Running on Empty* or *Stand by Me*. (Not the official synopses of these films by any means.) Or maybe, just maybe, in the right light, I was Winona Ryder in *Beetlejuice* with all my veils of melodrama, writing over and over again, "I am utterly alone." Despite my attempts at an arrested development through reruns and fantasy camp workshops in my own private cinematic void, in real life I played the vulnerable, shy small brown-haired boy coming of age as an adult.

Remember when Luke Skywalker is on Dagobah and asks Yoda, "What's in there?" And then Yoda says, "Only what you take with you." Well, that was sort of how I played out the rest of my contract until leaving Leaside (and the middle class) for good. As an adult, some twenty years later, in my cataloguing of childhood dregs, I sought other like-minded creative types as likely as the poet sitting next to me at Pivot, or as unlikely as Brendan

---

4   Many of the 1993 graduates from Leaside High School now work as CEOs for Kijiji, have their own medical practices, are engineers, lawyers, scientists, and Regional Vice Presidents of logistics firms. But none of them have won the ReLit Award for Best Novel!

Brown, the lead singer from Wheatus (authors of the 2000 Americana pop classic "Teenage Dirtbag"), whom I interviewed for a music magazine in 2010. During our back-and-forth of questions and commentary, he directed me to a *Rolling Stone* article from 1984: "That is the only place I have ever seen the term *dirtbag* used in the vintage suburban vernacular of the song's context." The article tells the story of a teenage satanic-ritual homicide that happened in his hometown, when a gang of "dirtbags" killed Gary Lauwers, a 17-year-old high-school dropout. According to the piece, the alleged murderers were Ricky Kasso and Jimmy Troiano. "Ricky and his douche crew chased me on my BMX bike here and there," Brown says,

> As a 10-year-old, I knew of The Knights of the Black Circle and was very scared. I wasn't allowed in the park they had commandeered at the end of Main Street here in Northport, which essentially meant that half of Northport Bay was off limits. They were noted for killing pets and digging up graves... and above all, for mass quantities of hard drugs. We're talking about high school kids, mind you.

I remember those years well; child safety in the early to mid-eighties was as big a topic as AIDS later on that decade. If you were in grade school in 1986, child murders in Ontario were more than mainstream news. If you were a paper boy, you were not far away from the eerie images of dead girls your own age. Every day I was reminded of the evils of men by the fates of Christine Jessop (raped and murdered in late 1984) and Nicole Morin (taken the following year from a high-rise elevator in the middle of the day).

Getting back to the Wheatus singer though—"When the murder happened," Brown says,

> a 'dirtbag' was a very bad thing to be. Heavy metal was suddenly a capital crime. Here I was, 10 years old, walking around with a tape case full of AC/DC and my ripped jeans. Ricky was arrested with an AC/DC shirt on. I lived for my tape case. To suddenly have it demonized, literally, well, that

sucked. When I wrote "Teenage Dirtbag" that was who I was talking about: 10-year-old me, branded a devil worshiper.

2. MY OWN PRIVATE DEATH OF A SALESMAN

By 1990, my father had been working in the insurance business for a decade and was about to head the environmental liability division at a prominent firm in downtown Toronto. This was around the time that the soft drink giants in Ontario increased their commitment to the province's recycling programs to $20 million over four years, while the total number of households with Blue Box service reached one million. Ontario was considered a global leader in recycling.

On an international scale, companies desperately wanted to avoid vilification in the media, with international examples being made out of Exxon Valdez, the oil tanker owned by the Exxon Shipping Company that spilled 11 million gallons of crude oil into the Pacific Ocean in March 1989. The spill was a visual metaphor of what not to do when transporting dirty merchandise in the age of what would become the planet's green movement.

One week, during a public-school strike, I accompanied my father to work to help him out. My job was to collate packages for a presentation on environmental liability—my area of expertise, of course. In all seriousness, however, I remember the toxic illustration that was on the cover: an oil drum with a skull on it, oozing some salacious material into the otherwise white space the design offered. The people on the fourth-floor office at 425 University Avenue were kind throughout my time there as a child labourer. Although evidence of this type of protection was in play in the late 1970s, the rollout of insurance for companies transporting toxins didn't enter my consciousness until I was collating that week.

Today, this particular type of insurance is commonplace, with over 100 different environmental insurance policies available. They cover property, transportation, personal injury, loss of rent, business interruption, clean-up costs, fungal or bacteria pollutants, midnight dumping on insured locations, reputational damages, transportation of pollutants as cargo, and non-owned waste-disposal sites. Looking back, the slightly disturbing potential to make money off this new trend of businesses not wanting to follow in the footsteps of Exxon seemed infinite.

With the rise of environmental-damage insurance, CBC's *The National* interviewed my father for a short segment. Dad relayed the afternoon interview over dinner that night, explaining how they asked him to use his phone and act casual, like he was working. So he phoned mom and had a conversation with her, which was captured in a cutaway. Dad's appearance was reduced to about fifteen seconds of speech, where he explained why companies need protection policies in his soft alto voice.

One cool autumn night a few months later, my father got hammered at an office function and told off his boss. Dad got canned right away but was kept on to train someone half his age to take over his accounts. He must have said something terrible to the man who was putting food on our table, because not only was he fired; the industry blackballed him all over North America. With a large mortgage, two growing sons heading to university, and other daily stresses in his life, dad was heading for a meltdown. My brother Jeff and I wouldn't be told about my father's unemployment for nearly ten months. And even then, all we were told was that dad lost his job and was doing temp work filing and moving boxes around offices for minimum wage.

"Look at this. Jesus."

"What?"

"This tape. The label. 'Daddy on *The National*.'"

We had taped the CBC program a year earlier, when, in January 1990, our father appeared in the five-minute profile. Now it was like watching a snuff tape. Mom was upset, but she was *always* upset. I wondered if she let him have it for screwing up so badly. I felt for him. When I found out the reason why he was fired was because he was drunk and told off his boss, it only confirmed the suspicions I had about my father's problems with alcohol. "Your father thought his boss would be a good Christian and just forgive him."

Recently, I did the math and determined my dad was 49 when he was fired by the insurance overlords. If my brother (who continues to make up for dad's vocational shortcomings by working in the Toronto insurance trade) follows our father's footsteps, then in 2029 he will come home to his wife plastered and freshly unemployed, saying, "It happened, Laura, it happened."

Should I warn him? Better yet—what condition will the world be in by 2029? Will we have our own environmental-insurance policies as part of our personal life insurance? What about protection from air pollution while gardening in our own backyards? No, I'm serious, don't laugh. If scientists are right, 2029 will see our planet narrowly miss being hit by an asteroid (if you consider 35,000 kilometres *narrowly*). Time is cyclical. If the Beatles can have a number-one record in 2005, then pedestrian environmental-liability insurance, my brother repeating his father's vocational fate, and an asteroid breezing by our collective scalps one crisp April evening are all possible.

Since leaving Toronto in the mid-1990s, my father has had his own need for environmental-damage insurance. One winter, his skin reacted to some plastics he was burning in his indoor stove, causing all the hair on his face to fall out. My brother and I looked in horror at his face, which had never been without its cowboy-thick moustache, nor, of course, his human eyebrows. Not only is there a continuous threat of toxins from his own domestic experiments, but my father's small mobile home is located within a few kilometres of Kingston's dump. Highway garbage, air pollution, and windborne pesticides poison his sparse tomato and zucchini garden. There's also the Kingston recycling centre, which last year reported that close to five per cent of the materials they receive are "too dirty to market, so they end up in a landfill." The centre says over time the numbers are staggering, adding up to about 500 tonnes annually heading back to the ground. Still, the biggest liability my father has going for him on a daily basis is his smoking.

One summer, not too long ago, my brother and I spent an afternoon in Elgin, scrubbing our dad's dirty, smoke-stained walls. My father, ever the polarizing figure in our lives, could be both a pro-smoking action figure and a living warning label against the addictive habit—depending on who was investing. He's been smoking since the age of 13, but he still eats three square meals a day and isn't (technically) dead. He doesn't have lung cancer—or any cancer for that matter—can still walk, breathe (sort of), and mill about doing the things that shrinking old men do in their retirements (weeding, puttering, reading the newspaper, and paying bills).

As we scrubbed, wearing masks and gloves and pushing our gag reflexes to the limits, we could tell that underneath the eons of nicotine were healthy white walls, painted sometime in the early 1990s, ready for whatever tenant they would embrace in their bright, vast arms. It was an intimate moment, witnessing the footprint our father had left on his small quadrant of the earth. While his own air quality suffered, perhaps his indoor smoking reduced the amount of toxins being expelled into the earth's atmosphere over the decades. The cross study of our father continues as his health dwindles. He still smokes, putters around, has a puffer, and tries his best to manage any accruing pain he endures along his particular journey from life to death.

3. POST-REALITY BITES

By the late 1990s, my father and I were each other's own unpaid publicists as we both went out of the way to describe to relatives our perceived decrepit fates—a man who once thrived (mildly) in Toronto as a homeowner and worked in the insurance racket and became a sad, chain-smoking, 55-year-old paperboy, and a twenty-something academic fuck-up who was estranged from his mother and baby brother. I shook my head at how my father had customised his retirement through a small investment he'd made from falling in a Beer Store, almost literally living out the first lines of a Billy Bragg song I need not quote here. ("Levi Stubbs' Tears" if you are curious.) His payout, coming in annually, was and is enough for him to eat canned foods until his last day on earth, as he is alienated from all, and apprentices to become one of those strange hermits rummaging amongst rusty dregs in some far-off apocalyptic town.

Over the last ten years, however, as my responsibilities have shifted intensely to my own domestic narrative, I have changed the landscape of my life's work as it relates to my father. My filter on his life was such a strong identity for me. At parties when someone would bring up their own father, I would say, "Yes, I used to do that with my father, until he'd start hitting and strangling me." My friend pulled me aside once and said, "Don't say that shit, it's crazy."

These days my dad is dying very slowly from his smoking. Not that I wanted to, but I always wondered when I could use the line from *Reality Bites* in which Ethan Hawke's character Troy, patient zero of the hipster class of jackassery, not only self-identifies as a narcissist, opportunist, and sarcastic shithead, but manages to paint his post-adolescent family life as a bleak tragedy in which, should he survive it, he would pull off a miracle of the human spirit. Some of you born in the late 60s up until the early 80s might recall the scene in which Lainey, the waif portrayed by Gen-X poster woman Winona Ryder, is given a used BMW by her father upon her graduation from college. Ever the charmer, Troy quips, "Yeah, just think about all those starving children in Africa who don't even have cars." When asked by Lainey's mother if Troy's dad lavishes him with such gifts, Troy offers this squirming digestive: "Well, actually, my father's dying of prostate cancer, so I don't really trouble him much for gifts."

In her 2014 article "I Re-Watched *Reality Bites* and It's Basically a Manual for Shitheads," Lindy West tears down the plot, the cast, and the way in which Gen Xers idealise unhealthy and abusive role models. West's negative take on the film is by no means inaccurate, but my former self is an ashamed fan of the film. (Before *Fight Club* came along five years later, Ethan Hawke's Troy was fast becoming a worn-out personality disorder I'm sure thousands of men my age were subconsciously riffing on, like a terrible living karaoke song that never ended...) In detail, West dissects Troy's falsehood and shallowness to a tee: "Hey, Troy, I get that it's part of your whole anti-consumerist shtick, and was likely the peak of wit in 1994, but do you ever say *anything* that isn't just a corporate slogan parroted back in a sarcastic voice?" Ex-girlfriends of mine literally said the exact same thing to me on the way out the exit door of my troubled late twenties. Perhaps not exactly, but more precisely: "You may as well wear a T-shirt that says NO ONE LOVES ME I SPEND ALL DAY MASTURBATING & MAKING UP STUPID LOGOS TO ACCENT MY LETTERS & THINK ABOUT CELEBRITIES INSTEAD OF REAL LIFE."

Again and again, West confronts Troy throughout the piece, asking if he's capable of normalcy, reminding him that other people in the world, who pay mortgages and have reality-based concerns, don't care about the opinions of a greasy unemployed 23-year-old poet. And then it dawns on me: this is who I was. Not only who I was, but who I *wanted* to be. Forget stability! I'll rent *Reality Bites* from Blockbuster and order a pizza. I'll make every girlfriend I have from now until I'm in an old-age home watch this film so I can say, "That is/was so me." Which calls to mind to another proverb from the celluloid tapestries of the late 20th century, *High Fidelity*, in which

Cusack, portraying Nick Hornby's Rob Gordon, says, "What really matters is what you like, not what you *are* like."

4. HARMONICA LESSONS

My nuclear family was always in a state of meltdown, but one relative who dared to visit us was my mother's Uncle Carl. "Such a lovely day," the kind-faced old man said with a denture click. His exaggerated smile was just rows of glinting, indistinct teeth, losing colour in the driveway shade darkness. It *was* a lovely day, a fine spring afternoon in 1991, as a matter of fact. In our driveway on Glenvale Boulevard, on which a decade's worth of hockey battles, garden tool fights, and Canada Post footsteps were counted, my Great-Uncle Carl posed with my brother. He was sitting on my brother's bicycle, which we all found comical, since our uncle was in his late seventies and probably hadn't been on a bike (let alone ridden one) in decades.

My Great-Uncle Carl was my godfather and took a special liking to me. I was by far his favourite nephew, and he was by far our favourite relative; he gave me money, took me on drives, introduced me to Dean Martin and my brother Johnny Cash (not literally—through cassettes), and enjoyed coffee and the odd slice of banana bread. More importantly, we didn't have to act stoic around him like we did when my dad's side of the family came over. We could joke around and be natural.

For my mother and me though, Uncle Carl's generosity was a source of comfort in our ever-changing economic world. My ridiculous hobbies were, on occasion, costly—the development of all my visceral and vapid Kodak moments as I insatiably documented games of driveway hockey, Han Solo poses, or prop Star Wars models, tarnishing evidence of my inability to socialize at normative levels. And mom, well, she had expenses that my father's new part-time grave-digging salary couldn't sustain. Mom talked out loud to herself in a walking list of errands, acting out conversations with Uncle Carl in which she would ask him for some more money. "See if he can help us out again," was more than a common rehearsal refrain.

In the bicycle photo, like always, Uncle Carl is wearing a dull-grey suit with old and new dandruff caked on his shoulders. A tattered red sweater vest can be seen underneath, while his dress shirt is light blue and accompanied by a crusty clip-on tie. He always looked like a vacuum-cleaner salesman from a 1961 episode of *The Twilight Zone*. His hair was slicked back (grey/black), cut extremely short on the sides. Sparse white hairs could be seen within his dark, neat coif.

So there we were, enjoying a visit with our great-uncle, who was sitting down on one of our matching pink sofas when my father turned to him and said, "Carl, you've got pink hair."

Our Uncle protested, trying to change the topic. "No, no…" he said in a low voice, embarrassed and probably more than a little uncomfortable.

"Your hair is pink."

Mom later told me that Uncle Carl dyed his hair with a tonic. "It's what a lot of elderly men do," Mom once told us. "It doesn't look very good, but we shouldn't say anything."

"So it's women's hair dye?"

"No, it's a special tonic cream," Mom told us without getting into clairvoyant detail. Perhaps in the confluence of his natural white hair and the tonic's darkening qualities, alchemy was achieved in which a pink tone was created. I'll never understand what response my father was hoping to elicit by calling Uncle Carl out, but I'm more than certain the two never saw one another again. As he and I said goodbye outside, I watched him hunch over and vanish into the early evening.

Over the next few months it became cringeworthy listening to mom cold call Uncle Carl, who you could tell was balking at the invite, saying his other niece had promised to bring him over some lovely turkey sandwiches and he would be busy for the rest of the weekend. Mom would go nuclear: it was her closest thing to sibling rivalry. She kept going on about how her cousin Judith was always upstaging her, and that "Uncle Carl never calls…" She once told me a story of how Uncle Carl was going to marry a woman and move to Florida in the 1960s. His brother, my Grampy, forbade him to do so. "Because Grampy helped raise the kids with my grandmother, and he was the oldest, and your Uncle Carl listened to him, even as an adult."

As the final dregs of 1991 sifted their way to our family of four on Christmas morning, my thirteen-year-old brother scowled, opening his stocking. "That's from Uncle Carl," mom said from the gauzy realism of her pink housecoat. I knew why Jeff was so pissed off on Jesus's birthday. He wore his faded Beaver Canoe sweatshirt, his braces glistened; you could see sad bags of early-teen angst in his chocolate-brown eyes. He was just going through a pantomime of Christmas morning, knowing full well the only present that mattered had already been bestowed on his chief rival (me). Uncle Carl, my by-now infamous godfather, World War II vet, and altruistic bestower of my RCA SuperVHS camcorder, which retailed at $1,244.33, may as well have given Jeff an unwrapped bag of barbecue charcoal. Jeff said nothing, obscuring the small object in his hand with his sweatshirt sleeve. "What is it?" Dad asked. Reviving the moment with her defibrillator tone, mom offered an encouraging, "Oh, look," oblivious to Jeff's tragic kingdom. "It's a harmonica," Mom said, doing everything short of saying *golly gee*!

Later that morning, Jeff's opening salvo set the tone: "So *he* gets a two-thousand-dollar camera and I get a harmonica?" The rattling of gifts, slurping of coffee, and shuffling of slippers across broadloom came to a choreographed halt.

According to a 1986 *Chicago Tribune* article, the chances of my owning a camcorder at this juncture were very high. "We predict that by 1988, one in five VCR purchases will be a camcorder, and by 1991 5 million camcorders will have been sold," said chief RCA rival and JVC marketing Nostradamus Steve Isaacson. Through Uncle Carl, I had become a mental tourist, photographing and videotaping the nothing around me. I had a passion for documenting the pale existence and quotidian evidence of our daily lives. Here, look, it's our backyard, or a family dinner, or a driveway with a hockey net, or, every once in a while, the odd family vacation.

Uncle Carl was always interested in cameras. I travel back to his 35mm footage from the late 1970s, looking at myself with glasses, gay cheeks, and fur-trimmed hood, running across the street in the minus-eleven December weather. Soon Uncle Carl lends me the camera to film him going to his car for… more film. Action sequence! Or then we're eating Chinese food: the foil plates filled with rice and chicken balls. These are silent films, with dialogue lost to history.

While I'm sure Uncle Carl regretted missing out on having a wife, we were lucky enough to be a part of his life up until his death in 2003. Always a fixture in the early days at family dinners, birthdays, and Christmas vacation, when not working as a pharmacist at Doctor's Hospital he traveled the world and lived the life of a bachelor. He ate when and what he wanted, bought what he wanted—a new Oldsmobile, trips to Egypt, Africa, France, Florida, Alaska, and Japan, where he was photographed next to giant lobsters as big as a five-year-old child. He'd help the family out with larger purchases like a VCR (which thirty years ago cost upwards of $600 Canadian) or hand me a few twenties for "pocket money."

Near the end he visited less. Not simply because of his age, but because, as he would shyly reveal to me, of my father: "He's always so serious and wants to discuss politics." Our uncle had been through WWII and survived (sort of) the strange and controlling presence of his older brother Wilf, so he didn't feel obliged to listen to our father pontificate and regurgitate the current events of the day. To be fair, my father was likely very excited to have another adult in the house to talk to about *anything*. I think he just got too worked up for my dear and very old uncle. Dad wasn't a social person. I never saw him with a friend the whole time I lived in his home as a young person. Uncle Carl always called our father "Dave," which I thought was strange since my mom always called him "David." But to be fair, so few people called our father by his first name that it shouldn't have seemed out of the ordinary to me.

In short order, the mid-1990s took me down a dark path of substance abuse—mainly pharmaceuticals. I had become, in my own chemicalized mind, professionally mentally ill. I remember the shame I felt when I showed my seventy-four-year-old Uncle Carl my fresh wrist scars. I told him about wanting to visit a friend who'd just started art school at Parsons in New York City. She and I exchanged flirty notes, and soon I was on a plane paid for by my Uncle, just in time to see the *Ghostbusters* car rip down Eighth Avenue on Hallowe'en. Nine years later, I remember visiting his house and finding, on top of his television along with a decade's worth of dust, my postcard from New York. To my great embarrassment, the note on its back told him how much fun I was having and how much I was looking forward to being hospitalized upon my return. What foreign stress I must have delivered to an elderly man who had survived the Great Depression, World War II, and decades of MSG in his favourite Chinese takeout dishes.

Before he died, Uncle Carl was in and out of the hospital with SARS. His second cousin Doug took me for what ended up being my final visit. We had to dress in our anti-contagion moon suits and stood looking pensive as the nurses led us into antiseptic visitation. Uncle Carl handed me his wallet and his watch. He was in considerable pain; the doctor later told us his stomach had grown so weak that his lungs were resting on top of it in a strange failed sculpture of organs collapsing from the inside, making it nearly impossible to digest any food.

All those times he had refused to stay for dinner, the meals, pieces of cake, were symptoms of a finality that would take him away from all of us prematurely, even if it was just by a few years. I waited to hear when the memorial for Uncle Carl would take place, since he had not left any instructions for his funeral arrangements other than that he was to be cremated without a plot or gravesite. In the end, my brother, mom and I, along with our estranged second cousins, said goodbye at a makeshift wake.

But he was the best. I can't hear a Dean Martin song without seeing his dentured smile, his big grin, and his hand extended to me like a real gentleman, ready to—for a moment anyway—elevate me from the reality I was living out on my syndicated family broadcast.

5. DRUGSTORE COWBOY

I remember going to my first real therapy session at nineteen and thinking if I just had $20,000 everything would be fine. It was the autumn of 1994, *Natural Born Killers* was in theatres, the Beastie Boys' *Sabotage* music video was up for an MTV award, and Kurt Cobain had been dead for six months. This was days after I'd hurt myself with a razor blade, in the dog days of summer. It would take twenty years, not twenty thousand dollars, for me to gain the stability I felt I was robbed of that year.

In my own twenty-something hysteria, I found myself abandoning my family, or being abandoned by them (whichever way you want to look at it), and washing up on the psychiatric shores of Ontario's mental health system. What meager shelter I had within my nuclear family was all I knew prior to leaving just after my twentieth birthday. The stigma of mental illness was more than permanent. Not able to identify with friends or family members who were not suddenly crippled by depression, unemployment, and pill dependence, I sought out kinship in popular film narratives of the day. I would become an expert, not an extra, in my own mentally-ill life.

In her essay "The Psychopathology of Cinema," Lauren Beachum writes, "When people have little real-life experience with mental illness, they draw more of their knowledge from films, resulting in more inaccurate and negative perceptions." Beachum explains that this stigma can arise concurrently with discrimination, which discourages people from socializing with those who are mentally ill.

The 1990s were a playground in cinema for bipolar and mood disorders. To name but a few films that deal with this: *Mr. Jones, Mad Love, Benny & Joon, Misery, What About Bob?, Shine, Color of Night, Angel Baby,* and 1999's *Girl Interrupted.* Combined with the mainstreaming of Prozac, there may not have been a more budding time to be mentally ill than the 1990s. Personally, I never took Prozac; I was a Paxil guy, and started taking them two weeks after my parents announced their divorce and the sale of our home. (Thirty-five years after Prozac was introduced, the name has entered the cultural lexicon and shaped how people think of mental illness.)

My mom, it turns out, had been on Prozac and other antidepressants since 1993, and at one time had even given me a single during the summer of 1994, thinking it was like offering me a Tylenol. "I started taking antidepressants in 1993–94 because I had lost confidence in myself and was upset all the time and it was difficult for me to work, and your father and I were in the process of getting divorced. So my psychiatrist suggested that my doctor put me on antidepressants, and it helped a lot."

"Back in the 1990s, Prozac achieved what few prescription drugs ever do. It was trendy," writes BBC magazine's Tara McKelvey. Just as the brand name Kleenex is used to describe all tissues used to blow one's nose, Prozac has claimed an impressive legacy in the zeitgeist. "What made Prozac good was not that it was potent, which it really was not, but that it had really good marketing," says David Healy, a Cardiff University professor and the author of *Pharmageddon.* "They made us overcome the natural caution most of us have about pills and convinced us that we absolutely had to have these things," Healy writes. In addition to Paxil, I would go on to be prescribed

Lithium, a drug popularized by a band from Seattle and its self-destructive lead singer Kurt Cobain. This drug was so potent, I had to (like anyone on it) get regular blood tests to make sure I wasn't absorbing too much of it into my system. To calm down from all the fun of the first two pills, I was given Lorazepam. This went on for the better part of two years.

Looking back on my wasted medication days, I don't feel sorry for myself. Humankind is inventive and prone to both self-sabotage and survival. On one hand, I was doing everything in my power not to get better, attempting to stay the course of being mentally ill because it allowed me a government wage on which I could survive and not be homeless. And I was surviving, no matter how ugly it looked to my judgmental family. Did I become mentally ill because I was a lazy student? A bad son? I couldn't believe how much my life was changing. Could I have done anything else with my life at that time—having come to terms with the abuse I received in my youth? I suppose I could have looked for a part-time job and an apartment somehow, or tried to go to school. I applied for jobs occasionally, thinking I could escape my dependence on the social service system of Ontario. I was also convinced I could just continue my life as a student. After all, I had come this far, never failing a grade from 1 to 13. Why would university be different? Like the other 300 graduates from my high school, I would continue my education. And then I would get a job, find a life partner, and eventually buy a house.

Only, that didn't happen. Instead, I proceeded down the path least likely to achieve anything resembling such a trajectory. In 1997, at the heights of my alleged battle between academia and mental illness, I watched the NFB documentary *Ladies and Gentlemen, Mr. Leonard Cohen*. Before a reading at a university, Cohen tells a story, transcribed here:

> The other time I was in quarters such as these was when I visited the Verdun Mental Hospital in Montreal. I was visiting a friend. He was on a top floor and I asked him, while he was still lucid, where I could get a coffee. He said, "downstairs," which was one of those famous last words. I commenced the descent of several similar stone corridors and I found myself in a kind of arena, which was surrounded by closed doors. It

had been a hot afternoon and I removed my jacket, as I have been moved to do. I left it with my friend who, though mentally ill, was no thief. I suspect he wasn't even mentally ill: he was doing this instead of college. I stood watching the four or five doors, wondering about all the possibilities except for the one that occurred. A door opened and two large men in white uniforms walked out. And they said, "Where are you supposed to be now?"

I said, "In the cafeteria." They nodded to each other.

"Where are you supposed to be now?"

"*In the cafeteria!!!*"

Well, as their questions continued, my answers continued. And although they started out innocently enough, now it began to sound as though I were protesting too much. In fact, after being interrogated three or four more times, I was shouting and pushing them aside, causing them to run after me down the corridor. It was only after a guard identified me that I was able to go back to the room of my friend, who had eaten my jacket.

While I'm no garment eater, I've been visited numerous times in hospitals by friends. These were never long stays, but they were significant enough stretches of time that I carried the stigma around. As the nineties lingered on, one friend would continuously tell others in our expanding social circle how he and I met. "You were in the loonie bin when I met you," he'd say with smug pride. Another would say, "You were contemplating suicide when I was introduced to you." The 1990s were stupid that way: everyone I knew was bipolar or suicidal, a slacker on the verge of extinction. And then there was Leonardo DiCaprio in *Basketball Diaries*, Drew Barrymore playing a bipolar free spirit in *Mad Love*, Angelina Jolie and Winona Ryder's valium run in *Girl Interrupted*, and Brad Pitt's memorable psych-ward tour guide in *12 Monkeys*.

Then one day, like a cancelled television show, the sound of a family clashing on multiple floors of a two-story home was replaced by soft street noises on Danforth Avenue. Stitched up from a recent superficial "attempt" on my life, a head full of pharmacy treats, I was moved into the smallest one-room apartment imaginable, a stone's throw from my father's new one-bedroom atop Ralph Day Funeral Home. His connections in the death trade were now paying off. I had my own tiny apartment to adjust to life on medication and unemployment. The sound of my mother's screams slicing into the static of our domestic storm was replaced by the echoing pop from my bottle of Lithium, newly prescribed to my traumatized psyche.

I moved into that apartment on December 1, 1994, and was on my own for the first time. Now firmly in my early twenties, I was the ultimate academic fuck-up in university. I knew that my mother had been on antidepressants for a couple of years and that my father seemed to be dealing with a type of depression; I considered his recent job instabilities and subsequent sale of our family home to be signs he was self-destructive, wanting to break up our family and be on his own to have his own thoughts, unmonitored by anyone. I certainly didn't help with my erratic fits that contributed to the overall unpleasant vibe the family lived under.

At 20, on welfare, a York University dropout, and given the ever-fitting moniker of "Psycho Nate," my fate seemed preordained as another casualty of the mental health system. My father's angry voice was now that of a soft-speaking loner, and our relationship shifted into a calm truce. We'd even go out and have a drink from time to time at the Black Swan Tavern, not two minutes from our new and strange spinoff places of residence. In March 1996, we both faced major life changes. My father had failed his funeral director licensing exam and would have to wait another year to take it. He immediately fell into a depression, saying, "I haven't felt this bad since my fiancée died."

It had been a year of struggle for my father since leaving Glenvale Boulevard. As if things couldn't get any more mythological, that was the year when my dad, who in my eyes would be forever associated with beer and Jesus, broke his hip while returning empties to the beer store one sloppy winter evening. I visited him a couple of times in the hospital and helped him recover at home too, picking up his drink and cigarette orders. He told me this might be it. "I can't take the exam again for a full year." He needed the higher-paying job to afford remaining in Toronto. "I can't become a funeral director, not without passing the exam. My nerves were so bad."

He had been living in Toronto for fifty years and no matter what shape it took, he had made a home here.

The beer giant agreed to shell out its small annual contribution to my father's upkeep. I couldn't believe it; I still can't. Only my father and his strange mythological life could find a way not only to fall and break his hip while returning empties, but to conjure up a second act in his mysterious life by way of cashing in on his favourite pastime. The Beer Store had set him free.

Early the next year, depressed and floating around on a series of mood stabilizers, I overdosed on Epival. My brother would share the answering-machine recording of my parents talking as my dad stood over my lifeless body:

"He took pills."

"He's supposed to take pills."

"He took a lot."

"Is he breathing?" *Beep.* (End of recording).

I recovered at my mom's place and couch surfed for the rest of the spring.

As I bounced from temporary home to temporary home, I wrote letters to my grandparents and tried to find a place to live. My father and I talked about splitting the rent at his apartment. I told him I'd think about it and a week later left him a message on the phone saying I was interested. However, the next time I spoke to him he announced, much to my surprise, that he was moving to Elgin, a small hamlet just outside of Kingston, and would live out his days in a trailer park. If I was going to live with anyone in our family it was going to be Dad, but those hopes were squashed immediately. With my brother and mother crammed into a tiny two-bedroom apartment near Mount Pleasant and Eglinton, my sense of home was now vapour thin.

Over the next two decades I took a break from pharmaceuticals save for a yearlong experiment with Risperdal, an atypical antipsychotic used to treat symptoms of schizophrenia or bipolar disorder in teenagers and adults, which turned me into a mute who craved sleep. When I could, I self-therapized through writing and relationships, putting everything I had into my friendships and creativity. For the past three years I've taken a mild anti-depressant at a low dosage, and I look back to early times in my life with gratitude. I could have wound up a foggy-headed drooling pharmacy-trade automaton. I escaped with my head up.

Today, I'm long past the uncertainty that swelled in my stomach sitting in the waiting rooms of a thousand doctor's offices, feeling as though I was applying for a job I truly didn't think I was qualified to do. I don't know what damage the pills I took in the 1990s did to my body—and probably never will. But I know that going off them cold turkey after I overdosed was the right thing to do. That marching into my doctor's office at 22 years old, the week after I OD'd, and saying, "That's it, I'm done, no more pills," was the beginning of a long solo journey of self-discovery and survival. My path was not going to be clear. But it finally led me to what I have now: a new family, a career, and the ability to empathize with anyone suffering from mental illness and the stigma of having to go to appointments, feel fuzzy, speak slowly, and dream about a day when they can finally feel stable, secure, and loved.

MY GRANDFATHER'S CULT ($100)

My grandfather, George W. Moore Smith, was born in Toronto in 1911. While his brother, Brigadier Morgan Smith, became a Canadian war hero—he fought at Dieppe and landed at Normandy—my grandfather chose religion. From a young age, he was captivated by the story of Jesus and his teachings, and as an adult, he devoted his life to serving God with the Anglican Church of Canada. In 1939, he was appointed rector in Dunnville, Ontario, on the shores of Lake Erie, where he oversaw three parishes. He and my grandmother, Violet, had five children in quick succession: David, my father, was the eldest, followed by Rebecca, Ann, Patrick, and Suzie.

In demeanour, my grandparents always reminded me of Thurston Howell III and his wife, Lovey, the genteel castaways on *Gilligan's Island*. They were proper, with an air of sophistication and intelligence. In appearance, Violet was mousy and petite and always subservient to her husband. My grandfather, who went by Moore, was large and imposing, just under six feet with broad shoulders and a square jaw. He had a soft voice that could accelerate to a furious boom when he delivered sermons, and when he sang, he sounded like a cross between Kermit the Frog and Leonard Cohen. Some people found him to be a charismatic leader, while others thought he was prone to histrionics. Growing up, my father rarely saw his dad. Moore was always doing God's work.

For most of the 1940s, my grandfather and his family lived in a square cinder-block house in Dunnville. It was ill-heated—the furnace seldom worked—and there was no indoor toilet or running water. It was a difficult life and so, in 1948, when Moore was offered the job of rector at St. Matthias

Church on Bellwoods Avenue in Toronto, he leapt at the chance. The family packed up and moved into the rectory next door.

In the coming decades, the major Christian institutions in Canada—the Church of England, United Church, and Roman Catholic Church—found themselves in crisis. By the 1960s, as the Beatles meditated with the Maharishi Mahesh Yogi, as the Vietnam War eroded trust in authority, as young people leaned toward cultural revolution, the oligarchies of the past lost their power. Church memberships plummeted. Between 1961 and 1981, the number of Canadian Anglicans dropped by almost a third, from around 1.3 million to less than one million. The church had tried to modernize, changing its name from the Church of England to the Anglican Church and permitting divorcés to remarry, but it was still perceived as aloof and stodgy.

The new ideologies of the era were libertarian, anti-elitist, often radical, spurring some parishes toward new, ecstatic forms of prayer. The Pentecostal movement preached that worship had to be experiential, not just ritual or intellectual. Its cousin, the charismatic movement, espoused the notion that Christ conferred gifts upon his followers, like the ability to speak in tongues or the power to heal with one's hands. In 1952, my grandfather discovered these new religious practices when he attended a sermon by Canon Bryan Green, a British evangelical preacher known as the "Anglican Billy Graham," who preached at the CNE Coliseum before 5,000 people. "Man is not a pathological case, as psychiatrists would have us believe," Green pontificated. "He is a guilty sinner."

Moore went through a conversion that day. He considered himself born again. "He became addicted to intense religious experience," my aunt Ann later said. "We—his children and family—had to buy into it. We had no choice."

After Green's sermon, my grandfather embraced rituals that were wildly different from the Anglicanism he'd practised before. He spoke in tongues. He performed the laying on of hands. Sometimes, he'd whip himself into a frenzy, flailing and rolling around on the floor. During sermons, he'd shake and howl unintelligibly. This kind of preaching extended to the home, where his children were exposed to odd spiritual behaviour. His ministry was a patchwork of influences, some of them self-contradictory. He described it as "Catholic in faith, liturgy, and worship, evangelical in Christian experience, biblical in teaching and witness, Pentecostal in ministry, proclaiming Christ in the inner city."

My Grandfather Moore's radical new dogma created a divide within the congregation. Around half of the members left the parish. But some were captivated. In 1963, he was invited to deliver a sermon at Grace Church on-the-Hill in Forest Hill. In the audience that day were Professor William Rogers, the chair of the French department at U of T's Trinity College, and his wife, Marjorie, who was particularly entranced by my grandfather's faith-healing practices. The couple were fairly well off, with a large house in Moore Park. After that first sermon, they joined St. Matthias and became my grandfather's most devoted parishioners. In turn, he confided in them about the difficulties he faced, describing in letters how busy he was with his ministry, how he often felt "off" and "on"—possessed by malignant energy—and how that resulted in cruel outbursts with his family.

As my grandfather's ministry evolved, the leaders of the Anglican Church remained hands-off and occasionally even seemed to indulge some of his beliefs. In 1958, he received permission to bring a British faith healer— who claimed to have cured his own son's meningitis—to the parish, largely at the expense of the church. At one point, he was also allowed to form his own healing committee. But behind closed doors, the diocese was trying to transfer Moore away from St. Matthias. They approached seven Ontario parishes between 1959 and 1964. All of them refused to take my grandfather as their minister.

In 1964, tragedy struck. My uncle Patrick, the favoured son, was killed. He was 14 at the time, on his way home from his job at a stationery store. As he cycled past the corner of Dundas and Shaw, a car collided with him and threw him from his bike, bashing his head on the concrete. He was rushed to SickKids but died the next day.

Everyone in the family fell into a depression after Patrick died. "He was always in song, and carried his guitar with him, always cheerful," my grandfather once told me. "He would say the most remarkable things about Jesus." After he lost Patrick, my grandfather relied increasingly on faith healing to help himself and his family get through the tragedy. At hospital visits and home visits, he insisted on healing the sick, praying and laying his hands on their wounds, whipping himself into hysteria. Within a couple of years, he had become obsessed with the idea of the devil and exorcisms. He often claimed to hear voices, to which he'd turn for guidance.

By 1966, he had formed a close-knit group of followers who subscribed to his form of faith-healing Christianity. He called it the Ministry of Healing. He was assisted by Doug Tisdall, a young Anglican priest whose father, Frederick Tisdall, was one of the inventors of Pablum. Doug had been involved in charismatic Christianity from a young age, praying in tongues and practising faith healing. The diocese bishop had encouraged him to pursue his Ph.D., but at my grandfather's urging, the young man was instead ordained as a priest in 1965. Marjorie Rogers, her brown hair in a tall bouffant, provided counsel for the Ministry of Healing's members and claimed to possess the ability to discern when someone was "off," or not listening to their holy guidance.

According to some members, she would perform what the group called "potting out"—going into a kind of trance, howling like a dog, and chanting. That behaviour indicated there was demonic energy in the room and helped her sniff out who in the group was possessed. She was reportedly only able to come out of it when other members laid their hands on her and prayed loudly until she was herself again. Once, she even suggested that my grandfather and Doug were off and sent them to a motel for the night until they were back to normal. (I reached out to Marjorie, now in her 80s, for comment on this story. She confirmed that she possessed the gift of discernment but denied that she ever entered trances.)

Many members claimed to be able to perceive evil: some described a "head," which was a kind of headache that would manifest when there was a demonic presence in the room; others could sense a "bad atmosphere" when an evil spirit supposedly infringed on the Holy Spirit. They believed in bad omens—a cut on the hand or a dropped dish might indicate the presence of evil.

My grandfather had a standard recruiting process. First he'd identify a troubled parishioner and counsel him or her late into the night. After a few sessions, he'd invite the parishioner to join his group. It seemed like a credible operation: it was associated with a real church, and there were two Anglican priests at the helm. Many members moved into the rectory, next door to the church. Others moved in with Marjorie and her husband,

William, in Moore Park. William, however, was starting to have his doubts. He was disturbed by his wife's fierce devotion and especially by the constant presence of my grandfather and Doug. In October 1966, he moved out, telling a friend their activities had driven him away. A few months later, Marjorie moved into Doug's house on Gloucester Street, which became a second headquarters for the group. They later married and had a daughter.

In its first months, Canon Moore Smith's ministry attracted around 50 vulnerable young men and women. Several of them were theology students Doug had met at the University of Toronto. My grandfather never called his group a cult, but that's what it was. He would insist that new members commit themselves fully to God's will, as he and his cohorts interpreted it, in exchange for the group's protection and support. They'd often have to cut off contact with their families—their fellow cult members would be their new family—and reveal all their secrets and sins to foster a sense of trust. They were encouraged to maintain a sense of serenity and goodwill towards all their fellow members but urged to be wary of outsiders. Many members suffered from depression or came from troubled homes. The more disturbed they were, the more opportunity they had to be healed.

One woman, a 19-year-old mother of two, brought her kids to live with Marjorie and Doug after my grandfather convinced her that living with her parents was evil. "He prayed all of the hell and atmosphere out of my clothes and belongings," she later said. During her first night at the house, she woke up convinced the devil was in her bedroom, which Marjorie confirmed. Right then and there, at 4 a.m., Doug baptized her with holy oils.

Another young woman had been married at 14 and later separated from her husband and two children. She'd attempted suicide by shooting herself, and the bullet had lodged in her spine, causing her to limp. Her ex-neighbour, a cult member, told her the residual pain indicated that there was evil in her body and introduced her to Doug. When he touched her leg, she claimed, the pain went away. While living at the rectory, she coughed up blood one night. "That's hell coming through you," Doug told her.

At a vestry meeting, my grandfather spoke openly about his new venture. He had become irrational after Patrick's death, and the members of his group had saved him. "I keep telling you that God rescues us when we are in trouble. You should believe me because I certainly needed help myself," he said. "The group came because they needed help, and the help was there... they saw the trouble I was in, and they stayed to help me."

The Anglican Diocese of Toronto was aware of the strange and mystical activities at St. Matthias, yet they seemed unwilling or unable to stop them. In March 1966, an archdeacon was assigned to investigate the ministry. He spoke candidly to the bishop about the dangers he perceived under my grandfather's leadership. But without concrete evidence of wrongdoing, the diocese was at a loss about what action to take. So they took none.

My aunt Ann, then 17, had been away from home for two years, teaching at a residential school near James Bay. While she was gone, she'd received strange letters from her father, proselytizing about the wonders taking place at St. Matthias. When she came home to Toronto, she found the doors bolted at the rectory. The church secretary passed on a message from her father: if she wanted to see her family again, she'd have to give herself over with complete dedication to the group and report to Marjorie Rogers. She had no choice but to acquiesce. Living at the rectory, she was often told she was off, and no one would speak to her for two or three weeks at a time. One time, during an off period, she ran to the basement, where her father and Doug stopped her. "You're filled with the devil!" they kept shouting until she went limp.

My grandfather often arranged romantic partnerships between members of his cult. He paired Ann with a young man at the rectory who was struggling with his homosexuality. One day, her father accused her of being cold to her new boyfriend. She was ordered to go to her room and take off her clothes. Moments later, Moore walked in. He was also naked, carrying a chalice and some bread and wine. He anointed her body with oils and celebrated the Eucharist. Later that evening, her assigned boyfriend came to her room and she was urged to have sex with him.

In the summer of 1966, Katherine Globe, a high school student from Burlington, joined my grandfather's cult. Her older brother Alex was already a member of the ministry; he credited it with curing his epilepsy. Their father, an engineer, had recently suffered a heart attack, and her mother had a history of mental illness. Alex worried his parents wouldn't be able to take care of Kathy, so he suggested she join Canon Moore Smith's group and finish high school in Toronto. My grandfather visited her father in the hospital, where he signed over Kathy's legal guardianship. (He later claimed Moore blackmailed him, threatening to ruin him in court if he protested.) The next day, Kathy moved to the rectory on Bellwoods Avenue, where she roomed with my aunt Ann. At 17, she was one of the cult's youngest members.

Kathy Globe had short brown hair, blue eyes, and a ski-slope nose. She was a typical teenager of the 1960s: she loved the Beatles, and according to her high-school yearbook, she dreamed of running her own household. Like other cult members, she was forbidden to speak with her parents, and my grandfather continuously reminded the Globes of the papers they had signed.

Soon after she joined the group, Moore set her up with my father, David, then 25. My dad had always been a proud and dutiful son, loyally supporting my grandfather's teachings. He was tall and thin and clean-cut, with bushy eyebrows that threatened to join in the middle. His eyes were hazel and deeply set in his head. Within a few months of meeting, my father and Kathy were engaged.

At the end of May 1967, a year after joining the group, Kathy developed an earache. At first, it seemed like nothing out of the ordinary. She had chronic ear infections and had been seen by doctors at Toronto Western Hospital several times. On her last visit, they'd found hearing loss in her left ear, a thick discharge from her ear canal, and a bloody post-nasal discharge. She was prescribed antibiotics. When she started complaining of new pain, her friends at the rectory thought she was exaggerating—many believed she was prone to melodrama—and her brother figured she was responding to tension from her high school finals. But the earache wouldn't go away.

Over the next week, her pain got worse. By mid-June, Kathy was mostly bedridden, moaning in agony. On Monday, June 19, Moore visited her room. Kathy told him how much she wanted to beat the illness, and he agreed to pray for her. As her complaints persisted, the other cult members assumed she was off and, as was the custom, they ignored her, intending to give her the silent treatment until she returned to normal. By the next morning, her moans had intensified. That day, according to several cult members, Doug and my father went into her room and spanked her across the behind. "It is our belief that illness is caused by Satan," my grandfather later said by way of explanation.

Her cries continued all night, and by morning, they'd turned into one prolonged shriek. It was so excruciating that my grandmother, Violet, ran upstairs, where a cult member heard her slapping Kathy across the face. (Violet later claimed that the sound must have been Kathy slapping her own face.) Then my grandmother calmly walked downstairs and prepared lunch. She never took Kathy's temperature or found out when she'd last eaten. When my grandfather went up to Kathy's room later, she was in hysterics. "God help me," she screamed out the window. He threatened her, saying that if she didn't calm down and get out of bed, he'd have to cancel an appointment he'd made with the ear specialist for that day. The noise continued, so my grandmother called Marjorie, who sent over Doug and Alex. No ambulances were called. No doctors consulted. No painkillers administered. On the way from the Rogers home on Gloucester to the rectory on Bellwoods, the men stopped to pick up dry cleaning and at the church to pray. By the time they'd finished running their errands, Katherine Globe was dead.

Alex discovered his sister's body at the rectory. She was lying in bed, dressed only in her underwear. After a failed attempt at mouth-to-mouth resuscitation, he called the police, and Detective-Sergeant Patrick Donovan arrived at the scene. When he entered the church, he saw members of the cult lying in the chapel's aisles. In Kathy's bedroom, the wall and floors were streaked with vomit. Her discarded clothing and bed linens were also soaked in vomit, tossed in a heap on the floor. In her hysterical pain, she had removed the contents of her drawers and thrown them on the ground. There was a broken water glass on the floor and a second glass under the bed containing a greenish liquid, likely vomit or bile.

Kathy's body arrived at the morgue that evening. Standing around her corpse, my father, my grandfather, Alex, and Doug formed a tight circle. Moore anointed her with oils. Then, as the detective looked on in astonishment, the four of them clasped each other's shoulders. My grandfather incanted a prayer, asking if it was God's will that Kathy be brought back to life. They were trying to revive her. Later, Alex admitted he didn't think the ritual would work. "But I do believe the power of prayer is strong enough to bring a person back to life," he said. "It's recorded in the New Testament."

When police interviewed members of the cult, many of them said Kathy's illness had been an emotional one, the result of demonic possession. According to the post-mortem report, it was something much more prosaic. Frederick Jaffe, the pathologist who performed the autopsy, determined that Kathy had acute meningitis and an abscess near her left inner ear, which had ruptured hours before she died. Ontario's chief coroner, Beatty Cotnam, later asked my grandfather if anyone had considered calling a doctor. "I realize it should have been done," Moore said. "Our judgment was clouded." An inquest was ordered to look into Kathy's death. The cult spent days trying to pray the inquest away, to no avail. It began on September 28, 1967.

At the time, Kathy's death was the biggest story in Toronto. Front-page newspaper headlines described the downtown cult, the girl who'd died, and the exorcism attempts that had killed her. People were shocked that such a thing could happen in Toronto, where the best hospitals in the country were just a few blocks away. Originally, the inquest was to be held at the city morgue on Lombard Street, but due to the massive amount of attention from media and the public, it was moved to the city council chambers at Old City Hall, where hundreds of spectators sat in the gallery. They heard testimony from the doctors who had treated Kathy's ear infections and the pathologists who performed the autopsy, then from members of the cult. My father testified that he believed Kathy was trying to get his attention, and that she only seemed to scream when someone walked past her door. He had spanked her across the behind several times the day before she died, claiming that if she was going to act like a child, he was going to treat her like one. During his testimony, my grandparents looked on with doting affection, proud of his loyalty to the family. He had stuck to the script.

I can't help but sympathize with him. All the attention was on the cult leaders and the Globe family. I never read so much as a single keystroke of sympathy directed at my grieving father. And yet he had lost his fiancée and was himself a victim of the cult. In a piece for *Saturday Night* magazine, the journalist Barbara Frum took an ill view of my dad. "He is dour, rigid, straitlaced, with an icy, glowering intensity," she wrote.

Toward the end of the inquest, Moore took the stand. He denied ever hitting Kathy and claimed he loved her very much. By way of defence, my grandfather presented himself as a deeply troubled and weak man, susceptible to the influences of others. He also confessed that he'd believed he could bring Kathy back to life at the morgue and had hoped to just take her home with them as if nothing had happened. Doug, for his part, called the whole inquest a witch hunt.

After a few hours of deliberation, the inquest jury delivered their findings. They concluded that my grandfather and his wife had been negligent to not seek medical care or hospitalization for Kathy. "We find their judgments were so clouded by the religious beliefs of the healing group within the parish of St. Matthias that they failed to give her adequate personal attention and similarly failed to recognize the obvious symptoms that she was suffering severe physical pain." They recommended an inquiry into this and other faith-healing groups in Toronto. A few hours later, the Anglican Church released a statement. "The Anglican hierarchy must decisively dissociate itself from the unusual faith-healing practices, which border on exorcism." My grandfather was asked to resign from the church but was permitted to remain in the rectory until the end of the year. No criminal charges were ever laid.

The bishop, an ultra-conservative Anglican called George Snell, selected a commission of seven men to investigate Canon Moore Smith's ministry. It included an Anglican priest, a canon, and a rector, as well as the head of psychiatry at Sunnybrook Hospital, a U of T medical professor, and a lawyer from the Bay Street law firm Strathy, Archibald, Seagram and Cole, which would later merge with Gowlings. In May 1968, the commission published the results of its inquiry. They noted that Marjorie had held the reins of power and was regarded as an "all-wise matriarch," the person everyone—including the two priests—would consult before any action was taken. My grandfather, who was then living with his family in a rented house in the east end, was deemed a "mere straw figure." He was to submit to a psychiatric evaluation and was placed under close supervision for two years before he could run his own congregation again. "What began as a bold experiment in Christian outreach gradually degenerated into a mystic cult," the report stated. "Satanic influence was believed to be incorporated into objects as well as persons. Given this premise, the need for exorcism followed as a logical consequence." My grandfather's only statement that day: "I have never left the church."

By January 1969, my grandfather was a visiting pastor to the Church of St. Michael and All Angels on St. Clair West, and regularly administered Eucharist at St. John's House, a community centre on Portland Street. He was in dire financial straits and dealing with the lingering trauma of Kathy's death. He decided his only solution was to leave the country. That year, he and my grandmother settled in the mountains in Jamaica. For seven years, he ran three thriving congregations. He never practised faith healing again.

After Kathy died, my father enrolled in the history program at the University of Toronto and later entered the insurance business. He renounced Anglicanism but couldn't shed religion altogether, and he eventually became a member of the United Church of Canada. In 1969, the same year his parents fled to Jamaica, he met my mother, Diane, who was 27 and working as an administrative assistant at U of T. As they got to know each other, she perceived the lasting scars the cult and Kathy's death had left. Soon after their marriage, he and my mom saw a psychiatrist several times to assess the damage. My father was haunted by guilt and shame, by the brutal shock of someone he loved dying because of his father, a man he worshipped. For years, he had recurring nightmares, and he'd often burst into uncontrollable sobs.

I was born in 1974, and my younger brother followed four years later. In 1981, the four of us settled in a modest detached house near Laird and Eglinton. Leaside will always be my Tatooine, minus the sand and droids. It's where I played out the years of my childhood with bike rides and toboggan runs in Serena Gundy Park, where I once put my Han Solo action figure in a cup of water in my freezer to re-enact his carbonite freeze moment on Cloud City.

To outsiders, we appeared to be the perfect nuclear family. But my relationship with my dad was always strained. Sometimes he could be kind, teaching me basic carpentry and electric skills for my Cub Scout badges. Other times, he could be unpredictably hostile. Once, when I was eight, he broke my hockey stick in half to teach me a lesson about cleaning up after myself. To get back at him, on the way into church one morning, I shouted at the top of my lungs, "DAVID GEORGE MOORE SMITH IS AN ASSHOLE!" He was so humiliated that he skipped the service and went home. I hated him.

I first met my grandparents in the early 1980s. They were stern but never cruel. They'd shout at my brother and me about tracking mud on the floors or about shutting up our noisy electric toys. Whenever they pulled up to our house, my mom would do her best *Poltergeist* impression: "They're heeeeere." Occasionally they stayed the night, but mostly they preferred to live in rural hideaways outside the city. "Grandfather doesn't like to spend too much time in Toronto," my mom would say cryptically.

By this point, they had left Jamaica and moved to Wilberforce, Ontario, where my grandfather ran a ministry at St. Margaret's church. Whenever we visited our grandparents, we would participate as guests at their Anglican parish. I can still remember my anxiety about taking communion and walking up in a line with my mother. She told me I didn't have to drink the wine, that she'd told my grandfather I was just to take the wafer. I looked back to see my mom sipping Christ's blood with a mixture of fear and curiosity. No one ever mentioned the cult. "You aren't to speak about that in front of my children," my mom told all our relatives.

Once, I attended a family reunion in Wilberforce. My grandfather was already going deaf at this point, and most sentences would either begin or end with a slightly elevated "Hmmmmmmmmm?" I was about eight years old, and the *Star Wars* craze was in full force. He presented my brother and me with matching Yoda action figures and explained how being a good Christian and believing in God were similar to the Jedi and the Force.

We went to Northlea United Church in Leaside every Sunday. We wore itchy sweaters, and my brother and I were never allowed to sit beside each other because we'd start fighting or making jokes. I was involved in the social aspects of church: the choir, the Christmas pageant, where I played one of the wise men. If my father was home, we prayed before every meal, blessing our fish sticks and meatloaf with the Lord's Prayer. But as I grew older, church and God became annoying chores I had to endure. I had no interest in the prehistoric ramblings of religious characters who were terrified of damnation and crops turning to dust. Deep down, religion also unsettled me. I was convinced that God wasn't really watching over us. Once I was so mad about something that I ripped a cross—given to me by my grandfather—off my neck and threw it out the car window. Another time, I took a gaudy wooden crucifix my father had given me and drove a nail into Jesus's stomach, then tossed it at my father's feet. "You're not hurting me when you do that," was his only reply.

I only knew snippets of my father's past. I knew that as a child he'd walked miles to go to school. I knew he'd had a dog and that he'd lived in a farmhouse with his parents and sisters before moving to Toronto when he was seven. He loved to sing and was in the church choir, but no one seemed to like his voice. He would sing off-key, which he seemed to do as a way of being heard. Most people try to stand out so they can reveal themselves to others. When my father did it, he was just alienating himself. He had few friends—the only people he knew were his family and the odd neighbour—and he never told us what he was thinking or feeling. He was always preoccupied and distant.

By 1995, my parents had split up and my dad was living in a one-bedroom apartment above the funeral home where he was working. That February, I got a phone call from my brother, telling me to read page A1 of the *Toronto Star*. My aunt Ann, who'd become a minister in the Anglican Church, had given an extensive interview to the paper about her father's cult. My grandparents commented for the story, too. "I take responsibility for the mistakes that were made," my grandfather said, adding that exorcisms should be avoided. On the subject of cults, he described "the separation, the isolationism, the pride and arrogance that goes with it. It happened to me. It was a dreadful time." My grandmother's take was eerier. "It happened in a gradual way; going into it, you feel God is guiding you, but you have to be very careful—it may be the other party." She meant Satan, of course. It was the first I'd ever heard of my father's ordeal, my grandfather's sins, and the death of Katherine Globe. It sounded like some twisted made-for-TV movie. At first, I was horrified, both by the story and at my aunt for airing it to the paper. The family figured she just wanted to drum up publicity for her new congregation. My father refused to talk about it.

And yet the *Star* piece was ultimately a blessing. I finally understood my grandfather. I thought about his fear of evil and endless regrets at being so weak. I recognized a genuine sadness at what had happened, the incredible remorse he must have felt. As for my father, everything made sense: his obsession with religion, his need to belt out a solo in the choir to impress his father and his simultaneous fear of him. A whole universe of tragedy seemed to predate my arrival in my father's life. How did he sweep it all under the table and start a family? After the article came out, my father and I never had any more confrontations. I saw him as a man burdened by his past. Our war was over.

These days, I live in Fredericton with my wife, Amber, and our daughter. My grandfather died in 2003, and my dad lives in Elgin, Ontario. We don't speak often. The last time I visited, earlier this year, my brother and I replaced his floors. I could sense that my father felt vulnerable—the process seemed invasive, and my brother wouldn't let him help. He was 76, suffering from emphysema, with a rake-thin Woody Allen physique. As he smoked in his lair, I found it hard to believe that this was the same man who'd seemed so overpowering when I was a kid.

In my father's bedroom, I saw the dresser he had bought in 1981 from the Art Shoppe, originally part of a set that included the bunk beds my brother and I slept on. Resting on the dresser was a tiny brass picture frame containing a black-and-white school photo of a pretty young girl with dark hair and a friendly smile. It was Kathy Globe.

Originally published in *Blood and Aphorism*

FEAR AND LOATHING ON PROTECTION ISLAND ($200)

My American great-grandfather, Thomas Linus Moore, who was an avid horticulturalist but mostly worked at 7-11 (which then operated under the name Tote'm Stores) as a night manager in the 1930s, once told my father, "The grass is always longer when you don't cut it, no matter what side you're standing on." I've always translated this Moore-ism as a bonified caveat to doing *anything*, period. Whether you do something, think about doing something, agree to do something, just remember someone somewhere will undoubtedly take notice and take it up with you, for good or for bad. But this isn't a story about ancestral advice passed down since the ice age—or in this case, the Slurpee age.

To start this journey properly, I need to talk about a certain feline gangster from the streets of Calgary named Bernie Mac. Bernie Mac is my family's first cat, who, by the time you have finished this epic, will have conquered no fewer than four provinces. His arrival came in the late autumn of 2013. My brother-in-law, my daughter's Uncle Taylor, was moving into a new apartment in Calgary with his then girlfriend, Sally, when they realized their building couldn't take pets. So one cold evening, Bernie Mac boarded a flight from the prairies and then took a cab to our walk-up apartment in downtown Toronto. He woke up our daughter, and soon we were all playing with the newest member of our tiny vegetarian brood.

Six months later, after our umpteenth winter of frozen parks and expensive cab rides and general misery commuting to work (my wife spent about three hours a day on the GO train), we decided to sell most of our belongings and move to a tiny island in the Pacific Ocean. At first, our equally poor and artistic friends in Toronto were like, "Come on, you're full of it." But it was true. The closer to the end of April 2014 we got, the less we had. I sold our books in slow motion before eventually donating the lion's share to a local hospital. We got Amber's mother to drive two hours to Nanaimo and take a small ferry to Protection Island, our future home.

Protection Island is considered a suburb of Nanaimo. It has Internet, electricity, and an overpriced pub, the only bar-restaurant on the island, where you can buy wine for double the price in town. We moved in one glorious, sun-emblazoned afternoon: I remember coming out of the airport, feeling the health in the air, and inhaling it greedily like fine drugs at a fancy party. Thinking we'd eventually do a larger grocery-store run, we picked up two small bags of food and ventured across the ocean, a 10-minute trip by ferry. We had three suitcases, a six-year-old, a jet-lagged cat, and, for some reason, an incredible amount of heavy pottery my mother-in-law had thoughtfully gifted us once we got off the plane. (Flowers would have been nice—a lei?)

The locals helped us with our gear, which now included a large dollhouse that Amber's grandfather had built, three large, heavy flowerpots, and the aforementioned groceries. After disembarking from the ferry and getting a lift in someone's pickup truck, we walked in dusty steps towards the house, where a small man was scything his way through the tall grass. Later that week we discovered the house had been built backwards and came with its share of odd and tacky décor—think *Gilligan's Island* castaway meets your uncle's midlife-crisis beach house with plenty of Phil Collins playing in the background. The rent was $995 per month, and it was situated on one of the busiest streets on Protection Island, Captain Morgan's Boulevard. (Foot and golf-cart traffic in this area can get up to 30 people a day). We soon discovered that all the streets had been named with a pirate theme in mind by a wild-eyed former mayor of Nanaimo, Frank Ney, who resembled the Hamburglar when he wanted to.

Local lore about the house we rented came in waves: we heard that the owners had kept switching contractors and had to add soil to the property, killing the trees in the process. "Wait until winter, you'll see; it's essentially built on a swamp," another neighbour told us. Still, we were in heaven: we had a month before we'd have to look for serious work, so we soaked up the sun and enjoyed slow jaunts to town and, of course, the swimming. Oh, the swimming. Private beaches at every turn, late-night campfires when the fire ban wasn't on. During the summer months, Finny wasn't in school, so there was no need to go to town each day.

To offset the cost of the local and very privately-run ferry, we decided to drop three grand on a speedboat none of us knew how to maintain. The boat would become an instant regret—the cost of buying it could have gone towards ferry passes for the next two years. We were desperate to not lose the small but significant fortune we had eagerly dumped into the ocean—literally! Sleepless nights filled with a short highlight reel of our time with our motorboat: the perilous trip across to Nanaimo (where the RCMP were doing helicopter-jump training into the ocean), the chaos of trying to cut the engine and gently guide the boat into a safe area along the dock while a thousand (six) gawking locals pointed and squinted in our general direction.

During our time on the island, we struggled to fit into the intrusive set, second cousin to the jet set. We eventually divulged (to the locals) our abilities to write things down for a living. Perhaps I should just switch to first-person singular real estate at this point and not drag Amber into it. So someone on the ferry says to me, "Oh, you'll have so much to write about, so many characters on the island!" And I want to barf. I can think of nothing more self-obsessed than sitting around like a Goth girl in black leggings, black lipstick, and medieval breastplate, carrying a notebook around and jotting down my neighbours' fumbling dialogue about groceries and tides. *Kill me now*, I thought. Here's a sample: "I didn't know Thomas very well, but heard later he had recently bought a new pair of tan slacks..."

I was getting regular work on the island as a handyman, a job that I essentially had invented one afternoon while cleaning someone's gutters. My daughter even joined the family business for a while, helping rake leaves until she was attacked by a swarm of wasps and ran howling down the dirt road like a cartoon character with its butt on fire. By the end of July, I was in high demand and found myself overthinking things. One morning before a job, I watched a YouTube video about how to safely climb down a ladder from a roof. Something in my brain must have made me memorize the incorrect method, because not half an hour into the job I found myself,

FEAR AND LOATHING ON PROTECTION ISLAND ($200)

Wile E. Coyote–style, dropping from the sky about 12 feet onto someone's deck. Thankfully, the ladder fell first, and it cradled my fall, protecting my head from a brain injury of any kind.

The next thing I remember, the men and women who frequently ran the ferry were in ambulance attire and lifting me onto a stretcher. Amber was soon at my side, and all of us boarded an emergency boat heading to Nanaimo, where the doctor said my eyes were too small, I was a bit overweight, and my organs were in the wrong place. (To this day, whenever my wife asks if I'm asleep I tell her, "No, I just have small eyes.") After running out of things to criticize about my body, the doctor informed me that I had a broken scapula and minor internal bleeding.

Amber picked up some of the work that was still on the docket for my handyman career, though a lot of clients withdrew their requests for my services after the island-wide news report of my fall. The client whose roof I fell from came by and handed Amber a few rolled-up twenties, hoping I wouldn't sue. I didn't, of course. This was a friendly island after all!

Things were still great. What to worry about? It's not like we needed to leave the island every day to take our child to school. That would be costly. Oh, wait! September rolled around, and work dried up. The boat wouldn't start. In fact, people were growing angry that our boat occupied a space on the dock, but they wouldn't tell us directly. Instead they left garbage in it, broke our windows, and cut our locks. Exhausted from the new twice-daily commute to town from Protection Island, we had to come up with a plan to make more money. I was helping some brothers on the island build a house (I should state clearly that all I did was dig the foundation—I would never recommend you read this article and hire me for any home repair), but my hours were constantly interrupted with the need to board a ferry, cross the ocean for several minutes, and walk 15 more to gather our daughter before heading back to Protection.

Our cat, Bernie Mac, was spending more and more time outside, on people's roofs and eventually in the wrong part of town. He came home one afternoon with a swollen leg, the result of a nasty bite from one of his cohorts. A costly trip to the vet followed, and soon he was back home with a cone around his neck, tubes coming from his leg, and a steady supply of morphine. He looked at himself in a mirrored closet door one afternoon and nearly fainted in depression. We would have to keep him indoors. So we got him a little friend named James, a silent, fluffy black cat whom Bernie Mac batted around several times before falling madly in love. They would be indoor cats together.

Despite the beautiful surroundings and lucking out by finding a used golf cart for $500, our life was not sustainable on the island. Sure, our daughter had friends, we had escaped Toronto, but my dream of working in publishing seemed as remote and fantastical now as our initial dream of leaving the big city for a simple life on an island in the Pacific Ocean once had.

After many action sequences, including my wife jumping off a dock onto a running motor, we were done with the speedboat. My missives on the island message board were comic gold, hinting at front-lawn fire sales: "This boat must go go go!" Finally we sold it to a young family for $600 (yes, that's a $2,400 loss), and I ruined my new leather getting the boat out of the water onto a trailer for them. I felt like Krusty the Clown after selling Homer the trampoline, waiting on my front porch with my metaphoric shotgun, telling anyone who dared attempt to return our boat to "just keep right on driving."

Over the year on the island, I earned close to $1000.00 in freelance fees from my magazine columns and reviews published in the *Georgia Straight*. The spring arrived, and our enthusiasm for renewing the lease on our ill-heated island home was comparable to a deer's passion for kissing the grille of an 18-wheeler. In case I haven't made myself clear, it wasn't very high. Nanaimo, the city we were technically a part of despite the bit of ocean between us, was driving me nuts. It was the Wild West—no rules, no mercy, and no major indie bookstore.

One morning at my daughter's school (she was in Grade 1 at the time), I had to confront the parent of a kid who had been strangling Finny in school. I told them they were raising a sociopath and that they should explain misogyny to their son. They were not pleased with me. They claimed their son was fine because he had two sisters and I was like, *that explains it perfectly. There is no balanced normative outlet for his masculinity, so he picks on small girls who can't defend themselves.* This boy stabbed her with a pencil!

At the time I wrote to a friend, "It's been a struggle, it's been paradise. We're happily stuck here and it's great. Though I don't have any friends, there isn't really time for friendship. Creatively I'm at the height of my powers." My joy for embracing what BC publishing had to offer was untested. After all, I was free of Toronto; I had a beard, a toque, cool hiking boots, and an island to live on, not too far from Vancouver. I asked my publisher Brian Kaufman (Anvil Press) if I could have a column in *subTerrain*, and so for about six issues I did. I wrote some reviews for the *Georgia Straight* and did a few readings, including *Books on the Radio* and Word Vancouver, where I saw the Harbour Publishing 40th anniversary booth and had a piece of cake. Foreshadowing!

A few months into my new status as British Columbia's hottest free agent, I wasted no time getting into the texts it had to offer. My first assignment—*From the Poplars*—was for the *Georgia Straight*; I wrote:

> Unoccupied for some time now, the revived (and displaced/homeless) Qayqayt First Nation has been working to regain control of the island as their traditional space. Qayqayt is the only such group registered in Canada without a land base. In *From the Poplars*, Cecily Nicholson excavates and exclaims these spaces for her readers both nearby and nationwide and brings a unique spotlight on New Westminister's growing history. While the collection is described as a long poem, it uses elements of style that range from lyric poetry to language poetry to the prose poem format, and finally the epistolary form. It is in the epistolary form that Nicholson delivers an engaging "found" dialogue between her subject and the reader.

Now back to the non-fiction of our geographic dystopia... By the end of 2014, it wouldn't be odd for me to hear any number of the following from my beautiful leader/wife Amber: "Nate, can you go bail out the boat?" "Nate, can you leave work on the island and go pick up Finny from school?" "Nate, I forgot my bank card—can you run it over to the ferry?" "Nate, someone cut the lock to our boat and left beer cans inside..." "Nate, I jumped off the dock today because the boat repair guy was about to let our boat float out to sea..." "Nate, Finny invited children over and they want soya sauce and spaghetti, and one of them keeps talking about poached eggs!" "Nate, Kate

wants you to buy her a new garden hose and fix a hole on her front porch..."
"Nate, the landlord is coming by to show the house, can you make sure to leave a note about not letting the cats out?"

Do you know how hard it is for a personality like me to be draped in satirical opportunity? Protection Island was nothing I was ever going to write about—I had so many other things on the go. But that didn't stop me from sending out the occasional island-inspired group email, *TMZ*ing my way into the hearts of a half-dozen close friends all shadowed by the CN Tower's stiff girth:

> Christian Bale stars in *Protection Resurrection*, the dystopian tale of a remote island, its squirrels, its people, and the fight for reasonable transportation and fairly-priced marble cheese. I mean, like weather and stock numbers, the price of cheese should be announced on morning radio: "And for those thinking about picking up 450 grams of Kraft cheese this morning, you're in luck, as the local average in downtown Nanaimo is only $14.50, while in the east you'll see fog patches breaking up by mid-morning, and the sun should make its way to us by lunchtime... Now with sports, we go to Matt..."

In June 2015, after a lot of bad mojo over a lease break and hiring the small boat to get us from one house to the next, we surrendered to the very city we feared the most: Nanaimo. It was a desert to us—at least the island had some colour. We had no choice—we couldn't afford to move back to Ontario, no matter how delicious the idea seemed. The idea of home didn't exist for us in 2015, not yet at least.

A buffet of emotional responses accessorized our exodus from the oasis by the sea. I seem to recall one long-time islander almost running out of room on their face from grinning when we told them we had no choice but to move. Soon I found myself in the running for a job as a publicist for not one, but three publishers at once. And get this: it was just across from Vancouver Island on the Sunshine Coast! They even flew me across the ocean from Vancouver Island for a six-hour interview (half of which was, of course, travel).

And so, I got the job and we had to find somewhere to live in Madeira Park. Quickly. Amber's dad came with a U-Haul to downtown Nanaimo where we were renting an apartment and helped load all our things, including a daughter and two nervous cats. We boarded a six a.m. ferry and headed to our new digs, sight unseen,[5] in the wooded world of Pender Harbour, the small community that's home to Harbour Publishing.

"When the going gets weird, the weird turn pro." That's what Hunter S. Thompson once said. Eighteen months since I'd said *ave atque vale* ("hail and farewell") to Toronto, I now found myself deeper in the woods, but surrounded by more books than ever. All because of my new full-time job as a publicist, of course, promoting books such as Tom Wayman's latest fiction collection, *The Shadows We Mistake for Love*. I never knew so many people had pot grow-ops, nor did I know the RCMP used special optics from their helicopters to discern the specific hue of green that distinguishes pot plants from forest. This space-age technology Big Brother uses reminds me of that tiny blotter tool in Photoshop.

Being a relatively new transplant made me feel a bit uncomfortable because I am from the centre of the universe. In fact, one of my contemporaries who was out for a literary function noted he couldn't imagine me living in the woods, that I was engrained in the Toronto scene like some terribly soiled copy of *The Grid* (a Toronto weekly that I only recently learned no longer exists).

It's nice to be surrounded by the energy of the Canadian publishing industry. It's a real force that awakens the mind, body, and soul. Sincerely. It's overwhelmingly organic. It sure beats falling off rooftops and raking leaves, or working in a pet store and having to take several buses just to sell people their overpriced gourmet dog food, as I did for the last six months of our stint on Protection (or as I liked to call it, Finnian's) Island.

The Sunshine Coast proved to be, at least for the first year and a half, much more fruitful, enjoyable, and stable. The family found modest accommodations in a mobile home that was not at all mobile, surrounded by giant trees and rolling hills. It was a beautiful rental we loved a lot. For

---

5   The names Harbour Publishing and Howard White hold a lot of water in these parts, and securing a rental was not so hard.

Finny's birthday that spring in Madeira Park, we had a packed backyard; sixteen children and even the interns from Harbour Publishing came wielding gifts for our daughter, and the local petting zoo came and set up shop. I invited my old friend Tavis, with whom I reunited after more than a decade, and soon we were enjoying the fresh spring air. Suddenly Rusty the mule got loose, and one of the zoo owners lit out haltingly after him. He was an elderly man who appeared slightly hobbled. As the children enjoyed the gated comfort of chickens and bunnies, the old man gave chase to the errant mule. Before offering help, Tavis reminded me to write this all down later. "This always happens to you," he said. Soon the mule, the old man, and everything settled in for what was the best birthday party in the history of time, with rides on Rusty and more than enough wrinkling bunny noses.

I loved working at Harbour, especially since much of my job involved talking to people on the phone about their books, including eighty-four-year-old debut author Barrie Farrell, who was turned loose all over Vancouver Island for his multi-city tour. The book, *Boats in My Blood*, was a bestseller for a few weeks as the energetic octogenarian shocked librarian after librarian with his stage-fright sense of humour. A few events into the tour, Howard White and I had a meeting and decided Barrie needed to tell stories rather than attempt to read from the book. So, his storytelling became a must-see spectacle. Almost a year later, Barrie was still itching to tour, but the book sales began to vanish. I had to explain to him that we couldn't keep sending him out without demand. He didn't understand.

"That was such a good book for you to start with," Howard White later told me. And he was right; the book was a lot of work, and Barrie was more than a handful at times. "He's almost ninety, I'm sorry that his jokes were shocking to some. I'll talk to him," was something I had to explain to more than a few confused administrators. My kid liked Barrie too: he let her tie his boat up one morning when he came to the coast for a visit. "You'll do alright, girl," he told her. I'll never forget Barrie Farrell, and if you want to read a real-life Canadian story akin to something you'd imagine one of Mark Twain's characters experiencing, I highly recommend *Boats in My Blood: A Life in Boat Building*.

Our adventures continued: bears knocked over our garbage and shook the side of our fragile home. A tree fell through our roof in the middle of the night. Our daughter made tons of friends and participated in Sechelt's Got Talent (she sang Taylor Swift's "Wildest Dreams" without accompaniment in front of 100 people). Amber published a book about our year-plus on Protection Island, which didn't go over very well with our former neighbours on their precious stretch of land, and she was hired on as an editor at Nightwood Editions. I was having a great time writing my own books and promoting others, but a nagging cough turned into half a year of bronchitis. We concluded that our rain-infested rental was the culprit and that the mould was doing serious damage to my breathing.

"We have to move out of this bomb shelter," I concluded. To be fair, Amber had already suggested this a month earlier, but in my World-War-I-like mustard-lung fog, I hadn't the faintest clue what she was saying. So we moved down the coast about 20 kilometres to a small neighbourhood called Halfmoon Bay. After we moved in, we realized that the arrangement we'd made with the landlord was less than ideal. The property included a warehouse in the back that had been rented out to a family of flea-market-furniture pirates who were supposed to limit their sales to twice a month. But as the weather warmed, the sales started happening three times a week.

Frustrated by the plethora of pickup trucks parking in our fenceless backyard (a fence had been promised when we moved in), I began to show my disdain for this family and their invasion of our general happiness by encouraging their customers not to park in our driveway or beside our lawn. This didn't work out, and soon a feud began between our two families, highlighted by me calling them hillbillies and them throwing our outdoor-sports equipment onto our roof. We called the city, and it turned out the property wasn't legally designated to contain a business operation, so they were forced to leave. Our landlord wasn't pleased, nor were we with our new vilified status in the community. When we saw a job posting for a book publisher in New Brunswick, we decided to throw our hats into contention and found ourselves figuring out how to sell our car, give notice to our employers, and tackle the gigantic task of moving 5,449.5 kilometres across the country, which cost us, in moving truck fees, about 56 cents per kilometre.

Less than a year after moving to Fredericton, we bought our first house, started a side publicity business, and got a third cat, Cider, who is orange and fluffy and was born and will be raised in Fredericton. Our daughter has a best friend around the corner whom she sees all the time, our parents love coming to visit us, and we love the Boyce Farmers Market on Saturdays. Libraries, galleries, quaint small businesses, and beautiful parks abound. This city is just right, having given us friends to read poetry with at events and quiet roads to play road hockey on. The province has also given us the intoxicating renewal of our favourite pastime—swimming in natural bodies of water. New River Beach is our favourite destination for catching waves and rays, but the cats have their own vacation too—frequent visits from the local pet-sitting service here in town.

Originally published in *The Maritime Edit*

PART FIVE: NO ALGORITHM, NO OVERTIME, NO MERCY!

MARK LEYNER: THE HOBOKEN KNIGHT ($100)

> Oops, Leyner has done it again. It's simply too much for this kiddie. You'll never listen to "What Have I Done to Deserve This?" by the Pet Shop Boys again without feeling like you've just lost your virginity. The master of everything good has returned to serve the planet another delicious martini. Et tu, Amazon?
>
> —My Amazon review of *The Sugar Frosted Nutsack*, 2012

A certain amount of ego-purging goes into writing about your favourite author, one with whom you feel a kinship. And unlike Catullus, whom I believe to be quite dead, Mark Leyner is alive, living on the east coast of America and, I'm sure, plotting his next big dip in the pool of his own brand of literary capital.

Autobiographies have always been in high fashion, dating back to the early 1990s when Mark Leyner meant to the world of contemporary fiction what threadbare tank tops mean to baristas. In *Et Tu, Babe*, Leyner's alter ego is his inner ego, setting on its side the concept of writer as self-God, writer as asshole, writer as sycophantic sexual maniac. The narrative voice in *Et Tu, Babe* works around the clock to ensure that Team Leyner makes a buck off readers and everyone with a pulse. He has millions of dollars, laboratories, assistants, and spends his days in high demand for his genius ability to write.

At the onset of the 21st century, while promoting his latest books, Leyner was interviewed by *Mondo* magazine, where he placed an effort at justifying his rather eccentric take on storytelling:

> From the beginning my impulse towards narrative disunity came from that desire for maximal input rather than from any sense of wanting to rebel against realism... I came from the fictional womb like I am. The postmodern battles had already been fought and won.

In his 2012 novel, *The Sugar Frosted Nutsack*, one can fall for the con of creativity and in that nanosecond, truly believe the author has served the story from his own stinking, sweet life. Leyner writes about masculinity as if he's doctoring a buddy-film script and adding more embarrassing asides and greater backstory so we can really enjoy watching the characters squirm. His lecherous depictions are at times unpleasant and grotesque, inappropriate in the age of, well, whatever age we are in, let's say the rage-age of information. But as we've imagined alien life forms interpreting our feeble life choices (fashion, politics, food, speech, driving habits) Leyner's vision seems refreshing and without bias. Take the opening moments of *Nutsack*: "A terrarium containing three tiny teenage girls mouthing a lot of high-pitched gibberish (like *Mothra*'s fairies, except for their wasted pallors, acne, big tits, and t-shirts that read 'I Don't Do White Guys') would inexplicably materialize, and then, just as inexplicably, disappear."

The novel tells the mystic story of Ike Karton, a New Jersey butcher who is currently out of work. Karton is continually harassed by a brutal brood of gods who have just returned from spring break. The novel is a creation story, but also a story about the dangers of worshipping gods. Just look at Elvis Presley or the Royal Family, stand-ins for gods but treated like deities regardless. Leyner reminds us that the image we recreate of our gods is one "endlessly reproduced in paintings, sculptures, temple carvings, coins, maritime flags, postage stamps, movie-studio logos, souvenir snow globes, take-out coffee cups, playing cards, cigarette packs, condom wrappers, etc."

I imagine the waitress in *Nutsack* (a minor character who slums in her part-time job but is more philosophical and nurturing towards the protagonist Ike Turner than a lot of his closest friends and family) to be an objectification fantasy but also a bait-and-switch tactic. Later in the novel, she is fired from a diner, and Leyner uses cold tabloid language to update readers on the waitress character's whereabouts as she quickly (and sadly) disappears from the book: "Inside her legal battle to regain her part-time job," Leyner writes. Like pretty much all the characters in the book, the waitress could be a subconscious attempt to escape the self and parrot an unlikely subject. Leyner could be revisiting his own early vocational hazards, perhaps not a waiter or waitress but something far away and depraved from the actual life he leads now. Or he's simply cataloguing the absurdity of existence, as if being a writer is the only noble pursuit, while those who are in the story are but examples of this strange world we live in. The idea, I believe, and I may be completely alone on this, is that there is nothing strange at all about Leyner's tone—he's just explaining the world as it's presented to him in all its plastic ventriloquisms.

No wonder then that Leyner is steadfast at keeping his fiction unique, a singular voice spoken by characters who are usually attempting to carve out paths for themselves that otherwise never existed.

Originally published in *subTerrain*

SINA QUEYRAS: TWENTY-FOUR HOURS ($175)

> How random the state of childhood, how the value of a childhood fluctuates.
>
> —Sina Queyras, *Autobiography of Childhood* (2011)

We can't escape childhood. It's not really an option. Every day, we are confronted with reminders and ghosts, and memory relaunches abound. One night this summer, while I was having after-dinner coffee in my sister's living room, my five-year-old niece, Sara, sidled up to me and said, "Nathaniel, someday I will get very old and die," and then shyly left the room. It was the same day I read the opening scene of Sina Queyras's debut novel, *Autobiography of Childhood*, in which a bold and telling recollection is declared from the outset: "She became aware of her own childhood one night in the middle of a very steep stairwell," as if the protagonist, Therese, is sifting through exhumed memories to determine that exact moment of initiation.

Mildly shocked from my niece's revelation, I was reminded of a short, ghastly fable called "Mr. Nobody" from *The Book of Knowledge*, in which an unnamed child meets a spectral figure on the stairs and throughout the house. To me, the fable is about understanding one's mortality and seeing its scope and finality. *Autobiography* does initially appear to encompass quotidian structure, telling its story from the point of view of each family member (siblings and a father) who must face the fact that Therese will die of a terminal illness in a matter of hours. From the beginning, Queyras reveals distinct portents with authorial panache: the past and its intricate seeds of pain, the power of this recognition, and the impossibility of distancing oneself from the present tense's acceleration. Queyras's prose is lyrically lucid, and as a storyteller she avoids the clutter of pedestrian minutiae and swelling her characters with heavy-hearted parlance. The choice for directness is evident with pared-down, kitchen-sink realities: "They aren't a family that has much to celebrate."

The individual portraits in *Autobiography* are reflective and connect to the book's entire emotional turbulence, allowing readers to form their own attachments from all sides, as if a day pass to visit the family saga's morbid trajectory has been issued. Take the absent father, Jean: insomniac, loner, armchair philosopher. "Life is so fleeting he thinks. Everything is loss. Even an apple. It has to be picked. It's useless if whole." The nexus of Jean's comprehension that he'll outlive his daughter comes from his recollection of his own childhood visit to his mother on her deathbed. Despite the ease of his recollection, he feels crowded by the familial voices who seek him out, voices "he no longer wants to hear."

The looming tragedy of the book—moreover, the way in which the time constraint adds to the drama's quick-burning wick—gives it a punchy suspense, a passionate, post-gritty glimpse into the human side of a dysfunctional family outgrowing its own familiarity. This is a family haunting its own identity and redefinition: "They are a family that once owned a house. They are a family that once stood at the kitchen table while their father inspected their newly washed hands. Or perhaps that was just once? Didn't he appear in a crisp white shirt, his hair freshly washed, face shaved, smelling of soap?"

Autobiography of Childhood is a sharp, post-millennial family novel with a purpose, a kinetic, shared trauma that investigates the parts and the whole, creating an uneasy tableau of life's arbitrary cruelties. The novel is a striking comment on tragedy and its place in the human jigsaw puzzle as the Combal family tries to cope with what everyone's family must someday face, collectively and alone.

Originally published in the *Globe and Mail*

LYNN COADY: *THE ANTAGONIST* IS THE ANTI-BUDDY FILM WE CAN ALL USE ($75)

If this review were a sports headline it would read, "Coady in the Time of [Sidney] Crosby." At least that's what I imagine some media factions coming up with over a three-thousand-dollar power lunch at The Keg Mansion as we learn that a book about a hockey thug's lexical revenge has just been shortlisted for the Giller Prize. Lynn Coady, who calls Edmonton home now, made a huge entry into fiction in 1998 when her book *Strange Heaven* was nominated for a Governor General's Award. She also won the Air Canada Award for most promising writer under 30. Her last major literary undertaking was *The Anansi Reader*, which she edited in 2008 for the press's 40th anniversary.

The first thing I thought about when I started reading Coady's fifth book, *The Antagonist*, was Oscar Wilde. In particular "De Profundis," the legendary epistolary piece that was published well after Wilde's death. This letter addresses Bosie, his lover and best friend, who betrayed Wilde and ultimately led to the bard's imprisonment and public disfavour. Flash-forward a century and some change, and we still have male entitlement running wild and dominating the psychic sphere in every property (both intellectual and vapid) known to world-kind. So why would Lynn Coady enter into the male-privilege cakewalk mindset of "hulking" Gordon Rankin (Rank Jr., actually, since he's named after his father) as he lashes out, not with the man-brutality for which he was famous as a youth, but with his mind? So she can emulate his oppressor (in this case a former school buddy), who cashed in on Rank's abject bully archetype and used it as fodder in his novel. Rank discovers he's been exploited in his former friend's fiction and begins his own oeuvre, which he arranges to send to his school chum via email. The book is the anti-buddy film, the anti-villain, the anti-hockey novel we can all use. Still, I'm puzzled by the fact that the water-cooler rep of this book is that it's a "hockey book," despite how hard Coady has worked to make this a unique take on what it is to be a man raging against a man and trying to use mind over matter.

I think gender studies students could talk until the milkman comes home about *The Antagonist*. Is Coady slumming it in male fantasy, male apathy? She thanks a few hockey studs in the back of the book. Will they in turn "pull Rank," so to speak, and start penning their own "De Profundis" with Lynn as the antagonist? Highly unlikely.

Still, *The Antagonist* should be commended for its quick singular voice that expands into other territories of inclusion and reflection, such as what Rank's father says to him and every minute detail Rank can recall to purge and rewrite history before the September deadline when he plans on going back to school. (Not exactly how most hockey jocks spend a summer, one would imagine, but that's just it—Coady lifts the stereotype veil long enough for the imagined character's purity to come out and declare war on apathy, war on its own cliché, war on acceptance of someone else's narrow view). Coady's book subverts the normative templates for the story-within-a-story routine by maintaining a singular voice that attempts to exorcise Rank's sense of betrayal and hostility.

Rank's response story, then, is the novel's entirety, as if Rank is leaving the reader a six-hour voice message. Sports take a back seat to character anxiety, purpose, and life reveal. Yet the atmospheres of *The Good Body* and *Twenty Miles* (both hockey novels) do surface from time to time, in the sense that one must imagine these physically-dominated characters are not known for emotional diplomacy or tact. *The Antagonist* is unhinged at times, cathartic, lyrical, and brave, especially when Rank describes a drug-dealer acquaintance from his past: "Imagine how any given small-town petty-criminal teen-age headbanger circa 1985 would decorate an apartment and—bang—there's your mental image of Croft's drug shack." Rank is, after all, typing to one person, with an emotional code at each stroke—that of revenge—and he is also at times buzzed on a few beers. The powder keg is lit from the very first page, the onset clear.

The reader must simply sit back and enjoy the unraveling and its breathtaking trajectory.

Originally published on *Rabble.ca*

ALISHA PIERCY: 2010: THE YEAR SHE MAKES CONTACT ($100)

Montreal writer and book artist Alisha Piercy arrives on the small-press scene with tales of rafting Boy Scouts, seaward romance, and fathoms of intrigue. It's been a pretty weird year for her. Well, maybe not weird so much as adventurous. Most people have book launches in darkened bars or the dusty corners of bookstores. But not Piercy. Take her combination art installation and chapbook launch in Montreal at the onset of the year as Exhibit A.

Each day for a month, Piercy added drawings to the walls of an art space that reflected the images she explored in the text of her impressively titled chapbook *You have hair like flags, flags that point in many directions at once but cannot pinpoint land when lost at sea* (Your Lips to Mine Press, Montreal and Berlin, 2010). The exhibit explores the perception of being lost at sea for 30 days. After 30 days of drawing (the exact length of the installation), Piercy erased the work she had done in the gallery by whiting the drawings out completely, as if washed away by the sea itself.

When it comes to conceptualizing, promoting, and even writing, there's a subtle duality to everything Piercy does. The origin of the ambitiously titled chapbook, according to Piercy, was the inspiration she felt after rereading her favourite novel, *Heroes and Villains* by Angela Carter. As Piercy explains: "On page 99, Jewel's hair 'blows like innumerable black flags.' I loved that and made it the conceit: to have hair like flags means daring, spirit, the will to push off from shore against all odds, among other things." The storyline concerns itself with all things nautical, but what fascinates is how much the entire project has in common with the sea itself: unpredictable and capable of erasing things, people, memory, and time. The narrative is about being adrift at sea for 30 days and experiencing "hallucinatory perception." And just like water can erase and take away, the drawings themselves ceased to exist.

Self-aware and at the same time enigmatic, the chapbook is not your average read. The book is a manifesto of sorts, a manifesto of the literary sea. "The fictional characters Pi [*Life of Pi*, Yann Martel, 2001] and Pym [*The Narrative of Arthur Gordon Pym*, Edgar Allen Poe, 1838] relate sea stories of horror filled with hallucinations that verge on the divine," Piercy says. Appropriating seaworthy characters from other texts and reimagining them in her own way, the work is at times romantic, didactic, and emotionally sparse. A literary investigation and infestation, *You have hair like flags...* won the 2010 bpNichol chapbook award in June of this year.

Exhibit B: On August 21, 2010, at 10 p.m. in Iceland, Piercy read from her chapbook with some Boy Scouts as a procession of burning rafts was set alight off the coast of Reykjavik as part of a performance installation created for Culture Night 2010.

Piercy says images from the story, such as the central image of a bonfire on a raft that keeps on burning, fuelled the images she would end up drawing for the installation, which she says included "processions of rafts, nets, 'northern' things, pink flares, and lots and lots of smoke and explosions." She met her Icelandic collaborator, a time-based artist named Oskar Ericsson, when he was having an exhibition in Montreal. "I told him about my piece and that I wanted to make a life-sized installation performance; I was thinking one or two rafts," says Piercy. Ericsson pushed her to develop the concept for the performance, and the rest is chapbook-launching history.

If all that wasn't enough for an auspicious debut, Piercy also released her first full-length book with Conundrum Press over the summer. *Icebreaker/Auricle* comprises two novellas as part of the press's reversible books series. While similarities between the two texts have been mentioned in interviews, I was struck more by how different they are.

Auricle was influenced by a real, yet unnamed, medical subject from the 1850s. In the story, a girl named Marie is born with growths on her neck, which are believed to provide her with extrasensory perception. When doctors suggest cutting them off, the story travels to Buenos Aires, where this procedure is to take place. It is here that Marie attempts to find a sense of cohesiveness within both herself and her family. "Is it because of my other tiny ears that I hear as if through a machine equipped with multiple openings?" Marie asks. Rounding out the adventure is Dr. Birkett, whom Marie is falling in love with. When she's not drunk, Marie's mother is obsessed with a pen pal named F. These characters pull the narration out of Marie's self-guided thought patterns and give the reader helpful insight into how she perceives the world around her.

Meanwhile, *Icebreaker* is a nostalgic romp via Alice, whose summer job is on an icebreaker ship that has been permanently docked and turned into a bed and breakfast. While working, she plays, hosting her drunken friends in the empty rooms of the ship. Though conflict presents itself through foggy romantic trysts on the boat, Alice's inner turmoil is just as ferocious and daunting. "Alice is shaking and running, tripping on the door-ledge, catching her ring on the jag of the lock. She cries out into the abandoned hallway, and feels a remote sense of embarrassment, feels her lungs gone wild. Then the empty, muffled feeling of the inside of the linen closet." Whether free-falling from barn rafters, tucking in crisp sheet corners, or getting drunk at Burger King with her friends, Alice's voice is distinct and detailed, but never bogged down in quotidian urban ritual.

While both of Piercy's novellas explore feminine connections to others, *Icebreaker* seems slightly more romantic, full of teenage melodrama and excess, mystery and lust, while there is more of an existential bent to *Auricle*: the offbeat and transplanted domestic relationship played out between mother and lovestruck Marie is a remix of the classic coming-of-age story, with the additional intrigue of a biologically-affected youth who feels singled out, freakish, and self-conscious.

With three separate stories released over the span of one year, some international romps, and a unique ability to present her work in both mysterious and unassuming ways that challenge the placidity of CanLit, hopefully Piercy can look back fondly on 2010 and recharge before her next creative call of duty.

Originally published in *Broken Pencil*

RACHEL ZOLF: A TORMENTED HISTORY ($177)

For some of us, 2015 is a time of heightened social awareness. Among the creative class in Canada, social issues are influencing arts projects. The reason could be an increased exposure to social media, which brings to light these injustices, in turn inspiring artists. The results, in any case, are evident in recent artistic projects nationwide: Toronto's Evan Munday has been tweeting images of missing or murdered indigenous women to Prime Minister Stephen Harper daily since January, and Vancouver poet Cecily Nicholson's recent book, *From the Poplars*, deals with the displaced Qayqayt First Nation, a people devastated by smallpox whose former home was transformed into a giant shipyard.

Rachel Zolf's latest book of poetry, *Janey's Arcadia*, fits nicely into the zeitgeist of social-justice art. The book is a case study of misreadings of historical texts that concern themselves with settlers and the Indigenous people they displaced, in particular from Manitoba. The book's deeper focus is the deaths and disappearances of over a thousand Indigenous women.

Using historical source texts such as antiquated brochure literature and newspaper interviews in almost collage-like fashion, Zolf eradicates the beginnings and endings of these texts and feeds them seamlessly into a loom of historical intolerance, racism, and colonial shaming. This only heightens the sense of urgency, despite the ordeals and struggles having taken place years ago. The confluence of this unravelling research and Zolf's own poetic voice-over reveals a tormented historical cross-section with all the power of an award-winning documentary.

Away from the bulk of remixed found material, the pared-down poems offer accessible narratives depicting a societal convergence in commerce as various ethnic groups coexist during a simple day of shopping. Zolf writes, "On the streets of Winnipeg, people smile at you in English, but speak in Russian." And later, in another piece, Zolf sheds light with a straitlaced lyric on rough childcare conditions: "The sisters run an industrial school where 250 orphans and Indign [sic] children are cared for at the horny sauce of discord." Zolf has exhumed an important and neglected cache of our country's sprawling history, and her ability to blend the personal, fact, tragedy, and shame, all while finding clarity and intent, is more than impressive.

Originally published in the *Georgia Straight*

JOEY COMEAU: A NIHILISTIC PARODY FOR OUR TROUBLED TIMES ($175)

Only in the dangerous water-cooler chatter that is small-press Canadian publishing can one discover a book brimming on the fake-wood edge of vocational apocalypse. Smack dab in the midst of global economic meltdown (where daily plant layoffs are as common on evening news reports as the weather) comes *Overqualified*, a collection of wry, clever, and demoniacal job-application letters, teeming with knife-edged malice and stomach-tearing hilarity.

At its micro-narrative core, *Overqualified* is a cover letter–based novel that negotiates a freedom for individual reaction to the oppressive routine of the job search. As a narrative arc, the epistolary form is used to isolate intent and focus on two characters: Joey and potential employer. Some pieces are picturesque snapshots, written around products that the author has or is using, such as a letter to Airwalk, a popular skateboard-shoe manufacturer based in the United States. Picking the mind of the shoe giant, Comeau tries to make a connection: "I want a piece of everything today. Do you get like this?"

Comeau shows a softer, more earnest side at times; take the lyrical letter to the University of Victoria for the position of linguistics professor. Coming off as a romantic bard, Comeau notes "that language's love is me, for real." Comeau's mind trick is hard at work, knowing full well the reader plays a hand in the con, that our minds are partially trained to imagine the hapless employer reading the sanity-chaffing letter stained with the author's personal back stories and barbed asides.

The author's letter to Yahoo Inc., for example, reads like an Internet prison letter, with inmate Comeau weighing in on his time logged on the information superhighway, where he pretends to be a 14-year-old "having relationship problems." He goes on to confess that he uses this identity and plays chess and makes lewd comments to other gamers. In another missive, he writes, "Corporations have been collecting from me for years. So I have started calling them. I'm tired of being afraid. It's time they were afraid of me."

Comeau's convivial prose, a confluence of faux naiveté and blatant intent to disarm, is controlled nicely throughout this mild temper tantrum. With that said, it is the timely subversion of consumer feedback and anonymity that is Comeau's best stroke, the classic "Is your refrigerator running?" joke turned into something inherently rude, yet an example of how Comeau's anti-hero tries to discover ways of relating to job descriptions through his own personal experiences. These experiences may explain how he would perform or understand the job requirements at hand, but the oversharing simply makes him seem strange.

The results, beyond hilarity, are a sense of relief that this person isn't working for you, and that you are not the person applying for the job. The nihilistic parody never tires (even Goodyear gets a turn in the hoax), because Comeau changes things on the fly for every one of these little nasties. The poet, like Prometheus before him, is playing with a medium he believes to be, in some ways, essential to survival: employment.

Overqualified successfully plays on the fear of the faceless corporate entity by empowering the faceless applicant who has nothing to lose except securing a job he or she probably doesn't want. If Comeau's rebel-yell manifesto catches on like old Prometheus's gift did all those years ago, human resources will never be the same again.

Originally published in the *Globe and Mail*

ROBERT ROTENBERG: TORONTO THE BAD ($250)

When I was 20, I worked at a funeral parlour on Danforth in Toronto with my father, a job that involved picking up bodies from the city morgue. Then, at 27, I testified in an assault trial at Old City Hall. Though unrelated, these two personal experiences vividly came to mind when reading *Old City Hall*, the crime debut of Robert Rotenberg, a top criminal lawyer.

Old City Hall delivers a rude good morning when its protagonist, Gurdial Singh, arrives at popular radio host Kevin Brace's home to deliver the day's paper, only to find him covered in blood. Brace calmly informs Singh that he has killed his wife, whose body is sprawled in the bathtub. In a gruesomely comic tableau, the police arrive to see the two men having tea in Brace's apartment, whereupon Brace is arrested.

Inevitably, what appears to be an open-and-shut case proves far more complex. What is Brace's motivation for killing his wife? How will the media, for which he works, respond to this dirty deed? And how will the Toronto public react to the length or brevity of his sentencing? Rotenberg expertly unveils the answers through witnesses, lawyers, police, and family members who step forward and root through the possibilities.

As the Crown builds its case, the story creeps into the crevices of its Old City Hall offices. Rotenberg shines here, in detailed descriptions that showcase not only his vast legal experience, but his architectural knowledge: "The Hall covered a whole city block. A massive stone structure, asymmetrical in design, filled with curling cornices, rounded pillars, marble walls, smiling cherubs, overhanging gargoyles, and the big clock tower to the left side of the main entrance which topped it off like a gigantic misplaced birthday candle."

The drama deepens when defence lawyer Nancy Parish discovers that her client Brace will communicate with her only through handwritten notes. With so much at stake, the reader is absorbed in their dissonant relationship. Brace's reticence to speak reflects the opaque process by which information is gathered in an otherwise uncomplicated case. His mute state—he even gets someone else to speak to his children from jail so his comments can't be used against him—is magnetic and draws attention to every aspect of his character, all the more for his refusal to explain himself.

Rich dialogue adds another layer, this time of gritty authenticity. Parish's wry sense of humour is self-deprecating, almost hip. When visiting Brace in jail, she jokes with a guard, "When you work for yourself, your boss is an asshole." The dialogue is just as potent among other characters: "Once a knife penetrates the surface, there's nothing in the stomach to stop it. It's like going through a feather pillow," one officer tells another.

These sound bites are prevalent throughout the book; rife with forensic intrigue, they deepen the psychological sweat, whether it's in the passive-aggressive Toronto parlance—you know who you are—or describing the not-so-fresh scent of the harbour: "There was a smell to the Toronto harbour which was foreign to the rest of the city. Pungent seagull guano, moist, coiled rope, and the whiff of outboard gasoline."

Originally published in the *Globe and Mail*

BURIED TREASURES ($0)

Obits.
by Tess Liem
Coach House Books

The Supreme Orchestra
by David Turgeon, translated by Pablo Strauss
Coach House Books

Not Extinct
by Marilyn James and Taress Alexis, illustrated by Tyler Toews
Maa Press

Examining the "mortal coil," to crib from Shakespeare, is an impossible task to say the least. Or to put it in more contemporary terms from my childhood: "Life's a bitch and then you die." Thankfully, Tess Liem's debut poetry collection *Obits.* never reads like a carpetbagger's manifesto, showing up to morbidly juggle funereal vernacular in clever ways. Instead, the poet deftly balances personal memories and source material, blending them into a highly engaging voice.

Early in the collection, in "Dead Theories," we see Liem looking back on what we can assume to be her callow youth, when she dyed her hair blonde. Without acrobatics or disturbing line breaks, the poet describes her affection for a female high-school friend with natural blonde hair: "All the boys who had crushes on her / would make out with me at parties / then offer to give her a ride home." Later the stanza ends with "All we all wanted was her sandy attention." What materializes for the reader is a living obituary for the poet's own adolescence. This self-focus is only temporary, however, and quickly vanishes as the poem rolls out a list of dead blondes and the objects of clothing they used to own.

I get an Anne Carson vibe from the scholarly tone and dreg-like atmosphere of some of the pieces, such as "After Baudelaire," with its litany of malice towards a certain dead poet, which gleefully ends, "a light in your awfulness." And the linguistic acuity of Obits. is so pared down at times that you can almost see the bone: "One written & not published / is a non-notice, / is anon."

Like Obits., David Turgeon's novel *The Supreme Orchestra* (translated by Pablo Strauss) is full of diverging nuance reassembled for a larger scope. Jewellery heists, erotic artists, subliminal messages in dance music, and temporary marriages converge in a distracting blitz of genre and tone. What do these variables all have in common? They're each components of life in constant movement and add to the novel's intrigue as everyone races towards the titular prize: a giant diamond, worth millions, called The Supreme Orchestra. While not a thief in the literal sense, Émilien Surville is a minor nobleman working to broker the purchase of the diamond on behalf of the Prince. He seems corrupt yet is also a meticulous and patient individual. The writing here exudes a tidiness befitting such a character: "The transaction would take place on the wedding day, early in the morning, in a discreet location to be determined. The diamond would be in a small black case." These exacting details written in another style might drag down the fun for the reader, but Pablo Strauss' translation of David Turgeon's writing keeps the novel aligned with a well-choreographed heist film or, more fittingly, reminiscent of Evelyn Waugh's convivial 1930 novel *Vile Bodies*.

Not Extinct: Keeping the Sinixt Way is a beautiful hybrid of story and art (its rectangular shape will, for some, harken back to illustrated primary-school books). Marilyn James and Taress Alexis and the Blood of Life Collective have collected First Nations stories, and Tyler Toews has enhanced them with illuminating artwork. In "Swarák'xn, Frog Mountain," Alexis tells a story learned from Eva Orr about an elder in the village who prayed for drought to end and a little frog, Swarák'xn, who appeared and promised that if the people dug caves, they would survive. And so they did. After the snow melted, the drought ended, and one of the tiny frogs grew into the Swaråk'xn mountain, a symbol of the love the frogs showed for the Sinixt people.

Not Extinct acts as a reminder of the need to respect not only fellow humans, but the environment we share, grow in, and often, unfortunately, destroy. In stories such as "Coyote Juggles His Eyes," Alexis tells of animals and humans working together to create a just society. In just a few short sentences, the world is revealed in new light. Countless species we may take for granted in daily life are given wonderful backstories, such as the mosquito, who bites in order to remember the dead.

Originally published in *Canadian Literature*

RATED "R" ($50)

Ricky Ricardo Suites
by Robert Allen
DC Books

The Richard Brautigan Ahhhhhhhhhh
by rob mclennan
Talon Books

Invisible to Predators
by R. M. Vaughan
ECW

A new trend in Canadian poetry is the reliance on more popular forms of entertainment. Yet perhaps no other type of writing has a more personal relationship with its reader than poetry. The first person or the projective "you" strikes a kinship with readers like an addictive pop ballad. Their cultural backdrop does, however, not shield these three books, dressed up in their modern plastic aesthetic. Even if mass by-products are sneaking in, they are harmless as grey nouns, and at worst give poetry a subtle endorsement by faceless giants. It's still the written world where these poets live and grow.

Robert Allen's *Ricky Ricardo Suites* is a prosaic blend of mood and voice. His thick language hangs heavy. Even the short Kentucky Fried Chicken™– enhanced "Cock Ale" is garnished with a deep visual buffet of "chicken limbs" that "were once eaten in a sauce of molten gold." The most common thread that resonates is tolerance and acceptance. Allen's short pieces are controlled and demonstrate a haunting presence in tone. Such is the case in "Stories:"

> If I toss you the knife to cut your blue pathways
> they will pour with the stories
> I came to this river for.

"Now that I have cable" paws at the conflict between literature and television, while "Fairy Tale of New York" pays homage to the Pogues' song of the same name. Another music-poetry crossover appears later on in collection with two Billie Holiday–inspired pieces. Right up to the end of the collection we are reminded how important music is to the poet. "It's been a Fred Astaire kind of century," Allen intones.

The long poem section "The Encantadas" is *Ricky Ricardo Suite*'s most ambitious moment, relentlessly digging crisp image after image fettered to a graffiti-like rage. Take "… / GALAPAGOS TURTLE GIVES BIRTH TO ELVIS'S HEAD / MIA & WOODY SACRIFICE YOUNGEST CHILD IN SATANIC RITE / ALIEN WROTE DYLAN'S LYRICS / MAN SNEEZES AND EYES POP OUT / NEW HUBBY FOR LIZ?" Or how within the same pages we find a new mood on the tongue: "women, timing their blood to rise simultaneously, when they all giggle and take cocktails at six. It's the least they can do, all being ex-lovers and ex-wives and ex-friends of someone, all hurting invisibly as only the conscious can."

Ottawa's irresistible force continues to churn out poetry books of considerable hype. rob mclennan's *The Richard Brautigan Ahhhhhhhhhh* is a humorous poetic carnival, with a narrative so discreetly and sincerely tucked into its sleeve one can barely sense the words being fed. "there's something about a heart that fools itself, holds out for hope & its dark in every city, wind thru the open window, blood & gravel in my eyes & i say fuck this, i say city flowers, i say, this could have been a poem," mclennan writes in "laundry & gin, tom waits, delaware avenue." In "hypnotic love poetry," mclennan uses his quick wit in compact passages, the narration less guided and more visual, using a tight-fitting stream-of-consciousness tone to produce lines

RATED "R" ($50)

like "blue clouds, lone star. suggestive huron winds, swirling like a deity," while in "after all" we are struck with a more sensitive thought-provoking scheme, a piece heavily grounded in the debate surrounding the remaining Dionne quintuplets of Montreal. Similar styles are used to provoke us in "lost poem for margot kidder" (who played Lois Lane in the 1980s), which ends with the terrifying "two suicides, car accident & a horse & lex luthor laughing."

Whether musing on Wayne Gretzky's father, Bogart, or trying to remember who sang the song in *Breakfast at Tiffany's*, the sly narration and invisible borders between voice and style creep in lowercase throughout *The Richard Brautigan Ahhhhhhhhhh*. And like Allen, mclennan gets prosaic in "(last leaves)," where the narration is much more grounded and personal. Perhaps the most haunting of mclennan's pieces are the quickest; appearing in Part 8 of "confectionary airs":

> o dennis,
> they should retire
> all the colours
> of the heart
>
> now yr gone

In some cases, popular culture references need not take the form of motion pictures or music. Such is the case in R. M. Vaughan's *Invisible to Predators*, where errands and groceries make an eerie appearance, while by-products from Nytol to Ruffles potato chips foul the senses in Vaughan's world. "In Camera," which begins with a nameless voice—"in this bed tell me a long, hopeless story to outlast me"—forces us into a bedroom crammed with intense pillow talk. "you dislike the pace of your ending, it's like travelling by car it's hours before you can stretch, move more than elbows and ankles no air between your legs, your only information from an open window," Vaughan writes.

His poetry is heckled by an erotic, deranged love balladeer who whispers filth like the voices in the prisons that fuelled Genet's novels and plays. For example, in "Six Love Poems for George-Jacques Danton," the reader is front row to puzzling exchanges of life and love that bring us that much closer to these undiscovered moments:

> While singing Sudbury Saturday Night in hollows of towers
> coins and dirt me thinking someday I may need
> to step over him, or him I
> remember your stemmed head in fresh red straw

The crafty Vaughan gets into the scent of things and makes us feel the dirt and prickles. At times he shows vulnerability in narration: "tears across the telephone, why is no one shocked? Electrically, hugging on College St. my face angled for kisses." Vaughan's strength is his unsympathetic self-revealing narrative—he's not cruel to himself in order to exhume a conflict, nor is he insincere about describing the flesh and tastes of the abject and counterfeit affections culled along the way.

Originally published in *The Antigonish Review*

SARAH EDMONDSON: HITTING THE RESET BUTTON ($0)

When I was an undergrad, I took a course on new religious movements, more sensationally known as cults. In our textbook, *Cults in Context: Readings in the Study of New Religious Movements*, Lorne Dawson noted, "the nature and evolution of charisma can thus provide opportunities for charismatic leaders to indulge the darker desires of their subconscious." This is the spoiler in all cults. It comes down to the dark desires of its leader and bending the will of members in need of structure and belief. "Charismatic leaders," Dawson continues, "may be able to render followers exclusively dependent upon them, eliminating constraints or inhibitions on their whims, leading to the possible emergence of unconventional sexual practices and violence."

Cults are as old as time, yet our reaction to their existence and capacity for sympathy towards those swallowed whole by their rigid and unorthodox grip is as divergent as their numerous forms. Countless podcasts, Netflix docs, and books come out each year emphasizing the sycophantic intrigues of cult followers. Viewers can't get enough of these mind-bending accounts of disillusionment and personal neglect. Nothing is more personal than that which occurs to us physically and emotionally. To relay these details to a friend or therapist is one thing; to regurgitate them on the page for all to see is another thing altogether.

Sarah Edmondson was a fledgling actress living in Vancouver with her filmmaker boyfriend David when she first heard of NXIVM (pronounced "NEX-ee-um"), a cult she would later become a key part of for more than a decade. NXIVM has been called everything from a "Hollywood sex cult" to a pyramid scheme to a multi-level marketing company that rewarded dedication and put its trainees through rigorous workshops called "intensives" that lasted up to fourteen hours a day and ran for two weeks at a time, costing thousands of dollars. These usually took place in hotels and hotel conference rooms. Founder Keith Raniere, an ambitious entrepreneur known as "Vanguard" to NXIVM members, has been in the news recently with horrific revelations of sexual slavery, food control, and human branding. What was set up to resemble a personal-development collective with pathological optimism has been exposed as something much darker, with Raniere recently found guilty of seven charges, among them sex trafficking, wire fraud conspiracy, and conspiracy to commit forced labour. (Another former cult member, Toni Natalie, wrote her own memoir, also published recently, called *The Program: Inside the Mind of Keith Raniere and the Rise and Fall of NXIVM*, and in recent interviews she admitted to finding peace and catharsis with the news that Raniere is now in prison.)

As readers dig into *Scarred*, they'll find that at first Edmondson's life in NXIVM appeared to be business as usual, a complement to her life and passion for self-care. The Vancouver-based actress's professional life reads like someone about to receive a Canadian Screen Award: voice actor for *My Little Pony: Friendship Is Magic*, *Transformers*, *Continuum*, *Dinotrux*, *Max Steel*, *At Home in Mitford*, and *Love at First Bark*, to name a few. At first glance her biography couldn't be further from describing someone engulfed in a mind-controlling cult; but then again, that's just what's so fascinating about these sects: they can prey on and influence susceptible people in all walks of life, ages, genders, and postal codes.

In 2005, at the age of 28, Edmondson, along with her boyfriend David, went on a cruise called the Spiritual Cinema Circle Festival at Sea. "I, for one, had been starving for purpose and fulfillment, and being a part of this kind of setting was what I needed to stay motivated," she told herself. The festival was also screening one of her boyfriend's films. Deeply interested in self-improvement, the self-described nerd, who spent her youth listening to self-improvement tapes instead of music, chasing spiritual bestsellers such as *The Artist's Way* and *The Celestine Prophecy* instead of boys, Edmondson saw the cruise as both a spiritual and a networking opportunity. And she was up for the adventure.

SARAH EDMONDSON: HITTING THE RESET BUTTON ($0)

On the cruise, a filmmaker the couple admired, in a not-so-chance encounter, told them about NXIVM, which he described as "a community of humanitarians who were spending their time and resources to shift the state of humanity." Edmondson and her partner became not only intrigued but borderline ecstatic. After worrying about the initial fee for their first seminar, they made their way to a Holiday Inn Express in Burnaby, sat on ripped chairs, and watched Nancy Salzman, the company's president, "who addressed the camera in a shoulder-padded suit and scholarly spectacles while seeming never to pause for a breath." Edmondson couldn't look past Salzman's 1990s Murphy Brown aesthetic and wondered why on earth she had paid over two grand to sit and watch a video. But things evolved, and Edmondson perked up when she read one of NXIVM's promises: "We are an ongoing program that helps you develop the necessary inner strength to achieve success. It's a team effort with team support." She liked the sound of that.

As a story, *Scarred* is the stuff of suspense and terrific drama, combined with the agony of witnessing humans at their most vulnerable, angry, and disrespected. Readers witness the slow build towards near-total self-abandonment as Edmondson's life was taken over by those she trusted. Then followed more than a decade of commitment, not to mention thousands upon thousands of dollars, missing friends' weddings because of "ethics breaches," and giving so much of herself that she arrived at her breaking point. Sitting naked in a room full of fellow women, all blindfolded, she was branded just above her pubic line. Enduring a pain she described as worse than childbirth, she realized she had, very carefully, to escape. While caring for her oozing scar, she saw that it was a sideways K and R, representing the founder's initials.

Soon Edmondson was meeting with the FBI and telling her story. Her emancipation was imminent, but the healing was only beginning. In late 2017, working closely with the FBI, she helped build a case against Raniere and began to work with the media as well, with every outlet from A&E to CBC, all the while cathartically journaling:

> I am clean again. I know that through this process I will have forgiven those who betrayed me; who threw me under the

bus. Who gaslit me and scavenged my delicate naive mind to replace my beliefs with theirs. I will let go of the rage, just dance in the breeze with that clothesline...swaying calm.

It's taken years, but in the end, with the help of her friends, husband, and daughter, Edmondson has navigated towards inner peace. *Scarred* documents that she has hit the reset button on a life where she is now in control and no longer the plaything of a sociopathic narcissist who was unable to respect anyone or to see people for what they are: individuals.

Originally published in *The Ormsby Review*

PART SIX: EXIT THROUGH THE GIFT SHOP

HOW TO BE YOUR OWN BOOK-PR DREAM TEAM ($125)

> Find out what you love about marketing, and then put your heart into it. Self-promotion without love and integrity can be really smarmy. Always be honest and transparently yourself. Promote out of love, not fear. People can tell the difference.
>
> —Sarah Selecky, Giller-finalist author of *This Cake Is for the Party*

Up until now, there has never been an instruction manual for how to exist as a writer in PR mode—that is, during the time just before and just after your book is released into the wild. This can be a tricky time in an author's life, never really knowing when things are starting or ending. You'll find yourself, towards the end, wondering just who the hell has bought your book anyway. When it comes to actual sales, I always tell my authors that they'll be surprised when they get their royalty statement (hopefully) because they will be seeing, for the very first time, evidence that their book has been purchased by people the author doesn't know. That feeling is worth holding onto should it arise.

DOS & DON'TS

> In Paris, a vampire has to be clever for many reasons. Here, all one needs is a pair of fangs.
>
> —Lestat, *Interview with the Vampire*, 1976

I've often thought of that line from the film *Interview with the Vampire* as it relates to publishing. Anyone can go get Microsoft Word, a Tumblr page, an author photo, and a new waistcoat (or whatever garment is suitable for a book launch where you're reading this). But a lot of unexplained details about being a writer and existing in a publishing community are not covered in your basic author-instruction manual.

In my job as a book publicist, whenever I get emails from authors saying something to the effect of, "I've asked around on advice as to just what a 'pitch letter' should include and have drafted one accordingly," I'm always curious as to whom the author has queried. Many authors want to be hands-on and get panicked without constant updates. On the other side of the spectrum are the rogue writers: those who you hear from regularly, but their updates are mildly baffling. "I've been pitching the newspapers and the CBC," they write; "my contact at the *Toronto Star* says I should send my poetry collection to the book editor."

It's my job to try to encourage these authors to curb their enthusiasm and stop contacting the media directly. I've had coffee with major newspaper book editors (this isn't a brag; lots of people have coffee with people with all sorts of jobs), and they expressed polite concern about one of my authors cold-emailing them and suggesting—in said email—a good reviewer for their book. So, dear writer, please commit this to memory on a list of DON'Ts: don't email book editors of national newspapers with a shortlist of authors/journalists worthy to review your book. Now, on with the rest of my list of Dos and Don'ts:

HOW TO BE YOUR OWN BOOK-PR DREAM TEAM ($125)

DO:

1. Record short audio-only clips of you reading from your book. These can be used online and in festival pitches as put together by your publicist—or if you've arranged to do some of your own promotional work such as connecting with festivals and reading series (with your publisher's blessing). An author's input into festival pitch letters and media letters is considerable. If your publisher asks you for details concerning a particular slant for your book, or your connections to the region the festival takes place in, you should take the time to really dig deep to make the most of it.

2. Compile a list of folks you think should receive your book for review purposes. Most publishers have extensive media lists, and it might be good to send your list to your publisher early so they can confirm any outlets that are new to them. Each author comes with their own cache of surprises. Communicate clearly, and let your wishes be known from the start so there are no disappointments later on.

3. Come up with launch and tour plans. Beyond your hometown, where you'll have your main launch, in what other places do you think you have fans/friends who would come out and buy your book?

4. Get some of your writer friends to support your efforts online (i.e., on social media). Ask them to do things on the street too: much covert operative work can be done behind the scenes. My advice is to enlist five to fifteen book besties to do the following for your book while you sleep:

> Reserve/request your book at their local library
> Reserve/pre-order your book from local indie bookstores
> Review the book on Goodreads
> Volunteer at your book launch (there's lots to do here, from being a greeter to showing folks where the book table is)
> Form a book club and champion your book

5. Post a weekly reminder about your book's existence in fun, non-annoying ways on social media. This can be a quick collage (in mid-to-late 2020, Camilla Gibb did a series of COVID collages that were quite eye-catching and a subtle means of surreptitious author branding), Instagram

post, or embarrassing photo of you when you were little with a caption that reads, "Who knew this person, dressed this way, with this haircut, would someday go on to write a novel?" But please, be mindful of the likelihood of your audience's Internet fatigue in your efforts at self-promotion. Also, keep in mind that your voice can carry your message further than just typing something out on Facebook or Twitter. Perhaps you could do an entire post that is your voice with an image of your book cover, and you could tell a short story that potential readers might find attractive. Says author Elizabeth Hay, "Today's media are making us stupider. Generally they're chatter-filled and audience-obsessed and less and less concerned with stimulating and deepening our thoughts. Radio at its best is still a wonderful thing. Like a good book, it can make you feel more alive, more connected to the world."

6. Have some fun. From the Claudia Dey archives: "I remember with my novel, *Stunt*, my friends played music outside of Pages bookstore (which is now sadly gone) to promote the book. Only two years later, everything is being done cyberly. For a girl who wishes she could ride a horse everywhere, this is a massive re-calibration—transactions and expression are immaterial." Remember to arrange your short-lived promo stunt with the bookstore before setting up the sidewalk people.

7. Visit your local library. Introduce yourself and ask the librarian if they'd take a look at your book with the notion of the branch ordering it for their collection. You may find your book is already in the system, but this might be a chance to get the library to order an additional copy or two, depending on how charming you are during your initial chat. You may also wish to do the same thing at a local arts or community centre. There can be opportunities to do class visits at community colleges and English departments at local universities too—think about what you could offer a classroom for a one-hour presentation and what you would talk about. Then get in touch.

8. Carry a notebook with you. You never know when you'll need to jot down an author name, a book title, or the name of a new venue that opened up in your neighbourhood that might be perfect for a book launch or reading.

9. Enter literary contests and subscribe to literary magazines.

10. Buy other local writers' books. Nothing says *I should support this author* more than your supporting other writers. If you attend a launch, buy

the book. It's an opportunity to snap a picture with a short comment about how excited you are to start reading the book. To avoid being perceived as a sycophant, I wouldn't suggest doing this very often, but once or twice a year seems reasonable.

DON'T:

1. Send book media giants 18-MB headshots of yourself with a side order of pixilated book cover demanding they review your book. Do not WeTransfer/email them a PDF of your unpublished/published manuscript or book proof. Consult a professional.

2. Beeline for someone you know who works in publishing and introduce yourself into their conversation to start talking about the projects you are working on. Read the room. (Publishers and authors are busy during launches. So unless they are really encouraging you to continue the schmooze, move along.)

3. "Like" everything an author you just met posts on social media as if you were best friends.

4. Overdo it on banter and introducing/contextualizing your work before you actually start to read it on stage.

5. Make a book trailer. (Short videos of you reading from your book are fine, but a book trailer, with its public-domain music, its snazzy font, and its possible inclusion of a book cover, is not required.)

6. Ask someone at a book event if they're a writer. (Almost everyone in the room is a writer, publisher, editor, agent, or otherwise in the industry.)

7. Ask writers about their work, or talk only about your own work.

8. Go overtime when on stage. Seven minutes is plenty for a reading. Unless the organizers have paid you to read for a set amount of time, less is more.

9. Send a potential publisher a complete layout of your book cover.

10. Cold-call a random publisher and ask them about submission policies.

HOW TO ORGANIZE A SUCCESSFUL BOOK EVENT

It's all about flow. Control. Mastering the art of less. You don't phone up a bartender and explain that you want to have a book launch at their establishment on their busiest night and proceed to read the first chapter to the hapless owner. Learn to make a clean pitch. Money is everything. So is people's time. Imagine delivering your message to a bar owner like a rehearsed, perfect scene in a high school play. You know your lines and you know how your stage partner will react. First off, tell them how much you love their place, and that you wanted to talk about a possible book event that would not happen during the busiest time of their business hours—let's say, for example, seven until eight-thirty. You say up front that you don't have a big budget, but you'd be willing to guarantee a certain amount of money in bar and food sales. They will ask about lighting and sound that might mean having to bring in extra staff that night. (The cost will vary city to city. Some bars now have minimums for events simply because there are so many events going on in larger urban centres).

A lot of first-time or even third-time writers over-plan their book launches. The best thing to do is pick a venue that everyone in your writing community knows. Make a big email and postal address list of everyone you know. Write a simple two-line event release for local weeklies and radio stations with the confirmed time and location. Leak a slightly larger press release online and send the links out to newspapers and other media outlets. Most writing communities in Canada are small, even Toronto, so it's best to publish your listings in the same few standard places as everyone else does.

You want things to go smoothly. Give journalists review copies of your book at the launch. Take note of their names and get your publisher to follow up (but email your publisher a week later—no need to jump on follow-ups immediately. Give the world some breathing room). While you're at the launch, enjoy yourself and take time to chat everyone up. If someone corners you, try to signal for help. There are gracious ways to evade domineering strangers who perhaps don't realise that this is your night, and that as much as it's all about the art, it's a business event as well. Thank your guests for coming when they leave and also in an email or message over social media the next day. (Don't thank the media for coming; save that for your publisher to follow up with at a later date).

When it's time for you to read, thank everyone for being there, but don't go on and on about how weird it is to be publishing your book and then say something about your third-grade teacher. Keep it light and just start reading a short section of about 3–4 pages. Don't read for more than ten minutes. Get some snack food, maybe a musical act and some other readers to share the lineup with you. Talk to your publisher. Ask them to walk around with copies of the book for guests you notice haven't purchased copies yet. After all, this isn't a casual hangout, but neither does it have to be high-pressure sales event. No one is working on commission tonight, but selling a few extra boxes of books to aunts and uncles and ex-roommates is nice.

Whenever someone is on stage, make sure they are holding a copy of your book. When I worked as a bookseller, we were told to practically put the book in people's hands; there is a power to physical contact with a possible fetish property. People love the smell of fresh ink.

> The book is an extension of who you are and what you do, so don't be afraid to talk about its greatness like the amazing thing that it is to everyone that you see, know, meet.
>
> —Sean Cranbury, Executive Director of BC & Yukon Book Awards; Host, *Books on the Radio*

THE CAMILLA GIBB EFFECT

In 2000, Giller Prize finalist Camilla Gibb bought up a chunk of the initial print run of her first novel, *Mouthing the Words*, and sold it out of her backpack for months, booking herself at every possible reading in an effort that eventually led to her winning the Toronto Book Award. While peddling your book doesn't always equal award glory, it's a nice little fable to think about, considering where Gibb is today.

In her charming interview with Susan G. Cole, Gibb can be seen as a confident PR maven, flitting around in pre-Twitter (heck, pre-Friendster)

Toronto. "She is in many ways a marketer's dream—someone with chops galore and, crucially, a willingness to sell herself."

Said Gibb about her first book: "I bought a hundred copies, read at every series, and sold the thing out of my knapsack. And I got my friends to go into Chapters and take it off the bottom shelf and put it on the Oprah's Picks table. I went to practically every independent bookstore in the city and signed copies." (I've always enjoyed this part of the story because when I worked at Indigo in 2005 or so, I would hand-sell dozens of Camilla's books and even got invited to the Random House paperback release, where I ate strawberries and drank champagne and talked to Team Camilla, which was quite pleasant and fancy.)

The point is: you can control your inventory and monitor personal author-to-reader sales in addition to relying on the traditional sales methods your publisher is taking care of. This approach also keeps you out of your publisher's hair and makes them love you more come grant time. Plus, you can negotiate a good deal with your publisher if you are buying in bulk and then selling at live shows or even on your own website.

BLURBS ARE ENDORSEMENTS, NOT REVIEWS

Blurbs, sometimes referred to as endorsements, are usually offered by more established writers who will lend your book some credibility. They are written before a book is published, and they appear on the front and back covers, as well as in catalogues and on publishers' websites. These are not reviews. Reviews appear when the book has come out, or are written from an ARC (Advance Reading Copy), which your publisher may decide to create (usually for fiction or nonfiction titles) and send out to media in advance of the publication date.

For *Jettison*, my debut collection of short fiction, published in 2016 by Anvil Press, I asked some of my closest writer pals to write mini-essays of about 120 words that would be used as blurbs (one for each story) to help spruce up the promotional material for the book. Working closely with my publisher, we decided to put these blurbs before the beginning of each story. The idea came when I was trying to imagine different ways my next book could be interpreted, not necessarily from a critical perspective, but a social perspective.

By starting these discussions with your contemporaries, you also get more out of an endorsement than a sentence or two that uses the words *daring* and *brave* and *fierce*. Blurbs are almost like little yearbook messages/intimate missives that add sparkle to your book. Of course, blurbs and how they are used ultimately comes down to your publisher and editor.

VIDEO KILLED THE POETRY STAR: THE DREADED BOOK TRAILER

In 2015, to "celebrate" the 10th anniversary of my debut book *Bowlbrawl* and its subsequent plethora of book trailers, I found myself nattering on in a column about a service I could provide authors who wanted an alternative to the book trailer: the Fake Book Trailer. Yes, a book trailer that appears online, but that also appears to be completely unauthorized and therefore slightly cooler. I mean, the last thing you want to be is that person who invites a bunch of friends over to watch a slow-motion slide presentation of your trip to Florida where it rained for three weeks straight. I wrote:

> Now, first off, I must dispel the rumour that I was hired by Coach House Books to write several thousand versions of the book copy for Christian Bök's long-awaited follow-up to his 2001 dance hit *Eunoia*. Well, it's complete rubbish—the rumour, that is. But here are several pull quotes that I am working on for my new venture Fake Book Trailer, as once advertised in *Broken Pencil* and *subTerrain* (see fakebooktrailer.tumblr.com).
>
> "*The Xenotext: Book 1* by Christian Bök is rooted in a firm belief in the solar system. Glugging along several light years away, *The Xenotext* is poised to return to earth in a searing ball of blue and gold flame this fall (2012), where it will enter the earth just below the surface and emerge as a giant insect with a translucent, seventy-metre proboscis. It

will then begin pollinating the young minds of college and university students who will begin chanting low-frequency sentence fragments while they chew on the sleeve cuffs of their alma-mater hoodies"; or, the following spring (2013), "Not since George Michael's *Listen Without Prejudice Vol. 1* has anyone waited with such faith and honour for a book of Canadian-published poetry. I, for one, won't be sitting this one out. This book is a living and breathing thing. Charge it rent if it's in your apartment!" Or from last summer's version, heavily influenced by the movie poster for *The Martian*, starring Matt Damon: "From nerf herders to astro girdles, this collection giggles along with the best line breaks money can buy. Born on another world, Xenia has come here to protect ours."

Based on that, it's not hard at all to imagine what a Fake Book Trailer for *The Xenotext* would look like. And it's not too late for you to get a Fake Book Trailer for your own book—no matter how new or old it is! This new-media venture is my gift back to Canadian and independent presses. As a pioneer of this ubiquitous MPEG practice in book promotion, I feel that I could Warhol this dead video-art genre into the next decade with some quality control and, of course, all the necessary feedback and paperwork from the authors and their myriad of think tanks. As it says on our website, "Fake Book Trailer is a new brand for your book trailer to remind you that the Internet is great, but it's not a bookstore, a great short story, a line break in a poem, or fun at a live reading or book signing. Nor is it the place or spirit that originally harnessed that which is the finality of your book. It's just a series of images, text, and sound. It is not a book. And it's not a trailer either, as those are in movie theatres to go along with billion-dollar feature films."

So far I've made trailers for Michael Turner's *The Pornographer's Poem* (Soft Skull Press edition) and my own *Jettison* (Anvil Press), with many more planned. As Johnny Rotten once said, "We invented punk and now we want to get paid for it." I, too, want to be paid for making your book trailer: anywhere from five to twenty dollars and I'll be more than pleased to make your backlist, frontlist, or sidelist 45-second promotional trailer under the Fake Book Trailer brand. I'll also be profiling authors and their publishers on the website.

The truth is, you're probably convinced a book trailer is going to make all the difference, so I'm not going to even attempt to stop you. I'm your friend, after all. Speaking of friends, a good video artist can help in the short term, if you want to do a short video of yourself reading from your book—better still, reciting a memorized passage.

A month before the launch of my poetry debut, *Let's Pretend We Never Met*, a freelance journalist emailed me to ask about my Catullus video. Did I pay out of pocket, or was there some kind of council funding available? (Keep in mind that YouTube was but two years old at this point, and Instagram a nonexistent napkin-sketch-in-waiting.) "I'm thinking of pitching *Quill* a short Omni piece about your YouTube trailer for the Catullus book. Obviously the intersection of Catullus, CanLit, and YouTube is an interesting marketing strategy, but I thought I'd check in with you first to see if there are any other newsier angles behind the creation of the video. How did it come to be? Who is the filmmaker? Any catchy stories there?"

(Doing a quick scan of my archives, I can see why they didn't take the piece: in the summer of 2006, *Quill & Quire* ran a short article on Conundrum Press turning ten in which I'm credited with presenting a "tongue-in-cheek" short film called *Dear Canada Council*, with video from Vitalyi Bulchev. The video depicts me addressing the Canada Council on fiscal struggle for artists and how they need to eat food to strengthen their journeys to meet one another at bars so they can come up with ideas to spend the money they hope to get.)

I let the journalist know that it was a friend in Toronto who had put the video together with me, and I reminded him that it was this same friend who had put together the *Bowlbrawl* trailers. "Video killed the poetry star" is about how people love watching videos a lot more than reading books, but the obvious irony is, they are being forced to watch literary-based videos, right? Right? Hook? Perhaps. I never heard from the journalist again, and *Quill & Quire* never wrote about my video, which is good, as I would spend the next decade renouncing my belief in book trailers, the combovers of the literary-art world. But listen: if you must, go ahead, make a book trailer. I promise to like it and share it. I won't judge. I mean, I've been making videos since the 1970s, I see the appeal. But can I just ask this one question: what is the plot of a book trailer?

THE GREAT CANADIAN LIT-MAG HUNT

Growing up as an aspiring small-press author as I did in the early 2000s, I was of course obsessed with literary magazines and journals. In 2002, small-press author Vern Smith wrote a thoughtful piece called "Pump up The Volumes" in the pages of *This Magazine*, examining the role of lit mags across the country and urging these creative outlets to consider becoming more diverse:

> Take *The Capilano Review*. It publishes "the best in fiction, drama, poetry and art from Canada and the rest of the world." Which sounds something like *Grain*'s "established writings from Canada and around the world." Which sounds like "the best of new and established Canadian and international writers" put out by *Event*. Just in case any of those aren't your thing, *The Antigonish Review* has "consistently published fine poetry and prose by emerging and established writers." *The Malahat Review* publishes "engaging and contemporary fiction and poetry by Canada's best writers." At *PRISM International* it's "the best in contemporary writing and translation from Canada." By defining themselves so broadly, are literary magazines selling themselves, and their readers, short?

Lately, however, I just don't know. Am I too old? At forty-six, is my time better spent playing a short game—book deals, grants, and take my chances on that level? Or follow the alleged time-honoured tradition of submitting my writing to magazines across the country to accrue some publishing credits to present to a publisher?

Or is it a whole new ball game? Online journals, short-run zines, chapbooks, and poetry podcasts have cropped up like satellites in space all across the zeitgeist of our marginalized wasteland of lexical excess. But are these destinations useful tools in the goal of moving ahead in the queue? A lot of writers don't like to talk about the fact that what we do is, well, sort of a business. It's not just for the sake of precious art that we're doing this. And I'm not talking about money—at least directly—but publishing work before it's in book form. Is that a noble pursuit in this day and age?

The reason I bring this up is that quite recently, I've discovered that many novelists are now getting published without a single publishing credit to their name. That means their very-first-*ever* publication is a completed novel. (This is *never* the case for poetry, at least from my vantage point. A poet usually has some obscure credit somewhere before they collapse at the door of their publisher for good).

Early on, I found that sending my work out was part of a ritual that all writers went through. You'd hear about a new zine or magazine at a reading, and someone would suggest you enter a contest, or send a poem for a theme issue. But in the ever-changing world of publishing, with so many different avenues, different geographies, an imbalance of funding, the overall cost to print and distribute, the landscape of literary magazine publishing in Canada is a bit of a wash. As Smith wrote in *This Magazine* nearly twenty years ago, it's pretty hard to tell the issues of [insert university-based literary journal here] apart based on design and ads. What is the value, then, of following the path of writers from generations before, when the leaps are so much larger now?

Fredericton poet Jennifer Houle, author of *Virga*, says the element of surprise is a big factor in the appeal of literary magazines:

> You never know what emerging author or new work by a longtime favourite you might discover. It's easy to fall into ruts where you stop seeking new work, especially if you're deep into a project or reading jag of your own. Lit mags are the way out of those ruts. I also appreciate the reviews and all the work

that goes into reflecting on and considering the immense creative output of writers. It's an irreplaceable service.

For a long time, the party line was *publish in literary magazines*; some over the years likened them to the farm system for sports teams. Michael Bryson, a fiction writer from Toronto and editor of *The Danforth Review*, sees things a bit differently:

> I'm not keen on the farm-team metaphor, because it has always seemed to me that literature is a marginal activity. That is, the lit mags and the small presses and the so-called margins of CanLit have always been the heart of literature in Canada. It's where the innovation happens. The farm-team metaphor works for sports, but the indie music scene is maybe a better analogy. Bands on the margins or coming up do weird, interesting things, but then get a major label and get flattened out (maybe not always, but often). In comedy, even the big comics go back to the small clubs to work on new material, stay fresh. Should we expect the same of big writers?

While completing her debut novel, *Daughters of Silence*, author Rebecca Fisseha approached literary-magazine publishing with a strategy in mind:

> I believed that it was a way to bolster my appeal to agents and publishers. And that was the general advice, something along the lines of *have something published elsewhere before you start sending out a full-length manuscript*, etc. Whether or not that made a difference, in the end, I'm not sure. Maybe it was the writing practice I got from writing and revising those stories that made the difference rather than having the publication credits.

Fisseha believes that submitting to journals is something she may do in between books, like "sending out signs of life." Since publishing her first book, the author feels more comfortable submitting her new work.

HOW TO BE YOUR OWN BOOK-PR DREAM TEAM ($125)

Veteran BC poet Tom Wayman says rejection is part of what defines a writer, as well as preparing them for greater disappointments in their careers.

> I think for any beginning writer, being steadily rejected by literary magazines helps them get used to the world not really welcoming their amazing insights and dazzling command of language. Since most novels, like most books, are in effect published straight into the warehouse, i.e., sink into oblivion with astonishing speed, I can imagine someone whose first publication is a novel being stunned and amazed at discovering after publication how little the real world cares about their work. Whereas a rejection-scarred writer, veteran of many submissions to literary magazines, is well prepared for the resounding silence and disregard that is the fate of most publications.

Wayman points out that technology has made it very easy for writers to submit to journals. "Poetry is the worst," says Wayman, who has heard that a magazine in the Los Angeles area, *Rattle*, claims they receive 120,000 poems a year and publish 150.

> In self-defence, many magazines have set up a screening mechanism consisting of grad students. Since these are often young people who haven't yet experienced full adult life (the main concerns of a post-secondary student's life are often far removed from those of a functioning adult out in the world dealing with a job, family, household, etc.), the danger is that a literary world develops whose main themes are those of interest to students, not the issues that absorb the Canadian population at large. A writer friend in California refers to the people who screen submissions as "the children." I'd add that the problem is compounded because screeners only know about those literary approaches advocated by instructors whose courses they've taken at the universities or colleges they've attended—a spectrum of literary possibility that can be quite narrow.

Years ago, *Frank* magazine characterized the Internet as "the vanity press of the deranged," and nothing I've encountered has led me to doubt this definition. People constantly send me jokes, memes, or funny YouTube postings that they've found online. But for the plethora of lit mags that have migrated online due to the dearth of institutional funding, I've yet to have anyone—student or colleague—refer me to a piece of writing they enjoyed that they found in an online mag. Whereas people do steadily point out writing in print mags that they've found personally meaningful and worthy of drawing my attention.

On balance, I'm grateful that people are willing to do the hard and essentially thankless work of producing print literary magazines. I subscribe at any one time to eight or nine of these, and I continually discover authors and poems and stories that I'm impressed by, even dazzled by, and thus find I can learn from. These are writers I would otherwise not encounter. If literary magazines disappeared, my only alternative would be word-of-mouth recommendations, and since the writers I talk to tend to be those whose aesthetics match my own, I believe that without literary magazines my sense of the possibilities for literature would be much, much poorer.

"As someone who is writing a novel at the moment and has been for the last couple of years, I have to say that I feel screwed when it comes to sending out prose," says Shazia Hafiz Ramji, author of *Port of Being*.

> There is no space for long form in magazines. Most stories cap at 2,500 or 3,000 words. How are novelists meant to publish without sacrificing the form and length of their work? It's common for novelists to appear out of nowhere and publish a book without publishing in magazines first, because there is no space for novelists in these venues. Even internationally, first-time novelists often publish a book and then get excerpted in places like *Granta*, etc.

Having spent a good chunk of time working for both publishers and magazines (sometimes at the same time), Ramji still feels that the vitality of literary magazines is something that should be supported and discussed. "I also think it's important to talk about contests, which are mostly hosted by magazines. Contests are still a way for a first-time writer to get published. Contests have helped me a lot. Contests often make up a lot of the venue's income. Without contests, many traditional lit mags could be dead."

I think lit mags are anything but dead. Lit mags are moving online and bring their own networks of people with them, which keep them alive and serve more than a magazine function. There is not enough incentive and infrastructure in Canada to have digital lit mags of the kind one sees in the States and elsewhere. We need to be questioning and revamping circulation-based and subscription-based models if magazines want to stay alive in Maple Land.

"I think there's still some cachet to being published in journals, especially the harder-to-get-into ones like *The Fiddlehead*," says poet Ian LeTourneau, who is also managing editor at the Fredericton-based literary journal. "Some publishers still read them to scout for talent. But my experience is mostly with poetry. My sense is that a lot of young writers try to build their resumes up by publishing in lit mags. Of course, young writers have always been in a hurry to publish, so I think lit mags serve a good intermediary step to book publication: you learn how to write cover letters, work with editors, etc."

Chris Benjamin, editor at *Atlantic Books Today*, hadn't published much before his first novel came out. "I've always seen lit journals as one route to a book, but not the only one. I'm not sure my novel would have been published if I hadn't won the Atlantic Writing Competition of the Writers Federation of Nova Scotia. That got some attention from publishers." Benjamin believes that journals have value in and of themselves. "I have a short story collection coming out, and almost every story was in a lit journal or an anthology first. I think short story collections are like poetry that way. I can't imagine submitting a collection of short stories without at least half of them having been published in journals or anthologies first."

But it's not so cut and dried: Benjamin does see the fine line on which an experienced writer dangles. "I do also feel weird sometimes submitting to lit journals, knowing that my work will likely be vetted (on first pass at least) by a young person without a lot of lived experience (or published work under their belt), let alone the kinds of experiences I put my characters through. I worry theirs will be a narrow and heavily theoretical lens. By and large, I like the results (as evidenced in the journals themselves), but then again, we don't get to see what's rejected. I wonder if there's gold in them thar slush piles."

Originally published in *Open Book Toronto*

AMAZON ISN'T THE ANTICHRIST. STILL, I WOULDN'T INVITE THEM TO MY BOOK LAUNCH ($100)

> The hand that stocks the drug stores rules the world. Let us start our Republic, with a chain of drug stores, a chain of grocery stores, a chain of gas chambers, and a national game. After that we can write our Constitution.
>
> —Amazon bestseller Kurt Vonnegut, *Cat's Cradle*, 1963

Plain and simple, if you are an author with a forthcoming book, I would encourage you to keep folks from chatting about Amazon online (read: your public social media feed). Amazon is a giant, and your cousins, coworkers, estranged aunts, and ex-boyfriends may wind up buying your book from them just out of habit alone; they need no encouragement (Amazon, that is; your estranged aunt, I have no idea). My thoughts are this: encourage friends nationwide to preorder the book from indie bookstores. Your book can be ordered by any store in Canada. After the initial launch is done, it's fine for folks to buy your book from Amazon.

My reasoning is twofold: Amazon doesn't always get their stock in time. Eager aunts and cousins and friends may think they're doing you a favour by pre-ordering your book, but then will they buy it at the launch? Will they bring their Amazon copies to the launch and have you sign them? It's best before, during, and a bit after the launch to encourage sales at the sponsoring bookseller.

For a living, I work with a dozen first-time authors each year. They are like children on their first day of school with fumbling baby goat–like steps to the bus and their nervous faces when they open their lunches to see what I've packed to sustain them. But to stir things up a bit, and get to the lecture at hand, I'm going to change perspectives, as I've walked away from the bus stop and am now working on their presidential campaign for the upcoming student council election, which we'll simply call a publicity campaign and drop the pedagogical gimmick completely. You see, dear first-time author (or author who hasn't published in a handful of seasons), publicizing the Amazon link to your book on social media is the equivalent to telling a journalist in an interview about your book that you used Microsoft Word to complete the manuscript: it's the most obvious gesture you could make, and it's not at all necessary.

It took a global pandemic to get mainstream book-buying culture in Canada to embrace indie bookstores. The CBC finally acknowledged they existed, as did everyone else (read: authors and their confused aunts and nephews). Suddenly, Amazon was seen, in some cases, as the big corporation it has always been—one not terribly interested in meeting the needs of publishers, who rely on indie stores for events, signings, and general browsing. Instead, Amazon let it be known that these publishers were not a priority. I finally felt like my twice-a-year battle cry to my authors was getting some nice back-up singers.

When the world went into lockdown in March 2020, bookstores across the country were forced to close alongside everything else. But the coronavirus-related closures threatened to have a particularly wrenching effect on Canada's independent booksellers, who have seen their share of challenges over the years. The average book reader doesn't necessarily imagine what is best for the book industry when buying a book on a whim. And this type of consumer isn't likely to dwell on the quarter-century-long struggle that independent bookstores have faced since the emergence of Amazon, rising shipping costs, higher rents, and other factors that affect the book industry. For decades now, generations of booklovers have been trained to buy their books from larger, less personal outlets.

Many book enthusiasts (whom I define as those who buy between five and 25 new books a year) have a limited understanding of how authors earn money. Hint: it's often not from book sales. While royalties do play a huge factor in the income for authors with household names, the average Canadian author earns far more money on advances, awards, and festival, conference, and academic appearances.

The average reader, by no fault of her own, might simply be unaware that buying books from Amazon doesn't have the same effect as buying from an independent bookstore. After all, the next time you shop at Amazon, notice: no one is coming up to you and asking how you're enjoying *Daughters of Silence* by Rebecca Fisseha, which might have been recommended to you because someone worked the book launch where they heard the author read. Another customer in the store overhears this conversation and picks up Fisseha's debut novel, and so on.

That's why I'm hoping to treat this essay as an olive branch to book readers across the country. Think of buying books from an independent store as an investment in a writer's entire career. Hand selling is one of the most successful means of selling books (I know from personal experience as a former bookseller that a lot of consumers love book recommendations). Festival curators often talk to booksellers on the regular. So, your enthusiasm at the indie-bookstore level can help an author's chances to make more money directly from an elongated period of hype. And guess who comes to festivals to sell books all day and night? Independent bookstores.

Things begin to build. Other stores may ask an author to come in to do signings. While a book signing doesn't pay anything to the author (save for those eventual royalties), it does raise the author's profile. A magazine like *Geist* may hear the buzz about a new author from a bookseller. Then *Geist* contacts the book's publisher, asks to run an excerpt, and is willing to pay a fee. That's more money for the author. The book's success will determine how much money the author will make on their next book as well: when their agent negotiates a new book contract, the publisher can look back and see how the sales were for their last book, and the agent can negotiate a larger paid advance.

While independently-owned bookstores are facing changing times during COVID-19, consumers can make their book purchases mean something more than blips on Amazon ratings. They can discover new stores in their hometowns that want to compete directly with these giants. And they can support Canadian publishing. In response, bookstores across the country, such as Fredericton's Westminster Books, Ottawa's Perfect Books, Montreal's Argo Bookshop, and Vancouver's The Paper Hound have been filling demands for special orders, regular requests by appointment, and delivering books within the city.

Mark Laliberte, publisher of *Carousel* magazine, says the owner of Biblioasis Bookshop in Windsor personally dropped off his order free of charge within a day or so, while Toronto author Maggie MacDonald didn't have to think twice when it came to her favourite store. "Type on Queen West offers curbside pickup. You call in an order and then walk over and get it. I love it because I have friendships with the booksellers in my neighbourhood and I can still ask them for personal recommendations. A brick-and-mortar bookstore is about culture and relationships, and the curbside model sustains that while we wait for the reopening."

"My experience buying books from local bookstores during COVID-19 has been a positive one. It has been easy enough to order via phone and conduct curbside pick-ups with Ottawa's Perfect Books," says Ottawa poet Ben Ladouceur.

> But I miss going into both of these places and others to browse around. And I can't imagine how bookstores will work, exactly, in the near future, when touching and handling and opening books is such a big part of the shopping experience. I have noticed myself reading book reviews more, which I think is my way of making up for long, luxurious, quiet visits to bookstores—form of stress relief I miss dearly. But it's a pale imitation.

Patricia Massy, owner of Massy Books in Vancouver, says that before COVID hit, the store was scheduled to participate in and host over 40 events in the months following, which were all cancelled. Each year, the popular store participates in over a hundred events, including festivals and book launches. These events translate to brand awareness and extra revenue in a shorter burst of time (the average book event is a two-hour affair, with sales usually at the beginning and tail end). "Events are a vital part of our business model and make up a large portion of our revenue. In one day, non-essential businesses were asked to shut down, we immediately lost an estimated $10,000 in revenue," Massy told me. The forced closure affected other revenue streams, including monies from the Growing Room festival, which the store was supposed to be part of. "Thankfully, *Room Magazine* and Massy did a social media promotion, offering to donate 50% of all sales from Growing Room titles back to Growing Room, and managed to donate over $600 back to the host magazine."

Now that events are not really an option for the foreseeable future, Massy is focusing on online orders, delivery, and online promotion. "We are selling an enormous amount of new books, which is getting us through this time! Lots of community support and excitement over reading, which is a beautiful thing to see."

While the uncertainty has been devastating for these businesses, it has provided these stores with insight into sales they would never otherwise have had. "It has certainly been a difficult period," says Jessica Paul of Munro's Books in Victoria, but she has been happily surprised with the overall adaptation. "We already had an online store, and our customers were quick to adapt to purchasing online while we were closed to the public for two months. We are now back open with a limited capacity, and it has been wonderful to see the enthusiasm that customers express for being able to browse the shelves again."

Originally published on *rabble.ca*

VIEWER DIGRESSION ADVISED: NETFLIX IS NOT A PUBLISHING COURSE ($0)

My wife and I have an ongoing game we like to play while enjoying our Netflix coma-as-you-go subscription. You can try it at home too. Keep a notepad next to you (or use your iPhone, I guess) to track how often a semi-main/main character on a random Netflix movie is identified as a writer. It's usually within the first ten minutes of a sitcom or movie. It doesn't take long to sort out. The importance of this declaration is usually low, and the character rarely exhibits the symptoms of being a writer in any real way. They seem to be eating regularly, without anxiety, laughing in slow motion on bicycle rides with loved ones, and, in general, displaying no forms of self-aggrandizement or literary envy.

Despite the prevalence of this doomed vocation as a character sentence on an unsuspecting script (and eventual Netflix audience), the average citizen of earth, who has not yet spent thousands of hours trawling the well-worn grooves of Canadian publishing online and in reality, doesn't have a clue as to how to properly submit a book to a Canadian publisher. Perhaps publishers and seasoned authors take this for granted, but poll those who answer phones at your average publishing house, or those who run Facebook pages for similar operations, and you'll get a pretty decent sampling of how ill-prepared authors are on their way to awkward forms of rejection.

What one never sees on Netflix is a nervous and confused self-identified writer navigating the Internet, trying to learn the basics of how to get a book published. You never see this character chatting casually with a friend like:

"So, main character, do you need an agent to submit your book to a publisher?

"It's different for every publisher."

"Maybe you could self-publish the book first?"

"Yes, I have the cover art and the book is all laid out."

"Maybe call a publisher and ask how much they charge to publish a book."

"I'm meeting with my friend tomorrow. We're having lunch; she knows someone who self-published their book then it got picked up by a publisher. She's working on her second book now."

Continuing this Netflix film that doesn't exist, you'd see someone who works for a publisher, let's say an assistant of some sort, who has to answer questions all day from people who dream of being writers, but do not have the advantage of an accurate depiction of how to be a writer in a handy format like a Netflix film. Over the course of the narrative, aspiring writers will drive the poor assistant insane; she'll spend much of the movie complaining about how time-consuming it is to answer misplaced/unprepared questions, and why does everyone who wants to publish a book know so little about publishing a book?

Other depictions are quite close to reality: *Limitless*, for example, is the story of every Canadian author at some point or another: finding designer, non-FDA-approved drugs via one's ex-spouse's brother; completing one's novel in a single evening; then finding one gets a bigger high off day trading and so becoming a stockbroker, all the while wondering why one ever bothered to be a novelist in the first place. Who among us in Canadian publishing, from André Alexis to Douglas Coupland, from Damian Rogers to Gregory Scofield, can't identify with that arc?

ReLit Award–winning author Daniel Scott Tysdal, one of Canada's best poets to catch on stage, says that he has been impressed with Netflix's recent writer-conscious offerings. "Three examples that really stuck with me are: the French TV show *Marianne*, the Spanish film *The Motive*, and the American film *The Kindergarten Teacher*."

These are three very different projects, but they are all linked by getting at the truth/reality of writing by exaggerating an aspect of the writing life or process. *Marianne* exposes the dark, horrific side of writing as possession, writing as casting a spell. *The Motive* plays with the real-world manipulations writers undertake to create fictional truths, the acts of appropriation they perform to give form to their visions. *The Kindergarten Teacher*'s character study/stalker narrative uses Maggie Gyllenhaal's protagonist to combine and probe two writer figures—the stunted artist and the questionable, abusive mentor.

Emma Rhodes, an up-and-coming poet, points out that fashion can play a huge role in the mainstream stereotyping of the writer. "The main guy in *Sinister* is a writer. I watched that a few years ago but remember being pretty upset that he was always in a knit sweater. Because how else would they show that he's a *writer*!? Can't be a writer unless he's in knit."

I recently watched the Coen Brothers' *Barton Fink*, which is about a writer. Fink is pretty self-obsessed, wants to write for and about "the people," but is super disconnected, privileged, self-pitying, and a terrible listener.

While it would be great to blame Netflix for releasing so many films where a writer struggles with some romantic problem whilst never finishing their book, the trouble truly lies within Canadian publishing, for it is there that the world of books has become a murky terrain of general incomprehension. In an email from the fall of 2013, I recall soliciting advice from an unfortunate/unsuspecting retinue of writing friends. Here I rant about the near two-decade groan that is the e-book discussion, the Cassandra-like warnings from everyone's mom, aunt, and cousin that the e-book has replaced the traditional, physical reality–based book. I can only interact with this Nostradamian notion with anxiety-based humour.

I talk to my mom all the time and she is constantly telling me about e-books and Kobos. I have no idea what those things are. To me, in Canada anyway, the mass class (read: your mom's generation) will buy the same five to ten books each year. These are books that win awards or are advertised on the TTC or win the Oscar for best picture. That leaves the rest of us (small-press author #13, small-press author #56, small-press author #2,324, and me) to fend for ourselves. We publish books but are not considered real writers. We are seen as amateurs. And this whole electronic book thing? It's just a discussion. Kobo and the like seem to have had a direct conversation with the 1940s- and '50s-born retired Canadian book lovers. I have no idea what they have said to each other, but the stats are there: old people are adapting to different forms of books.

The main trouble with the book industry is quite simply, it's so uncharted, vast, and complicated that plumbers or architects only have time to hear about one book a year—not the grand narrative of the book industry, nuts and bolts and all. So what happens is, the book industry gets a mysterious reputation as something complicated and weird. Like when my landlord talks to me about books. It's like *Planet of the Apes*. Even people who are very book-friendly have no knowledge about the difference between genres (poetry, fiction, cookbooks), formats (hardcover, paperback, electronic) or the publishers themselves (multinational, independent, imprints of larger presses, academic, foreign). You couldn't find a more complicated industry.

When I switched publishers to one operating out of Vancouver, people said, "So will you have to go to Vancouver?" and "How will the books be distributed?" I suppose indie filmmakers and musicians have it worse. I mean, you won't see their films at the giant mall's theatre, nor will you find their music at...wait...are there even record stores anymore? What is most frightening about the book industry is that it employs thousands of people who ship books, stock books, do all these things. But the layman on the street has no idea.

Regardless, you have a huge portion of the population with money, who like books but do not in any way comprehend that they exist on this level. [Male Canadian writer], for example, who is two years older than me, has published the same number of books as I have, lives 3 blocks away from me, makes about $100,000 dollars more annually, and was recently interviewed on CBC. My mom asked, "Do you know him?" This is how books find audiences: you have to be extremely lucky. I'm not criticizing anyone. This country is gigantic! But I am starting to have a punk mentality about my career. In a documentary on The Smiths, a guy likened the early '80s scene to a bunch of guys robbing a convenience store for the money to release a single. Then they'd break up. That's how I feel about *Savage*. Though *Savage* has been to date my biggest payday ever, I don't see this ability to keep what I already consider to be a marginalized fanbase interested.

Now, back to Netflix. I'm not talking about movies like *Shakespeare in Love*, *Adaptation*, or *Misery*—films in which writing is the key element of the plot. I'm talking about weird, esoteric rom-coms, squatting in their thumbnail cache on a giant network, in which the director has forced a top character to be a writer for no apparent reason other than to dress them in plaid, have them be able to wander aimlessly around New York for two hours, and not have to go to work or comb their hair. I'm talking about beautiful objects of romantic obsession who conquer the writing workshop, then succumb to murder at the hands of the ultimate book-sales spiker (nothing beats a dead author for sales).

As a writer, if you're lucky enough to hear things like "foreign rights" from your publisher or your agent, the notion of inking a Netflix deal isn't that far-fetched—though I have yet to see a Canadian small-press book adapted. When I interviewed Neil Smith for *Books in Canada* in the mid-2000s, he said that selling his book internationally took some of the pressure off. "I feel I have less to prove now because the Americans and British have embraced my book." The publications in Canada, the United Kingdom, and the United States were staggered over a year, and each country marketed the book differently. "I still marvel that *Bang Crunch* had multiple readers, never mind multiple covers."

CREATION MYTHS: HOW TO SHAPE YOUR WORK-IN-PROGRESS ($0)

While I have no idea what project it is you are currently working on, I can give you some thoughts as to how I would maintain intensity as you go along. In addition to your main Microsoft Word/Google Doc which contains your draft, create a junk file where you can put all your cut-and-pasted research material (make sure you include where you grabbed it from). For my most recent work-in-progress, a novelisation of a true-crime story that happened to a few of my family members six years before I was born, I created a junk file called WIFE PALES, which was a newspaper heading that described a court case and my grandmother's physical paling when she heard the verdict read. In this file I can work in isolation from the main chunk of text and then slowly, bit by bit, import more polished paragraphs into the final document.

"I map out a graphic novel or comic strip in fits and starts," says Montreal artist Billy Mavreas.

> I may see a sequence in my mind's eye and sketch it out, followed by another sequence. I then "fill in the blanks," so to speak, bridging the action with quieter moments. The story emerges as more and more is drawn. Sometimes I work intuitively and improvisationally; sometimes I have little bits planned out that I know must make an appearance in the story. Mostly, though, it's just a collection of happy accidents.

When it comes to showing family members your writing, take some advice from Elizabeth Hay, whom I interviewed shortly before the publication of her novel *Late Night on Air*. "Before publication I feel spasms of embarrassment when I imagine members of my family reading certain lines, certain scenes. It's part of the cloud of anxiety that settles over me. It's hard to have a writer in the family. I understand if they choose not to read what I write, even though I want them to read it and like it. My only way of coping with the awkwardness is to work on something new."

And speaking of family, how does one get to slice off time to isolate and invent a completely different world from that in which they live? "Easily. My problem is getting too excited and overwriting," says author Robert Hough.

> Left to my own devices, I'd write all day every day, but whenever I do this I tend to collapse and develop a whole slew of emotional and physical problems. For me, the discipline involves only writing in the mornings, five days a week. As for my family, that's one of the things I've liked about being a writer most: I'm always at home. I have breakfast, lunch, and dinner with my wife and two daughters, and they're by far the most charming people I know.

Author Paul Carlucci says that while real-life issues affect his writing, the subject has to inspire him in some way:

> I probably won't write about economic migrants or political intrigue or similar sorts of human experiences that shape the news narrative, just because I've never had any direct contact with that stuff, not even as an observer. The modern-life themes I write about are usually what I've rubbed up against, again not necessarily as an actor or agent, but at least as an observer, like I've gotten close enough to have a sense of the details. Power dynamics, class, work, certain kinds of displacement, addiction, conflict, insecurity, isolation. That's not to say I don't try writing about things that are totally abstract or foreign. I do, but stories come together better when I have some sense of how they play out in real life, facial expressions and lighting and smells and so on.

CREATION MYTHS: HOW TO SHAPE YOUR WORK-IN-PROGRESS ($0)

For me personally, my character's origin stories, their trajectories, memories, and potential remain in my cavernous mental factory. They are my beloveds, and to get even more grotesque, cheesy, and possibly maudlin, I can call on them at any hour. They pick up, and we talk, we linger and think of ways of bringing them back into a brand-new adventure on the page. My sister character Holly from *Savage 1986–2011* (Anvil Press), for example, is one of my all-time favourite creations. She may get recast into a new book sometime soon, probably with the same name. Charles, the neurotic anti-hero from *Wrong Bar*, was also very romantic. He's someone I could see bringing back. And, of course, my family get recast over and over again in every domestic-themed story or poem I write; it's never really them, but an imagined family, with a set of behaviours, a setting, a time frame, and the mystery of my initial intentions with their fates. I have to care about my characters from the beginning. To quote the late half-Greek poet from the United Kingdom, Georgios Kyriacos Panayiotou, in his 1987 poem "Father Figure," "I will be the one who loves you/ 'Til the end of time"

R. M. VAUGHAN: THE SELFLESS GIANT ($300, DONATED TO THE ARQUIVES)

And I'm just so bored of wasting my time
Love and death always on my mind.

—The Stills, "Love and Death," 2003

If anyone were to be the inspiration for a reboot of Oscar Wilde's classic story "The Selfish Giant," it would be my friend Richard Vaughan. But the title would have to go. To fit his legacy properly, and to modernize it for the current climate, perhaps we could go with "The Selfless Giant," or "The Gregarious Crafting Giant," or "The Community-Building Giant." Yeah, that might work all right.

When the police told my wife the news about finding Richard's body on Friday, Oct. 23, 2020, she came into the garden and told me to go speak with him—the officer standing in our kitchen. I didn't want to talk to a stranger about someone who meant more to me than practically anyone else in my life.

Richard Murray (R. M.) Vaughan, 55, was one of my closest friends, confidants, and collaborators. Two decades after I first met him while growing up in Toronto publishing streams, Richard came home in January to New Brunswick, where I had been living for three years—he had been appointed Writer-in-Residence at the University of New Brunswick. It was a sort of CanLit relocation program, and I was happy to see him. He was here only a short while before COVID-19 hit and he was booted from his digs in downtown Fredericton, so we asked him to live with us—which, thankfully, he did—on March 1. My wife, 11-year-old daughter, four cats, and new puppy were soon familiar with his hilarious personality and his love of crafting—which would greet us in many forms every few days. Sometimes a collage would appear on my desk, left as if by a proud grade-school child bringing home work he'd made during art class.

After receiving his Bachelor of Arts degree and his Master of Arts in English from the University of New Brunswick, Vaughan moved to Toronto and became a fixture in the city's art and literary scenes in the '90s and 2000s, working in visual art (video, performance, collage) as well as being a regular arts columnist and critic for newspapers and magazines. He was a board member of *This Magazine* and still has a large section of filing cabinets at the Gay/Lesbian archives just teeming with his work. (He took me there once).

His recent projects included editing a collection of poetry by queer New Brunswick writers for Frog Hollow Press, and he had recently published a chapbook called *Contemporary Art Hates You* with Anstruther Press.

His vast bibliography includes the poetry collections *A Selection of Dazzling Scarves, Invisible to Predators, Ruined Stars, Troubled*, and *Ve1Xe*; the novels *Quilted Heart* and *Spells*; the plays *Camera, Woman* and *The Monster Trilogy*; and *Compared to Hitler: Selected Essays*, which came out in 2013.

He was taught by his mother to be a kind and well-mannered Maritime boy. Young man. He once cancelled a sushi date with me because he had to interview Freddy Krueger actor Robert Englund—oh, the laugh we had because he was ditching me to talk to Freddy Krueger. Always there were the laughs and the anecdotes. They helped define our friendship, as they did with so many others—the amount of personal mail Richard received every week, from friends across Canada and beyond, attests to his ability to keep in touch, to draw people towards him, and his dedication to and pride in those he loved, dated, admired, and collaborated with.

When he wasn't working on his poetry, his novels, or writing his widely loved columns and articles, he was in our large lovely garden, nurturing life, planting seeds, and proudly watering his towering sunflowers. He also grew potatoes for the first time this summer, and he shared his bounty with us. More than once a day his phone alarm would sound, and he'd be off to talk to one of his many friends across the world on Skype. He treasured his connections to "my gays," as he'd call them affectionately. We were his "straights."

When a television reporter came to talk to me for a story on Richard's death, they cut out what I felt was more important than what he meant to me personally: I talked about his impact on the queer creatives who were so oppressed when he came of age in the 1980s and '90s; how important his work and advocacy was to their empowerment; how the mainstreaming of queer culture is because of the efforts of icons like him.

He's like Andy Warhol and Douglas Coupland, Truman Capote and Kathy Acker all in one, with just the right splash of his favourite actress, Jodie Foster. Richard was a true pioneer and made a joke of being what he called the "token gay"—"We need a gay? Let's get Richard!"—but it really meant he was always in demand.

He carried an undercurrent of sadness—about his mother's death in 2015; for the abuse he faced as a child from his father for being chubby; for being different—that sometimes clouded our bonfire conversations. He would drift away, only to recover again quickly, picking up another train of thought, making us laugh again. His gregarious personality created a curtain for his pain; his heart was big; he connected people. "You should talk to…" he'd say. "I'll introduce you."

The writing community is full of hotheads and saints, egoists and divas. But it's changing, becoming filled with influencers and those without experience. Last week saw both the retirement of beloved Brick Books publisher Kitty Lewis and the announcement that Pedlar Press will cease printing this year.

In an interview, Pedlar founder Beth Follett talked of her fears of leaving the publishing world in the hands of those who don't know it intricacies. "There's a lot of expertise in the small-press world, and if there aren't excellent succession plans getting worked up then it could be really dicey in a couple more years," she told *Quill and Quire* recently.

R. M. Vaughan's death is that kind of loss. Who can possibly replace his ability to make everyone feel welcome, loved, curious about the world of creatives around them, all the while making them spit their drinks out from laughter? You can't go to charm school to learn any of that.

When Richard first went missing, I prayed we'd find him. He'd been suffering bouts of isolation, sometimes staying in his apartment downstairs for four days at a time, not even leaving to check the mail. I prayed he was holed up in a motel with a cute boy and some weed and was just taking a break.

I'm so sad that he wasn't.

I dreamt recently that I found him with cuts on his body. Again I thought of Wilde's story, the part where the giant finds a little child he had loved standing in his garden, with his wounds of crucifixion, and the child says, "These are the wounds of Love."

I hope Richard is in his garden, in Paradise, covered in white blossoms. I pray that, like the boy in Wilde's story, his wounds are the wounds of Love.

Originally published in the *Star*

ACKNOWLEDGEMENTS

I would like to thank Aimee Parent and Jim Johnstone for their encouragement to bring together essays from my past and present. I am aware of how lucky I am to have published so many books since 2005, and to be able to look back, and hopefully shed some light on a few dozen old Canadian books that might get some new readers, well, Jeez, it's once again an honour, so help me Margaret Atwood. Where was I? Oh yes, the team at Palimpsest: Aimee, Jim, Ellie and Carleton. Thank you for taking such care with me on this weird ride. It is an honour to be publishing once again with an Ontario publisher. Some of these essays wouldn't exist without support from publications across the country, who agreed to publish my work, and continued to publish my work for years to come. I'd like to thank my wife and partner Amber McMillan and our daughter Finny. Most of all I want to thank the writers I connected with in the pages of these essays. And finally, thank you to the industry who continue to put food on the table for all of us: the publishers, national, provincial and municipal funding bodies, book loving book buyers, charming festival curators, burnt out magazine editors and designers and of course, the angelic booksellers who deserve our daily thoughts as we continue to bring new and old voices to readers from the Paper Hound in Vancouver on Pender Street (see cover photo) to Broken Books in St. John's Newfoundland on Duckworth Street.

PHOTO CREDIT: AMBER MCMILLAN

ABOUT THE AUTHOR

Nathaniel G. Moore was born in Toronto in 1974. He has lived and worked as a writer and book publicist in Quebec, British Columbia, Ontario, and New Brunswick, where he now lives with his wife and daughter and runs moorehype, a boutique publicity operation. His books include *Savage 1986–2011*, winner of the 2014 ReLit Award for Best Novel, and most recently, the poetry collection *Goodbye Horses*. His writing has appeared in *Toronto Star*, *Toronto Life*, *This Magazine*, *The Berkeley Review*, *The Georgia Straight*, *The National Post*, *The Globe and Mail* and *Edit*.